LAURENCE STERNE AND THE
EIGHTEENTH-CENTURY BOOK

Scrutinising Sterne's fiction through a book history lens, Helen Williams creates novel readings of his work based on meticulous examination of its material and bibliographical conditions. Alongside multiple editions and manuscripts of Sterne's own letters and works, a panorama of interdisciplinary sources are explored, including dance manuals, letter-writing handbooks, newspaper advertisements, medical pamphlets and disposable packaging. For the first time, this wealth of previously overlooked material is critically analysed in relation to the design history of *Tristram Shandy*, conceptualising the eighteenth-century novel as an artefact that developed in close conjunction with other media. In examining the complex interrelation between a period's literature and the print matter of everyday life, this study sheds new light on Sterne and eighteenth-century literature by redefining the origins of his work and of the eighteenth-century novel more broadly, while introducing readers to diverse print cultural forms and their production histories.

HELEN WILLIAMS is a Senior Lecturer in English at Northumbria University, researching eighteenth-century literature and book history. She has co-edited John Cleland's *Memoirs of a Woman of Pleasure* (2018) and has won a British Academy Rising Star Engagement Award (2019) for her work on the novel in the hand-press period.

LAURENCE STERNE AND THE EIGHTEENTH-CENTURY BOOK

HELEN WILLIAMS

Northumbria University, Newcastle

CAMBRIDGE
UNIVERSITY PRESS

Shaftesbury Road, Cambridge CB2 8EA, United Kingdom

One Liberty Plaza, 20th Floor, New York, NY 10006, USA

477 Williamstown Road, Port Melbourne, VIC 3207, Australia

314–321, 3rd Floor, Plot 3, Splendor Forum, Jasola District Centre, New Delhi – 110025, India

103 Penang Road, #05–06/07, Visioncrest Commercial, Singapore 238467

Cambridge University Press is part of Cambridge University Press & Assessment, a department of the University of Cambridge.

We share the University's mission to contribute to society through the pursuit of education, learning and research at the highest international levels of excellence.

www.cambridge.org
Information on this title: www.cambridge.org/9781108822602

DOI: 10.1017/9781108904162

First published 2021
First paperback edition 2023

A catalogue record for this publication is available from the British Library

Library of Congress Cataloging-in-Publication data
NAMES: Williams, Helen, 1986– author.
TITLE: Laurence Sterne and the eighteenth-century book / Helen Williams.
DESCRIPTION: New York, NY : Cambridge University Press, 2021. |
Includes bibliographical references and index.
IDENTIFIERS: LCCN 2020022778 | ISBN 9781108842761 (hardback) |
ISBN 9781108822602 (paperback)
SUBJECTS: LCSH: Sterne, Laurence, 1713-1768. Life and opinions of Tristram Shandy,
gentleman. | Literature publishing–England–History–18th century. |
Book design–England–History–18th century. | Printing–Great
Britain–History–18th century.
CLASSIFICATION: LCC PR3714.T73 W55 2021 | DDC 823/.6–DC23
LC record available at https://lccn.loc.gov/2020022778

ISBN   978-1-108-84276-1   Hardback
ISBN   978-1-108-82260-2   Paperback

Contents

Contents

Figures

vii

Acknowledgements

Back in 2009, I was lucky enough to begin studying at Northumbria University and The Laurence Sterne Trust at Shandy Hall on an AHRC-funded Collaborative Doctoral Award. With the support of the board and with partner Chris Pearson, curator Patrick Wildgust welcomed me into his museum, also his home, where I was offered every opportunity and all of the archival matter I could cope with. Through his infectious enthusiasm, the books, manuscripts, artworks and artefacts over which he is custodian have shaped the kind of research (book history) and teaching (literature and heritage management) that I find most enjoyable. Without the wealth of experience opened up to me there, where my earliest research began, this book would not exist.

Beyond my friends at the Trust I am beholden to a huge number of archivists, librarians and curators at institutions such as the British Library, the Huntington Library, the Beinecke, the Pierpont Morgan, the Borthwick Institute, Cambridge University Library, the Museum of the History of Science and the National Portrait Gallery. Special thanks must go to Dr Gillian Dow and librarian Darren Wood at Chawton House Library for their support of part of this project during my time on a library fellowship there, where I found true friends in fellows Megan Peiser and Aran Ruth. A grant from the British Academy Rising Star Engagement Awards has brought me into contact with printers, print curators and academics with whom I have been able to put my print historical theories into practice. Those experiences would not have been possible without Northumbria University's English Department recognising the value in external collaboration. The book would have taken much longer without the research sabbatical I was granted in the Spring term of 2016, during which the bulk of the research and writing was completed. I spent that term as Visiting Fellow in the Department of History at the University of Ulster and on placement at the Communities Department of Government Northern Ireland, which was a rich and rewarding time for me thanks to the kindnesses of Ian Thatcher and Bethany Sinclair, allowing me the space to write, run, consider the wider potential impacts of book historical work and, most of all, to think out loud with interested and interesting colleagues.

This book looked quite different to its earliest audience, Clark Lawlor, Judith Hawley and Moyra Haslett, to whom I am grateful for their recommended change in direction which brought me squarely into the design history of the eighteenth-century novel. I would like to thank friends and colleagues who have assisted me over the years, Mary Newbould, Paul Goring, Siv Gøril Brandtzæg, Elinor Camille-Wood, Ashleigh Blackwood, Katherine Aske, Mary Pickin, Richard Keogh, Jamie McKinstry, Claudine van Hensbergen, Katherine Baxter and Ann-Marie Einhaus. I am particularly indebted to friends who read parts of this manuscript for me – Allan Ingram, Peter de Voogd, Geoffrey Day and Lindsey Eckert – as well as the anonymous readers of the final manuscript for their care and attention. To Fiona Robinson, Kelly Haswell and Vicki Wilson I owe respite and laughter. Perhaps unwisely I hope one day to repay the book-debts that have accumulated against my name to Richard Terry, who still has the patience to be my collaborator, mentor and friend, after a decade of pondering over my prose.

I'm one of three first-generation students in a family who have backed this project since before it began: many will understand the love and support that got me here. My mother deserves her name on the cover for childcare alone, and my parents and siblings for their ongoing interest and patience. My partner Kyle Hughes has coloured this project as one that I will be sorry to complete: his humour and sensitivity have made the writing easy and the downtime a dream, both before and after the birth of our daughter. To our typographically curious toddler, Ida, this arrangement of 'alphabets' is dedicated.

Introduction

In 2010 a new publisher, Visual Editions, launched its first book, Laurence Sterne's *The Life and Opinions of Tristram Shandy, Gentleman*. The volume, by London-based graphic design studio A Practice for Everyday Life (APFEL), was shortlisted for 'Designs of the Year 2010' in the graphics category, securing for Visual Editions a reputation for stylish experimentation. In their version of *Tristram Shandy*, APFEL pinpoint Sterne's innovations in the first edition (1759–67) and then reconceptualise them.[1] They expand one paragraph of dashes representing Tristram's skim-reading to ten pages of orange lines; the fading cries of Amandus and Amanda literally become fainter through being represented in paler ink; pointing hands gesture boldly from the very edge of the paper; and the 'T' of 'to a T' looms large and fluorescent beneath the rest of the text on the page.[2] APFEL also treat Sterne's nine duodecimo volumes as three-dimensional artefacts, much as he did ('do, Sir, sit down upon a set').[3] The designers have changed the shape and the feel of the petite volumes, making their own weighty tome distinctive by carving into its contours. The point at which Tristram demands that the reader

————————————Shut the door————————————

is perhaps the most arresting, as APFEL print this line in orange, on a folded-down edge of paper, creating a physical divide in the volume between those pages addressed to simply anyone and those that remain reserved for the privileged readers admitted into Tristram's confidence.[4] APFEL tear out Sterne's 'torn-out' pages, leaving a toothy gap in the

---

[1] For the Visual Editions' *Tristram Shandy* as an experimental text in its own right, see Alison Gibbons, 'Multimodal Literature and Experimentation', in Joe Bray, Alison Gibbons and Brian McHale (eds.), *Routledge Companion to Experimental Literature* (Abingdon: Routledge, 2012), 427.
[2] Laurence Sterne, *The Life and Opinions of Tristram Shandy, Gentleman* (London: Visual Editions, 2010), 7.544–54; 7.536; 2.116; 6.443; 2.99.
[3] Ibid., 6.426.   [4] Ibid., 1.19.

codex and a margin-width stump with a perforated edge in the place of each page.[5] In response to Tristram's invitation to the reader to 'paint' widow Wadman 'to your own mind', they overlay Sterne's blank page with a mirror created from a smooth, reflective oval of varnish, thereby coproducing with each reader a self-portrait.[6] These pages surprise, and they cry out to be touched.

APFEL's methods are wide-ranging, as, indeed, were Sterne's. And like Sterne, who exploited the range of technologies available to him and his contemporaries in the print shop, in the Visual Editions version of the novel the designers have similarly used widely available print and graphic technologies in innovative and surprising ways.[7] In an interview they revealed that 'it was key that (like the original) all our interventions would only use the graphic language and existing "tools" of a book: typography, symbols, line, figures, paper, plates, printing ink'.[8] The mirror is made from a varnish commonly used in book production and printing, while the marbled page is lithographic whereby the moiré of dots created through the superimposition of the printing plates mimic the random design Sterne's marbling technique.[9] Through APFEL's innovation with existing tools and processes, their *Tristram Shandy* is in keeping with the author's legacy of innovation. Their edition of Sterne's novel reminds us what seemed original about it, despite being created using existing and even traditional print practices, when it appeared in 1759. Like Sterne APFEL use punctuation, typography and illustrations in surprising ways while also adding new visual pages and graphic devices, such as a frontispiece to Sterne's interpolated text, Slawkenbergius's Tale.[10]

It was impossible, however, for APFEL to recreate the delight that the earliest readers of *Tristram Shandy* must have felt in finding themselves in the unusual position of perusing a first edition novel featuring a number of visual effects. In this period, the most common graphic elements of eighteenth-century fiction tended to be illustrations, often produced by copperplate printing which required use of a different press, and such

---

[5] Ibid., 4.321–33.   [6] Ibid., 6.485.
[7] In this study of book design elements in Sterne's fiction, I will not be addressing the issue of whether or not *Tristram Shandy* is a novel, and I use the term throughout in the modern sense. The latest word on the subject is by Tim Parnell in an article which also historicises the problem: 'Sterne's Fiction and the Mid-Century Novel: The "Vast Empire of Biographical Freebooters" and the "Crying Volume"', in Alan Downie (ed.), *The Oxford Handbook of the Eighteenth-Century Novel* (Oxford University Press, 2016), 264–81.
[8] APFEL, cited in Helen Williams, '"Looking and Reading Simultaneously": APFEL on *Tristram Shandy*', *The Shandean*, 23 (2012), 134.
[9] Ibid., pp. 131–2.   [10] Sterne, *Tristram Shandy* (Visual Editions), 3.275.

productions being therefore appended to literary texts after the fact. Illustrations were most often commissioned for reissues rather than first edition works, as they inevitably required extra investment on the part of publishers.[11] *Tristram Shandy* is rich in visuals, including illustrations by William Hogarth in the second (first London) edition of volume 1 (1760) and the first edition of volume 3 (1761). But it also includes graphic features anchored within the book, such as woodcut engravings printed within the line of type. Purchasers of the first edition of *Tristram Shandy* would not have known about the engravings, or the marbled page; these unusual and potentially saleable features of the books were not included in the newspaper advertisements for the novel or on its various title pages.[12] The novel's graphic features, therefore, were surprising to readers, even to those approaching later volumes accustomed to the visual experimentation of earlier instalments. Sterne's consistent inclusion in *Tristram Shandy* of visual effects rewards readers loyal to the serial publication of the novel at the same time as it demonstrates his capacity to continue innovating and surprising his audience within a work which had been experimental from its very beginning. Sterne's lavish investment in four coloured inks for the marbled page, for example, at a time when books sold with colour illustrations were luxury collectables,[13] enhances the value of his work and presents the novel as a design product with integral visual qualities. Woodcut engravings, page design and idiosyncratic typesetting are central to the very concept of *Tristram Shandy*, with the latter rendering troublesome any straightforward definition of 'accidentals' in historical bibliography.

In treating the history of print as central to the development of the eighteenth-century novel, this study joins a scholarly tradition inspired by David McKitterick's influential claim, in *Print, Manuscript and the Search for Order* (2003), that authors of this period were the earliest to shape the appearance of their books.[14] James McLaverty was perhaps the first to undertake an author-length study combining book-historical research with

[11] See, for example, Sandro Jung, 'The Other *Pamela*: Readership and the Illustrated Chapbook Abridgement', *Journal for Eighteenth-Century Studies*, 39 (2016), Special Issue: *Picturing the Eighteenth-Century Novel through Time*, Christina Ionescu and Ann Lewis (eds.), 513–31.

[12] Siv Gøril Brandtzæg, M-C. Newbould and Helen Williams, 'Advertising Sterne's Novels in Eighteenth-Century Newspapers', *The Shandean*, 27 (2016), 27–58.

[13] Sarah Lowengard, 'Colour Printed Illustrations in Eighteenth-Century Periodicals', in Christina Ionescu (ed.), *Book Illustration in the Long Eighteenth Century: Reconfiguring the Visual Periphery of the Text* (Newcastle: Cambridge Scholars, 2011), 58.

[14] David McKitterick, *Print, Manuscript and the Search for Order, 1450–1830* (Cambridge University Press, 2003).

close reading, in *Pope, Print and Meaning* (2001). Paddy Bullard and McLaverty's edited collection, *Jonathan Swift and the Eighteenth-Century Book* (2013), undertook a similar project for Pope's companion, contextualising Swift's productions through their source genres: miscellanies, epistolary fiction and mock editions. Janine Barchas was pioneering in her analysis of the graphic qualities of this period's prose fiction in *Graphic Design, Print Culture, and the Eighteenth-Century Novel* (2003). There, she reads the novel's design history as integral to its production of meaning, using such case studies as Swift's frontispieces, Sarah Fielding's dashes and Samuel Richardson's fleurons. Christopher Flint's *The Appearance of Print in Eighteenth-Century Fiction* (2011) was one of the foremost fruits of what Barchas rightly identified as a burgeoning field. The manner in which novels confront their own materiality, Flint suggests, shaped the way that readers thought about print. However, these print-historical treatments of eighteenth-century authors largely ignore non-fiction intertexts, and genres other than fiction also have an important role to play in understanding a printed work's meaning. Analysing a broader range of source materials opens up new avenues for critical inquiry and for better understanding the meaning that arises from print devices in mid-century literature. And there must be no other author in that century who more explicitly, and more creatively, engages with print than Laurence Sterne. In designing a bestselling novel renowned for its visuality, which helped establish as it simultaneously overturned the printed appearance of the developing genre, Sterne is overdue a book-length study of his graphic and typographic ingenuity. As an author cum book designer, he theorised and criticised print production even as he manipulated and commented upon it, always drawing it to the attention of his readers.

Despite regularly referencing the process of book design, Sterne is notorious for rarely citing his sources. Nevertheless, the range of intertexts from which Sterne directly quoted and borrowed is nowhere better documented than in the Florida Edition of the Works of Laurence Sterne, under the general editorship of Melvyn New. The third volume of the Works, *The Notes* (1984), co-edited with Richard Davies and W.G. Day, demonstrates the astonishing degree of *Tristram Shandy*'s intertextuality, identifying a huge range of source texts, including literary, religious, philosophical and scientific works.[15] But the Florida annotations are

[15] *The Life and Opinions of Tristram Shandy, Gentleman: The Notes*, Melvyn New, Richard A. Davies and W.G. Day (eds.), The Florida Edition of the Works of Laurence Sterne (Gainesville, FL: University Press of Florida, 1984), vol. 3.

unusually patchy in their coverage when we expand our search for literary allusion to include not just textual but also visual echoes. One exception is their treatment of Yorick's death, where the editors refer readers of the epitaph, 'Alas, poor Yorick!', to the anonymous novel, *Life and Memoirs of Ephraim Tristram Bates* (1756), first identified as a source by Hester Thrale Piozzi: when Bates dies, the anonymous author centres the line, 'Alas! poor Bates'. We get the sense, however, that the verbal echo, rather than the visual emphasis, is of most interest here. The editors omit any mention of the black leadings surrounding Yorick's epitaph, but they do remark upon early seventeenth-century visual sources for the black page.[16] The apparatus fails to record any visual precursors of the marbled page or the diagrammatic plotlines in volume 6; and the visual innovations of the ninth volume, including the blank chapters and Trim's flourish, do not attract comment. Most surprising of all is that the image of Yorick's handwriting (his annotation of his sermon with the term 'BRAVO', as discussed in Chapter 1) remains unglossed, despite the editors' obvious efforts to approximate this visual effect.[17] Given the justified influence of the Florida apparatus, the effect of these omissions has been to obscure Sterne's true contribution to book design, with the immediate print context from which his innovation emerged being under-represented both here and further afield. Only by investigating the wider context of book production in the eighteenth century, including the book's graphic qualities, can Sterne's engagement with the novel form and the print culture of his day be fully appreciated.

This is the first monograph devoted to Sterne's creative manipulation of the eighteenth-century book. It draws upon a long history of scholarship exploring the meaning of Sterne's visuals, especially in articles of the 1970s and 1980s by Peter de Voogd, W.G. Day and Roger Moss, and by

[16] Robert Fludd's *Utriusque cosmi maioris scilicet et minoris metaphysica, physica atque technical historia* (Oppenhemii: de Bry, 1617), and Joshua Sylvester's commemorative volume, *Lachrimæ Lachrimarvm, or the Distillation of Teares Shede for the Untimely Death of the Incomparable Prince Panaretus* (London: Lownes, 1612). I explore these precursors in more detail in Chapter 3.

[17] *The Life and Opinions of Tristram Shandy, Gentleman: The Text*, Joan New and Melvyn New (eds.), The Florida Edition of the Works of Laurence Sterne (Gainesville, FL: University Press of Florida, 1978), vol. 2. The strikethrough effect appears at 6.11.516 of the Florida Edition; there is no corresponding note. The note on the marbled page refers readers to W.G. Day's bibliographical essay on its creation ('*Tristram Shandy*: The Marbled Leaf', *Library*, 27 (1972), 143–5) and to Eric Rothstein's discussion of an earlier textual reference to a marbled page: Rothstein, *Systems of Order and Inquiry in Later Eighteenth-Century Fiction* (Berkeley, CA: University of California Press, 1975), 66. The signatures beneath the plotlines, i.e. their being '*invenit*' and '*sculpsit*' by Tristram, come in for commentary, but not the lines themselves.

Christopher Fanning in 1998.[18] Longer Sterne studies, with the notable
exception of W.B. Gerard's *Laurence Sterne and the Visual Imagination*
(2006), tend to treat *Tristram Shandy*'s graphic elements only briefly.
Gerard analyses the art of Sterne's illustrators, however, while I limit my
study to first edition graphics. In fact, many – if not most – of the
monographs that have emerged in recent years are more concerned with
what Sterne's imitators and adaptors can tell us about Sterne's works, than
with his own print context, as his distinctive graphic-narrative style and
experimentation with typography would go on to inspire the cultural
phenomenon of Sterneana, vibrant from 1760 through to the nineteenth
century.[19] This study is concerned with identifying the intertexts for
Sterne's work which would have been available to his earliest readers. In
focusing mainly on the period in which *Tristram Shandy* was serially
published and the decade preceding its appearance, this book follows on
from the work of Thomas Keymer, who has positioned Sterne squarely
within the literary marketplace of the 1760s. His monumental study,
Sterne, the Moderns, and the Novel (2002), is one of few to read *Tristram
Shandy* within its own print cultural moment, foregrounding mid-century
literary works as potential source texts for Sterne's experimentation. Some
of Keymer's sources also feature in my own work, such as William
Toldervy's *Two Orphans* (1756), Thomas Amory's *John Buncle* (1756)
and the works of Samuel Richardson, the novelist and master printer.
But Keymer's study, like Bullard and McLaverty's treatments of Swift and
Pope, is limited to literary texts, whereas my own approach is deliberately
broader. I explore the print-production circumstances which gave rise to
the startling originality of *Tristram Shandy*, through a detailed focus on the
print history of the first editions of Sterne's works.

Sterne's innovative novel was produced in a cultural moment characterised by a paradox: this was a period of relative stability in the development of print technology and yet it witnessed increasing demand for books
of all kinds of designs and formats, and ever more elaborate and surprising

[18] Peter de Voogd, 'Laurence Sterne, the Marbled Page, and the "Use of Accidents"', *Word and Image*,
   1 (1985), 279–87; Day, 'The Marbled Leaf', 143–5; Roger B. Moss, 'Sterne's Punctuation',
   Eighteenth-Century Studies, 15 (1981–82), 179–200. These influential articles were followed by
   one much later by Christopher Fanning: 'On Sterne's Page: Spatial Layout, Spatial Form, and
   Social Spaces in *Tristram Shandy*', *Eighteenth-Century Fiction*, 10 (1998), 429–50.
[19] Studies of Sterne's visuals in regards to *Tristram Shandy*'s reception history include: René Bosch,
   Labyrinth of Digressions: Tristram Shandy *as Perceived and Influenced by Sterne's Early Imitators*
   (Amsterdam: Rodopi, 2007); Warren L. Oakley, *A Culture of Mimicry: Laurence Sterne, His Readers
   and the Art of Bodysnatching* (London: MHRA, 2010); and M-C. Newbould, *Adaptations of
   Laurence Sterne's Fiction: Sterneana, 1760–1840* (Aldershot: Ashgate, 2013).

visuals. Novel readers, including Sterne, were well versed in the print conventions of a wide range of books, and Sterne not only borrowed from those books when designing his own novel but also self-consciously commented upon the publishing trends in which he was participating. His method of selecting interesting graphic techniques strikes the modern reader as unusual in the pages of an eighteenth-century novel, but would not have appeared unusual in other print genres of the period. The central questions addressed here will be: where did Sterne get the inspiration for his idiosyncratic printed pages, and what does exploring his potential source material contribute to our understanding of *Tristram Shandy*? As well as novels and poetry, the sources explored here include dance manuals, closet drama, letter-writing handbooks, newspaper advertisements, medical pamphlets and disposable packaging. Much of this matter has evaded critical analysis in relation to fiction and challenges existing preconceptions of the eighteenth-century novel as an artefact which developed in isolation from other media. Within such a diverse body of work, *Tristram Shandy* emerges as a hybrid product of the eighteenth-century print shop, and the innovation of its author lies in importing into the novel sometimes standard printing practices from other popular and widespread genres, bringing with them their own varied associations.

This study is organised around Sterne's major visual innovations, many of which would have been (and still are) perceived to be 'firsts' within the context of the novel: printed strikethrough; a performed sermon; a suite of mourning iconography; the marbled leaf; wholesale disruption of the order and packaging of the book as a physical artefact; and engraved diagrammatic lines. The book is largely chronological, dealing with each print element as it appeared in Sterne's serial publication of *Tristram Shandy*, charting Sterne's literary interventions in a fast-developing, and historicised, print market. So, to be clear, Chapter 2 deals with the black page (vol. 1; 1759), Chapter 3 with the sermon (vol. 2; 1759), Chapter 4 with the marbled page (vol. 3; 1761), Chapter 5 with footnotes and catchwords (mostly in vols. 4 and 9; 1763 and 1765) and Chapter 6 with engraved lines (vols. 6 and 9; 1765 and 1767). Each chapter takes one of Sterne's iconic visual experiments and analyses its associated meanings through tracing its production history. This involves the treatment of largely printed sources from a wide variety of disciplines, the vast majority of which were produced during Sterne's lifetime but before (or during) the publication of *Tristram Shandy*, though there are some which date from earlier periods. The chapters often offer combinations of source materials which may seem perverse to modern readers (such as wrapping paper and anatomical drawings, in the case of the marbled page). But this seeming incongruity is one of the fruits of this study, which elucidates the wide field of visual reference that Sterne shared with his contemporaries and the associated meanings these visual elements may have brought with them to early readers of the novel. Modish visual effects often emerge from unusual, multiple and sometimes contradictory sources. In its assortment of source material, this study reveals a whole host of resources that the eighteenth-century book trade offered to an author looking to create a text with graphic and material qualities which not only help facilitate meaning and humour but which also frequently become (integral to) the message itself.

The first chapter, on hands and handwriting, provides a historical and theoretical framework for reading Sterne's visual effects. In practical terms, this is a reading of the six instances of printed manicules in *Tristram Shandy* and a bespoke woodcut of Yorick's handwriting. It aims to demonstrate Sterne's attempts to control every aspect of book production and his engagement with the copyright debates of his day. This chapter establishes Sterne's position in the print shop, his desire for his own works to have idiosyncratic visual attributes, and identifies beneath that desire his anxiety over the potential invasion of his copyright. It establishes my argument which will develop across the rest of the volume, that Sterne's book design manifests both creative and anxious responses to the borrowing of print practices and therefore the idea of originality more broadly. The chapter sets up this study as one which positions Sterne as a book designer well versed in codices from multiple disciplines – handwriting manuals, newspapers and fiction (Samuel Richardson's Clarissa [1748]) – and their varied experiments in the printed presentation of data. The ingenuity of the woodcut, the first instance of printed strikethrough that I have encountered, along with Sterne's time-investment in signing each copy of the first and second edition of volume 5, and of the first editions of 7 and 9, reveal the efforts in which Sterne engaged to inscribe *Tristram Shandy* with examples of real and fictional handwriting to set apart his own work from that of his precursors and secure his literary ownership.

Chapter 2 explores the black page commemorating the death of parson Yorick, often perceived as the pre-eminent symbol of Sterne's experimentation. I suggest that with the black page Sterne participates in a long-standing tradition of woodcut ornaments and mourning typography in funeral publications from the seventeenth to the eighteenth centuries. He comments on how far this form of typographic commemoration had by this time become clichéd, by referring to two recent typesetting trends: the representation of major funeral processions in national newspapers and gravestone-like pages in the mid-century novel, as evidenced in *Tom Jones* (1749), *Peregrine Pickle* (1751) and William Toldervy's *Two Orphans* (1756). Through considering the rarely studied mourning borders around Yorick's epitaph alongside the black page's double-sided covering of black ink, this chapter sees Sterne engaging with past and contemporary print practices of commemoration while playing upon – and pushing to its limits – the novelistic epitaph's self-conscious manipulation of the printed page.

Reviewers and imitators immediately hit upon the subject of chapter three, Sterne's 'Abuses of Conscience' sermon in *Tristram Shandy*, as a remarkably innovative formal device. In spanning forty-eight pages, it is certainly his most sustained visual effect. Sterne's sermon had been in print for almost a decade before it featured in *Tristram Shandy*. The sermon, read aloud by Corporal Trim to a disruptive congregation of Walter, Toby and Dr Slop, is reprinted in full, but appears interwoven with and fragmented by parentheses indicating the varying reactions of its Shandean auditors. Printed sermons had long featured square brackets for emphasis, where they sought to fix the meaning of potentially blasphemous words. But in *Tristram Shandy*, Sterne uses the marker in ways much more in keeping with the print history of drama in order to highlight the origins of his own dramatic style. This chapter analyses the 'Abuses of Conscience' sermon, whose pages depend for their graphic distinctiveness as well as their comprehensibility on innovative typesetting, as a melange of print genres. When Sterne (unsuccessfully) pitched to Robert Dodsley the first two volumes of *Tristram Shandy*, which include the 'Abuses of Conscience' sermon, he was directing his novel to the very man whose career had been built on writing and publishing texts which sat on generic boundaries. Dodsley's high-profile play, *The Toy-Shop* (1735), was much more successful in print than performance, and worked best as a reading text. This chapter contextualises Sterne's experimentation with *mise en page* in the 'Abuses of Conscience' episode within a wider mid-century fascination with hybrid print forms. As well as Dodsley's play and closet drama, it explores experimental precursors such as Jane Collier and Sarah Fielding's *The Cry: A Dramatic Fable*, published by Dodsley in 1754, and Richardson's *Sir Charles Grandison* (1753), which imported dramatic devices into mid-century prose. By analysing Sterne's sermonic punctuation and linking it to his development of a mid-century aesthetics of typesetting the novel, I suggest that sermonic printing is central to the plot and construction of *Tristram Shandy*. Sterne drew from Anglican works published from within his professional context, which themselves had a theatrical heritage, while responding to a 1750s fashion for printing closet drama and dramatic novels.

Sterne inserts his most startling innovation, the marbled page, into the third volume of *Tristram Shandy*. This volume is almost entirely concerned with the publication and collection of medical books: Tristram uses his father's library, the contents of which theorise the value of large noses, to explain Walter Shandy's distress when baby Tristram's nose is broken by forceps delivery. Chapter 4 situates Sterne's remarkable visual device within a history of colour book illustration dominated by scientific works of the kind treasured by Walter. It also recounts the history of marbled paper, commonly recognised as bookbinding material but less well known as medical packaging for nostrums prescribed to treat wounds and ailments. As a colour illustration in the instalment of *Tristram Shandy* addressing a wounded nose, the marbled leaf would have been surprising, but such imagery was more familiar in colour-illustrated medical books and distinctively packaged branded remedies. The marbled page, therefore, references a full range of paper materials seeking to theorise, diagnose and treat malfunctioning bodies. The field of reference for Sterne's graphic ingenuity is, perhaps unsurprisingly, at its widest and most inventive when we consider his most dazzling contribution to book history.

Chapter 5 takes as its subject the more functional face of book history. By mid-century, the novel had inherited from other book genres a certain printed appearance. Readers began to expect a printed framework for reading prose narrative consisting of cues such as page numbers, catchwords, chapter divisions and notes. These navigational elements aimed to facilitate reading while remaining in the background; they were simultaneously visible and invisible, read and unread. But navigational elements in Sterne's works rarely remain invisible for long. This chapter tells the backstory of the navigational framework of the eighteenth-century novel which Sterne disrupts, before analysing his experimentation with the *mise en page* of the novel in a manner that foregrounds those elements of book production rarely scrutinised. This study of Sterne's manipulation of seemingly untouchable conventions of the printed page, such as pagination and catchwords, complements an approach to his more widely recognised interference with footnotes and chapters, and reveals the full extent of his pioneering disruption to the format of the eighteenth-century book. Sterne's innovations with footnotes, catchwords, chapters and pagination combine aspects of Scriblerian satire with more recent but perhaps lesser-known interventions in the codex by Thomas Amory in *John Buncle* (1756). Both Sterne and the Scriblerians use multiple voices in footnotes to obfuscate meaning, satirising the infinite process of searching for a more perfect and authorised edition. Unlike Swift and Pope, however, and like Amory, Sterne deploys footnotes in the first edition of his work, encouraging the reader to approach at once all sections of the page in search of meaning and raising questions about literary authority from the outset. The confusion of narrative and delay of catchwords in *John Buncle* anticipate Sterne's own experiments with those very paratexts in *Tristram Shandy*. Whereas the Scriblerians often satirise scholastic pedantry in order to attack specific enemies, Sterne's targets, like Amory's, are the all-too-human creators of the eighteenth-century book.

The final chapter of the book considers Sterne's use of engraved lines as visual and verbal illustrations of digression. Chapter 6 begins by contextualising printed zigzag lines, examining the history of the dance manual, which, like that of *Tristram Shandy*, is one of innovation. Dance manuals were by necessity visual texts, and had to be ever more experimental in their attempt to teach movement by means of the printed page. *Tristram Shandy* shares with them diagrams which become demystified through labelling and instruction: the four zigzag lines closing volume 6 and Trim's flourish in volume 9. Sterne defers annotating these lines to encourage the reader to encounter the digressive text in a looping and non-linear manner. We dance around the text, rehearsing, learning and then perfecting our reading of his graven lines. Trim's flourish is remarkably like the symbols which in the Beauchamp-Feuillet dance notation system represent arm movements or dance steps, and the serpentine progress of a dance such as the minuet, one of the most popular dances of the mid-eighteenth century. Like Sterne's use of dance in *Tristram Shandy* – featuring in the novel both as content and as a metaphor for circuitous narration – Trim's flourish, when read alongside eighteenth-century dance notation, signifies both the one-off movement of his stick and the inability of anyone in Sterne's novel to progress in a straight line.

In a final Shandean subversion of order, this monograph closes with a coda analysing *Sterne's* extra-textual collaboration with Joshua Reynolds and William Hogarth on the frontispieces for his *Sermons of Mr. Yorick* as well as for *Tristram Shandy*. These images were both free-standing as well as bookish ones bound within Sterne's works, and served as important marketable visuals to prospective buyers. This final discussion of design elements beyond the narrative proper of *Tristram Shandy* demonstrates how, for Sterne, his literary project spanned print media, constructing an image of the man as well as the book as a print commodity.

This book locates Sterne's sources in a wide range of eighteenth-century printed materials. It contributes to his reputation as a highly original author by interrogating and attempting to measure the extent of his appropriation and departure from precursors. Landmark innovations, such as the black page and until-now unnoticed devices such as the strikethrough woodcut, can be fully appreciated as original by looking closely at the sources which underpinned them and from which Sterne often, though not always, departed with imaginative aplomb. This study thereby brings to light not only new precursors to *Tristram Shandy* in the sense of individual titles but also new print genres as previously unconsidered catalysts for Sterne and his contemporaries' experimentation with the form of the novel. Measuring the extent of Sterne's innovation and his engagement with a wider print culture requires exploring formal innovation by writers other than Sterne at mid-century, and in genres other than the novel. Sterne's graphic design interventions encourage us to consider the ways in which other eighteenth-century authors, too, might have creatively worked with the technology available to them and the print conventions established and establishing in a wide range of genres during that period. Analysing a work so inherently aware of its own mechanical production as *Tristram Shandy* necessarily entails exploring the wider print culture of the eighteenth century, including and especially non-literary works such as, in this instance, dancing manuals and non-books such as medical packaging, revealing a dynamic and interactive print history. *Tristram Shandy* is a serial work, responding to a vibrant trade in printed artefacts, and the distinctive modes of Sterne's various visual experiments are dependent on the particular moments in which they were produced. The process of setting the textual experiments and bookish features of this iconic novel within a wider context of print history has therefore resulted in a wide-ranging study, the first to deal with Sterne's design choices in the varied print contexts in which he made them. It is hoped, therefore, that this project demonstrates how far the history of the novel can be an interdisciplinary pursuit, considering a much broader print culture of the eighteenth century and offering new angles to historians of print culture and eighteenth-century literature alike.

CHAPTER I

Hands

The serial publication of Laurence Sterne's *Tristram Shandy* between 1759 and 1767 (two volumes at a time until the final ninth volume) gave an opportunity for hack writers wishing to take advantage of the novel's instantaneous success to churn out spurious volumes. The author responded to this invasion of his copyright by signing the first and second editions of volume 5 and the first editions of volumes 7 and 9. He might be perceived as having gone to unusual lengths to claim ownership of *Tristram Shandy*, but Sterne was not the only eighteenth-century writer to express his property rights in this way. Teresia Constantia Phillips signed each copy of her *Apology for the Conduct of Mrs. Teresia Constantia Phillips* (1748), as she said, 'to prevent Imposition'.[1] Charles Churchill would also take this approach in 1764, leaving a blank space on the printed title page of his poems 'The Times' and 'Gotham' to sign, instead of print, his name.[2] Like Phillips, and anticipating Churchill,[3] Sterne inscribed *Tristram Shandy* with the hand, the origin of its production, renouncing the anonymity that once characterised his title pages.

The autograph, of course, differs very slightly in each copy due to the idiosyncrasies of the hand and the body that directs the pen, but its authenticity arises from its ability to be reproduced. As Jonathan Goldberg points out, drawing on Derrida: 'To be legible . . . it must be repeatable. From the discipline of copy, then, the authentic signature takes its cue: it is inscribed within domains of repetition that (de)situate the hand.'[4] Sterne's attempt at authentication required an assiduous degree of replication: Peter de Voogd estimates that he must have had to sign 12,750

---

[1] Thomas Keymer, *Sterne, the Moderns, and the Novel* (Oxford University Press, 2002), 115.
[2] Churchill's use of print and handwriting causes difficulties for bibliographers, as in the case of ECCO, where his poem 'The Times' is recorded as 'The times. A poem. By [blank]'.
[3] Volumes 5 and 6 of *Tristram Shandy* were published in 1762, two years before Churchill's poems.
[4] Jonathan Goldberg, *Writing Matter: From the Hands of the English Renaissance* (Palo Alto, CA: Stanford University Press, 1990), 236.

copies.[5] And Sterne did not stop there. In *Tristram Shandy*, when one of Yorick's sermons is threatened with editorial misrepresentation, Sterne, associating handwriting with literary ownership, creates a visual joke about the safeguarding of an author's copyright which has thus far escaped the attention of *Tristram Shandy*'s modern editors. He prints an example of Yorick's handwriting: 'BRAVO'.[6] Like Sterne's signature, this engraved, printed image of Yorick's handwriting relies on its duplicative status for effect. In *Tristram Shandy* Sterne questions the possibility of authenticity after the development of a print market while playfully acknowledging his dependence on what Elizabeth Eisenstein calls 'the duplicative powers of print'.[7]

This chapter reads Sterne's innovation with representing script in print through his use of the printed hand: the typographic manicule. The manicule is a print icon which reminds us of the manuscript origins of the literary work – the hand – at the same time as its printedness underscores the eighteenth-century book trade's dependence on print technology. As we shall see throughout this study, Sterne often combines old manuscript and printing techniques with new ones in pioneering ways. In drawing from the handwritten, Sterne problematises the concept of print being uniform and replicable, and makes a bid for each copy of his novel to be considered as a unique artwork. The ideologies which led him to commission an original woodcut device to create the image of handwriting also underpin his desire to sign each copy of his novel, and culminate in his design of the marbled page (the subject of Chapter 4). This first chapter establishes Sterne's position in the print shop, his desire for his own works to have extremely specific material attributes, and identifies beneath that desire his anxiety over the potential invasion of his copyright. In revealing the author's attempts to control every aspect of book production and his engagement with the copyright debates of his day, we see Sterne as a book designer well-versed

---

[5] Peter J. de Voogd, '*Tristram Shandy* as Aesthetic Object', in Thomas Keymer (ed.), *Laurence Sterne's Tristram Shandy: A Casebook* (Oxford University Press, 2006), 108. He also suggests that Sterne employed manicules in *Tristram Shandy* 'to score a point'.

[6] Laurence Sterne, *The Life and Opinions of Tristram Shandy, Gentleman*, first edition (York and London: The Author; Dodsley; Becket, 1759–67), vol. 6, ch. 11, 53. Because of the nature of this study, all subsequent references to *Tristram Shandy* will be to the first edition and will be given in parentheses within the text, in the form vol.chap.p., unless a footnote is indicated. A first edition of *Tristram Shandy* is available via Cambridge Digital Library. M-C. Newbould and Helen Williams, (eds.), *Laurence Sterne and Sterneana*, available at https://cudl.lib.cam.ac.uk/collections/sterne/, last accessed 1 October 2020.

[7] Elizabeth L. Eisenstein, *The Printing Press as an Agent of Change: Communications and Cultural Transformations in Early-Modern Europe* (Cambridge University Press, 1979), vol. 1, 113–14.

in codices from multiple disciplines and their varied experiments in the visual presentation of data.

I   Marking Hands

In volume 3 of the first edition of *Tristram Shandy*, Sterne creates a typographic pun by means of a small printed hand: '☞ Mark only', says Tristram, '—I write not for them' (3.20.109) (Figure 1.1).

The audience to which Tristram declines to address himself is comprised of those he calls the 'graver gentry' or 'great wigs', about whom he admits 'I may be thought to have spoken my mind too freely' (3.20.107; 3.20.109). The typographic hand that appears at this moment, with its stretching index finger, slightly cocked thumb and visible shirt cuff, was a device located in this period both in manuscript and print cultures. Sterne's manicules are always printed mid-line, and this manicule's presence here reminds the reader that the term 'mark' may refer to both handwritten and printed symbols. The hand beckons the general reader but also paradoxically prefaces a statement of exclusion towards a specific category of unwelcome readers. Aiming the finger of the typographic device towards a statement of control over readership ('I write not for them'), Sterne playfully invokes an idealised image of manuscript culture in which circulation and reception are much more clearly anticipated and delimited, but which he recognises is a fantasy: he cannot know that the 'great wigs' will not read his work.

Sterne was well aware that the act of printing necessarily involved a loss of authorial control. What is ironic about this recognition is his tendency to express concern about that loss through the very medium of print itself: that is, through creatively embracing typographic effects designed to preserve or mimic the intimacies of manuscript dissemination. As Thomas Keymer reminds us, although '*Tristram Shandy* is among the defining successes of eighteenth-century print culture, it also retains prominent features of an earlier manuscript culture'.[8] One very specific manifestation of this might be seen to be Sterne's employment (six times in the novel in total) of the pointing hand, used as a symbol of the slipperiness of assigning literary ownership of printed works.[9] As early as 1762, an

---

[8] Keymer, *Sterne*, 191. Christopher Fanning has noted that 'there remains within *Tristram Shandy* something of a nostalgia for the manual production of manuscript culture' ('Sterne and Print Culture', in Keymer (ed.), *The Cambridge Companion to Laurence Sterne* (Cambridge University Press, 2009), 133).

[9] The hands occur here: 2.12.80; 2.17.100; 3.20.109; 4.25.164; 4.26.164; 6.11.48.

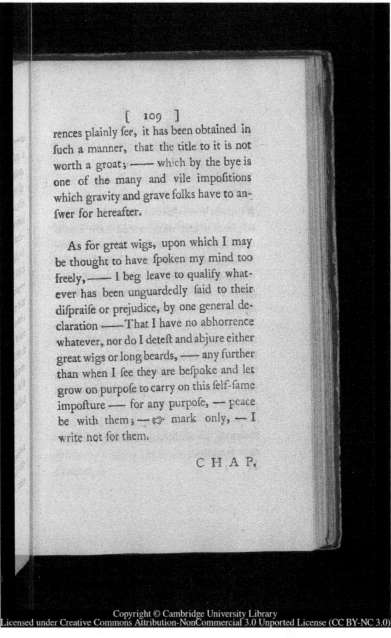

Figure 1.1   A pointing hand in the first edition of *Tristram Shandy*, 'Mark only'
(3.20.109). Image courtesy of Cambridge University Library

anonymous author capitalising on the success of *Tristram Shandy* liberally scattered the symbol through the pages of *The Life and Opinions of Christopher Wagstaff, Gentleman, Grandfather to Tristram Shandy*.[10] In 1781 Leonard MacNally also associated the typographic hand with Sterne's narrative art, employing the icon in a tribute to Shandean style in his *Sentimental Excursions to Windsor*.[11] In the 2010 Visual Editions *Tristram Shandy*, APFEL enlarge and highlight the hand in fluorescent orange ink, printing it in the margins of the text for greater impact.[12] However, despite A.E. Dyson listing the hand among the typographic effects that distinguish *Tristram Shandy* as 'one of the most boldly experimental novels ever conceived',[13] as well as brief mentions by Peter de Voogd and Eva C. van Leewen, no study so far has analysed Sterne's printed use of the symbol in any detail, or explored the extraordinary measures he takes to retain a sense of the handwritten in *Tristram Shandy*.[14] In line with a growing reluctance to associate Sterne unqualifiedly with print culture, in this book I adopt a position similar to that of Christopher Flint, who has argued that an authorial figure arose in early modern publishing 'that both embodied print culture and often resisted it passionately, producing fame through the mechanics of the print industry while emphatically reserving the imprimatur of the author's name'.[15] In this chapter, I consider Sterne's treatment of the hand, handwriting and their representation through the print medium to illustrate this underexplored element of Sterne's relationship with print: his longing for the accuracy of the manuscript copy and his valorisation of the primacy of authorial intention.[16] He employs typographic hands and a bespoke

---

[10] *The Life, Travels, and Adventures of Christopher Wagstaff, Gentleman, Grandfather to Tristram Shandy*, 2 vols. (London: Hinxman, 1762), 1.23.115; 2.14.59; 2.28.123; 2.34.186; 2.41.193.

[11] Leonard MacNally, *Sentimental Excursions to Windsor* (London: Walker, 1781), 168. Kenneth Monkman has suggested that the hand devices 'become almost a trademark' of Sterne's. When he wrongly attributed a pamphlet to Sterne based on the author's apparent obsession over printed presentation, the presence of a manicule in the text was, for him, the defining factor: 'Sterne and the '45 (1743–8)', *The Shandean*, 2 (1990), 54.

[12] Laurence Sterne, *The Life and Opinions of Tristram Shandy, Gentleman* (London: Visual Editions, 2010), 6.443.

[13] A.E. Dyson, *The Crazy Fabric: Essays in Irony* (New York: St Martin's, 1973), 33.

[14] De Voogd suggests that Sterne employed manicules in *Tristram Shandy* 'to score a point'. 'Aesthetic Object', 114. Eva C. van Leewen states that the single instance of the device in Sterne's *Journal to Eliza* marks a change of thought: *Sterne's* Journal to Eliza: *A Semiological and Linguistic Approach to the Text*, Studies and Texts in English 2 (Tübingen: Narr, 1981), 143–4.

[15] Christopher Flint, 'In Other Words: Eighteenth-Century Authorship and the Ornaments of Print', *Eighteenth-Century Fiction*, 14 (2002), 632.

[16] Recent years have seen an increased scholarly interest in and theorisation of the finger and the hand. See, for example: Goldberg, *Writing Matter*; Katherine Rowe, *Dead Hands: Fictions of Agency, Renaissance to Modern* (Palo Alto, CA: Stanford University Press, 1999); Sotaro Kita (ed.), *Pointing:*

woodcut representation of handwriting to make his mark as an innovative book designer while calling attention to the origins of the printed work: the hand; manuscript. In so doing, he stakes a claim for his literary property while conveying a sense of the problematics of literary ownership in this period.

II The Manicule

William Sherman's pioneering research on the pointing hand resulted in his finding no fewer than fifteen English names (some incorrect) for the same device: 'hand, hand director, pointing hand, pointing finger, pointer, digit, fist, mutton fist, bishop's fist, index, indicator, indicule, maniple, and pilcrow'.[17] As he has pointed out, the ornament 'may be the most pervasive feature in the history of textual culture that does not have a standard name'.[18] Like Sherman, I prefer the term 'manicule' because it refers to both hand-drawn and printed devices, as opposed to 'fist' or 'printer's first', for example, which most often refers to the latter.[19] Paul McPharlin dates its first instance to the 1086 Domesday Book.[20] The earliest known printed manicule occurs four centuries later, in Paulus Florentinus's 'Breviarum totius juris canonici', printed by Huss at Lyon in 1484.[21] Even in early printed texts the function of the manicule remained largely the same: an indexing device, as implied by the term 'printer's index'. In addition to this, the manicule has served a range of purposes. Manicules have been used by medieval scribes within the main body of the text to mark paragraph breaks, by Elizabethan schoolchildren to mark sententious or epigrammatic sayings and by authors to suggest that a corresponding note could be found in the margin or nearby.[22] When appearing without annotation, however, manicules were used by both printers and authors to simply point out notable material.[23]

Where Language, Culture, and Cognition Meet (London: Erlbaum, 2003); Goldberg, *Shakespeare's Hand* (Minneapolis, MN: University of Minnesota Press, 2003); Raymond Tallis, *The Hand: A Philosophical Inquiry into Human Being* (Edinburgh University Press, 2003); Tallis, *Michelangelo's Finger: An Exploration of Everyday Transcendence* (New Haven, CT: Yale University Press, 2010); and Angus Trumble, *The Finger: A Handbook* (New York: Farrar, 2010).

[17] William H. Sherman, *Used Books: Marking Readers in Renaissance England*, Material Texts (Philadelphia, PA: University of Pennsylvania Press, 2008), 33.

[18] Ibid., 33.   [19] Ibid., 34.

[20] Paul McPharlin, *Roman Numerals, Typographic Leaves and Pointing Hands: Some Notes on Their Origin, History and Contemporary Use*, Typophile Chap Books, 7 (New York: Typophiles, 1942), 47, 47–50.

[21] Sherman, *Used Books*, 32.   [22] Ibid., 32–3; 44; 43.   [23] Ibid., 43.

Manicules have also been used as advertising devices from the early modern period, when they were printed on the title pages of texts to emphasise their titles.[24] During the late seventeenth and early eighteenth centuries, the manicule served a similar purpose in printed ephemera, particularly newspapers, emphasising individual notices or calling attention to the key line in an advert.[25] By 1710 this practice had become so familiar that Joseph Addison featured manicules in a spoof guide to composing advertisements:

> The great Art in writing Advertisements, is the finding out a proper Method to catch the Reader's Eye; without which, a good Thing may pass over unobserved, or be lost among Commissions of Bankrupt. Asterisks and Hands were formerly of great Use for this Purpose.[26]

Addison's reference to a 'former' use of typographic symbols such as asterisks and manicules suggests that by this point they were old-fashioned in newspaper advertising; he recommends instead a more modish use of 'N.B.', images or italic (the 'blind *Italian* Character') to catch the reader's eye.[27] In a letter to Lord Fauconberg of 1767, Sterne mockingly fashions himself as a journalist publishing the gossip of the day, and includes a manicule as a joking reference to its use in the press, revealing his awareness of the most popular usage of the device at this time. The letter shows Sterne's self-consciousness about his inclusion of town gossip to entertain the ladies at Newburgh, signing off as the 'most unworthy Gazetteere that ever wrote': '☞ (all this is for the Ladies)', he writes.[28] In another letter of 1767, Sterne informs his wife of the whereabouts of several letters for posthumous publication:

> ☞ Hall [John Hall-Stevenson] has by him a great number wth those in this book & in my Bureau—& those above w^{d} make 4 Vo^{ls} the size of Shandy—they would sell well—and produce 800 p^{ds} at the least—.[29]

<hr>

[24] Ibid., 41–2.

[25] Jill Campbell, 'Domestic Intelligence: Newspaper Advertising and the Eighteenth-Century Novel', *The Yale Journal of Criticism*, 15 (2002), 264. See also Monkman, 'Sterne and the '45', 54.

[26] [Joseph Addison], *The Tatler* 224 (14 September 1710).   [27] Ibid.

[28] Sterne, 'To Thomas Belasyse, Lord Fauconberg' (9 January 1767), in *The Letters, Part 2, 1765–1768*, Melvyn New and Peter de Voogd (eds.), The Florida Edition of the Works of Laurence Sterne (Gainesville, FL: University Press of Florida, 2009), vol. 8, letter 189, 520.

[29] Sterne, 'For Elizabeth Sterne' (end of December 1767), New and Voogd (eds.), in *The Letters, Part 2*, letter 237, 639–40. A third instance of Sterne employing the manicule in his correspondence is 'To Robert Foley' (29 March 1763), in *The Letters, Part 2*, letter 111, 321–2. No manuscript exists for this letter.

Although simply a note, Sterne wrote it foreseeing that his letters (and perhaps this one) might one day appear in print. The duality that the device represents in *Tristram Shandy* informs Sterne's use of the device in his letters, where he identifies the icon as a device crossing print and manuscript by specifically employing it in those letters that address aspects of print culture.

Aside from its familiar appearance in printed works, the manicule continued to be used as a handwritten device throughout the eighteenth century. It appears in many letter-writing manuals of the period, such as the *English Spelling-Book* (1719), which defines the manicule as follows: '*Index*, the Fore-finger pointing, signifies that Passage to be very remarkable, against which it is placed.'[30] In *The Compleat Letter Writer*, first published in 1756 and going through twenty editions before the end of the century, the manicule is included in a chapter entitled 'Of Stops or Points, and Marks or Notes', prefaced with the following introduction:

> As in Speech or Discourse there are often several Motions made by different Parts of the Body, in order to excite Attention, and transmit a more clear and perfect Idea to the Hearer of the Meaning and Intention of the Speaker: So Writing being the very Image of Speech, there are several Points and Marks made use of in it, not only to mark the Distance of Time in pronouncing, but also to prevent any Confusion or Obscurity in the Sense of the Writer whereby it may the more readily be distinguished and comprehended by the Reader.[31]

The author emphasises the role of the body during speech, suggesting that punctuation performs the same function as physical gesture. In this context, the manicule becomes a gestural device, assisting the transmission of the 'Sense of the Writer' to the reader by pointing towards an important passage, just as a speaker would, 'in order to excite Attention'. In *Tristram Shandy* Sterne does not employ the manicule to clarify meaning, as this manual suggests is the role of the hand-drawn device. Instead, he draws attention to the symbol's inherent ambiguity, arising from the variety of its functions (annotative, structural, indexical) and its users (reader, author, editor, typesetter). Through the manicule – literally, a hand reproduced by

---

[30] S. Harland, *The English Spelling-Book*, 3rd ed. (London: Taylor, 1719), 49. Similar (largely derivative and abbreviated) definitions appear in *The Compleat Letter Writer: or, New and Polite English Secretary*, 3rd ed. (London: Crowder, 1756), 16; Jean Palairet, *A New Royal French Grammar* (London: Nourse, 1733), 31; William Leekey, *A Discourse on the Use of the Pen* (London: Ware, [1750?]), 31; John Marchant, 'Of Punctuation', in *A New Complete English Dictionary* (London: Fuller, 1760), xlv.

[31] 'Of Stops or Points, and Marks or Notes', *The Compleat Letter Writer*, 14.

print technology – Sterne practises a style of literary production which draws from a wide range of print and non-print sources, making use of the tools of both the print shop and manuscript production. He explores what happens to the sense of the writer, and the potential ownership of the text, when not only handwriting but also print is involved in its transmission.

III   Literary Property

At moments in *Tristram Shandy* when the issue of literary property arises, Sterne uses typography to emphasise his own innovation and highlight how far he departs from earlier experiments in printed texts. He voices anxiety over his literary property most explicitly in 1759, just months before he would begin work on *Tristram Shandy*. In a memorable letter to his publisher Caesar Ward, regarding the production of *A Political Romance* (1759), he airs concerns about the mediation of his text by print:

> I have only to add two Things:—First, That, at your Peril, you do not presume to alter or transpose one Word, nor rectify one false Spelling, nor so much as add or diminish one Comma or Tittle, in or to my *Romance*:— For if you do,—In case any of the Descendents of *Curll* should think fit to invade my Copy-Right, and print it over again in my Teeth, I may not be able, in a Court of Justice, to swear strictly to my own Child, after you had *so large a Share* in the begetting it.[32]

Sterne worries that his text may be disfigured by the publisher due to an unsympathetic handling of his spelling and punctuation, as he warns Ward not to change even so much as his commas and tittles (the tiny diacritics and dots of lower-case Is and Js). He hints at his apprehension by invoking the name of the notorious Edmund Curll, described by Jonathan Swift as 'a prostitute bookseller'[33] and perhaps best remembered for his pirated edition of Alexander Pope's correspondence, which resulted in legal action and lengthy debate surrounding the ownership of literary property.[34] Sterne is concerned that, if his own work were pirated by a publisher like Curll, he would not be able to claim the text as his sole property in court, considering the influence a publisher may exert over the text's appearance. He later reused the idiosyncratic idiom of this letter to express the same concern

---

[32] Sterne, *A Political Romance* [1759](Menston: Scolar, 1979), 50.
[33] Jonathan Swift, *A Tale of a Tub*, in *A Tale of a Tub and Other Works*, Angus Ross and David Woolley (eds.), Oxford World's Classics (Oxford University Press, 2008), 10.
[34] For details see Mark Rose, 'The Author in Court: Pope v. Curll (1741)', *Cultural Critique*, 21 (1992), 197–217.

about *Tristram Shandy*, claiming that the story is 'so nice and intricate a one, it will scarce bear the transposition of a single tittle' (8.7.20). In this repeated emphasis on tiny printed dots, Sterne reveals how far literary meaning is shaped by punctuation. As scholars we have been accustomed to referring to tittles as the 'accidentals' of a printed text, a term which suggests that they are merely accessory to a work's meaning. Sterne emphasises time and again that what happens to a work in the print shop is not merely the objective transmission of a literary text but a creative, and therefore potentially threatening, means of meaning-making.

Desiring to direct the printing process in creative ways, Sterne oversaw the production of every edition of *Tristram Shandy* during his lifetime. In his correspondence with Dodsley in 1759, Sterne had offered to correct each proof himself.[35] He was not unique in his desire for mastery over the printing of his works. David McKitterick has suggested that the eighteenth century witnessed a distinct change in the attitudes of authors and readers towards book production.[36] Despite print technology remaining relatively stable until the end of the century, changes to the discourse surrounding print and printers occurred throughout the century, with mid-century in particular becoming a period of adjustment and experimentation.[37] McKitterick records the fact that a familiar element of the early seventeenth-century book, the printer's note, became a rare component of the eighteenth-century work. These notes were a particularly personal aspect of the printed book, consisting of an address to the reader from the printer, acknowledging errors or complaining about uncooperative authors. Their disappearance suggests an increasing reluctance to acknowledge the human side of printing in the eighteenth century.[38] Lisa Maruca has charted a similar change in attitudes to print between the publication of two seminal printers' manuals, Joseph Moxon's *Mechanick Exercises* (1683) and John Smith's *The Printer's Grammar* (1755). The greatest disparity between these texts lies in the description of the print shop workforce, who mutate from specifically corporal figures in Moxon to ghostly abstractions in Smith.[39] Such a difference in the representation of

---

[35] Sterne, 'To Robert Dodsley' (5 October 1759), in *The Letters, Part 1, 1739–1764*, Melvyn New and Peter de Voogd (eds.), The Florida Edition of the Works of Laurence Sterne (Gainesville, FL: University Press of Florida, 2009), vol. 7, letter 36, 97.

[36] David McKitterick, *Print, Manuscript and the Search for Order, 1450–1830* (Cambridge University Press, 2003), 166–7.

[37] Ibid., 190.   [38] Ibid., 139.

[39] Lisa Maruca, 'Bodies of Type: The Work of Textual Production in English Printers' Manuals', *Eighteenth-Century Studies*, 36 (2003), 335.

printing reflects how far the concept of literary property was changing at mid-century, when a growing discourse arose around the author's originality and genius.[40] Maruca describes how, for Smith, even spelling and punctuation are 'part of the Author's near theological immanence'.[41] This reduced emphasis on the printer's body, a product of the mid-century aim to minimise the perceived mediation of the author's original words by those involved in printing the work, bears witness to a corresponding shift in discourse surrounding authorship and copyright.

During the copyright debates taking place at mid-century, the writing body became valorised as a means of proving that the printed work belonged to its author. From as far back as Galen and Aristotle, who first described the hand as the 'instrument of instruments', the body and specifically the hands have been associated with agency and, by extension, the rights and authority of the self.[42] Invoking the embodied image of the writer at his desk with pen in hand, those fighting in the legal battle for the consideration of literary property as an author's right drew on John Locke's *Second Treatise of Government* (1690):[43] 'Though the Earth, and all inferior Creatures be common to all Men, yet every Man has a *Property* in his own *Person*. This no Body has any Right to but himself. The *Labour* of his Body, and the *Work* of his Hands, we may say, are properly his'.[44] In *Tristram Shandy* Sterne reworked this idea to comic effect, extending the image from one of material goods ('The *Labour* of his Body, and the *Work* of his Hands') to also include intellectual property, before bathetically comparing it to a pair of breeches: 'the sweat of a man's brows, and the exsudations of a man's brains, are as much a man's own property as the breeches upon his backside' (3.34.159). Legal discourse began to represent intellectual property as belonging to the writer in part because it was 'the *Work* of his Hands', designating authorship through hands and hapticity: the sense of touch. The printer effectively stood in the way of an author making a straightforward claim for ownership of a printed work because such works could also be seen as products of the printer's rival pair of hands. At the height of the debates over literary property, as authors

[40] Ibid., 337. For further information on the relationship between copyright and the rise of authorial genius, see Martha Woodmansee, 'The Genius and the Copyright: Economic and Legal Conditions of the Emergence of the "Author"', *The Printed Word in the Eighteenth Century*, special issue of *Eighteenth-Century Studies*, 17 (1984), 425–48.
[41] Maruca, 'Bodies of Type', 336.   [42] Rowe, *Dead Hands*, 3–6, 12.
[43] Rose, *Authors and Owners: The Invention of Copyright* (Cambridge, MA: Harvard University Press, 1993), 4–6.
[44] John Locke, *Two Treatises of Government* (London: Churchill, 1690), 245.

became more and more demanding regarding their copyright, printers had a better chance of securing successful authors if they made less visible their role in the production of the work.

If printers at this time underplayed their handiwork, Sterne loudly pronounced his, especially in the many scenes of Tristram crumpling paper and scrawling drafts. He uses the image of the hand during episodes addressing issues of literary property, where it expresses his fear of an unknowable and therefore uncontrollable response to his own work. He hints at the manicule when describing Walter's hands-on reading practice:

> My father shut the book,—not as if he resolved to read no more of it, for he kept his forefinger in the chapter:——nor pettishly,—for he shut the book slowly; his thumb resting, when he had done it, upon the upper-side of the cover, as his three fingers supported the lower-side of it, without the least compressive violence.—— (5.33.118)

Sterne depicts Walter's reading as an intensely embodied experience, with the intricate account of Walter's 'forefinger in the chapter' also invoking an image of another 'forefinger in the chapter': the manicule. Sterne mimics one of the functions of the manicule in the description of Walter's fleshy fingers: reluctant to lose his place in his book, Walter dextrously handles the volume, using his forefinger as a bookmark or index. But this human manicule reminds us of an earlier instance of Walter's hands-on reading, when he deformed a book by scratching away at the text with a knife to change the meaning (3.37.173). In *Tristram Shandy*, reading, like writing, functions as a haptic and therefore empowering experience, and annotation is a profoundly subversive act. For Sterne, it is not just the printer who gains control over the author's work but also the reader, who, handling the printed text, may read particular sections out of context or place emphasis on passages of their own choosing. Through images of Walter's hands-on reading Sterne muses on the degree to which readers and printers creatively engage in the production of literary meaning in ways unforeseen by a text's author.

Sterne asserts control over the process of reading in the famous Toby and the fly scene. Here he plays on one of the manicule's readerly functions as a handwritten marker of sententiae. Tristram tells the reader that he learned one half of his philanthropy from this episode, which consists of a fly pestering Toby all dinnertime until, after 'infinite attempts', Toby finally catches the fly in his hand and releases it out of the window, exclaiming, 'why should I hurt thee?—This world surely is wide enough to hold both thee and me' (2.12.79). A manicule then materialises to point out that this story can be used as a lesson independent of its textual context: '☞ This is to serve for parents and governors instead of a whole volume upon the subject' (2.12.80). But rather than directing the manicule towards the passage which is 'to serve for parents and governors', Sterne points it at the commentary. He subverts the reader's expectation that the device would be used primarily to clarify the organisation of the text.[45] Instead, Sterne proposes a kind of hermeneutic challenge, requiring the reader to reread the text in order to identify and extract the relevant passage. Here he mocks the traditional use of the marker as a facilitating device from the commonplacing tradition; instead of using it as a cue to attend to the text, he gestures with the manicule towards the fragmented, decontextualising mode of its consumption. Furthermore, underlying this episode is the clichéd but succinct expression 'wouldn't hurt a fly', which would serve as a much more efficient replacement for a whole volume on the subject, or even just the passage.

The novel is well known for generating such self-reflexivity, most perceptibly in the numerous images of Tristram writing in his study. By reminding the reader of the physicality of textual production, Sterne makes a claim for his novel as his literary property, as deriving from the work of his hands. Sterne frequently highlights the corporality of the creative act by describing his hapless narrator wielding his pen or tearing up his paper:

> Every line I write, I feel an abatement of the quickness of my pulse, [...]——And this moment that I last dipp'd my pen into my ink, I could not help taking notice what a cautious air of sad composure and solemnity there appear'd in my manner of doing it.——Lord! how different from the rash jerks, and hare-brain'd squirts thou art wont, Tristram! to transact it with in other humours,——dropping thy pen,—spurting thy ink about thy table and thy books,——as if thy pen and thy ink, thy books and thy furniture cost thee nothing. (3.28.139–40)

Tristram can be excessively corporal in his clumsiness, all fingers and thumbs, depending on his humour. Here Sterne has him produce two forms of script: a solemn, composed hand and a messier scrawl made up of 'rash jerks' and 'hare-brain'd squirts'. Tristram's mood affects his handwriting, evoking the physicality of the experience of writing as the body's motions throb through the pen.[46] The idiosyncrasies of the handwritten

---

[45] Sherman, *Used Books*, 41.
[46] In fact, the creative process is frequently sexualised in *Tristram Shandy*. For further information see Dennis W. Allen, 'Sexuality/Textuality in *Tristram Shandy*', *Studies in English Literature, 1500–1900*, 25 (1985), 651–70. Frank Brady argues that Tristram perceives writing as masturbation, in '*Tristram Shandy*: Sexuality, Morality, and Sensibility', *Eighteenth-Century Studies*, 4 (1970), 41–56.

text are rendered invisible, Sterne hints, in the printed work, and yet through these self-reflexive scenes they are rendered visible again. Christina Lupton has argued that such images of Tristram's hands literally employed in the act of writing 'work to reintroduce the body to a process from which it appears severed when print introduces the written without writing'.[47] By including scenes of Tristram at work, Sterne not only provides an insight into the author's practice usually lost as a result of the mediation of print, but also hints at the inspiration behind some of his most innovative printed experiments.

IV   Richardson As Precursor

Samuel Richardson, the sole author – to my knowledge – employing the manicule in the main text of a novel published before 1759, anticipates Sterne both in his typographic experimentation and in his regular presence in the print shop: he was a master printer as well as a novelist.[48] In *Clarissa* (1748) Richardson draws on the pointing hand as a manuscript device and its use in contemporary letter-writing. Lovelace intercepts a letter from Miss Howe and, responding angrily to the contents, annotates the text with the manicule showing the extracts with which he is most dissatisfied.

To Miss Laetitia Beaumont.

☞ My dearest Friend,   Wednesday, June 7.

YOU will perhaps think, that I have been too long silent. But I had begun two letters at different times since my last, and written a great deal each
☞ time; and with spirit enough, I assure you; incensed as I was against the abominable wretch you are with; particularly on reading yours of the 21st of the past month (a).
☞ The *first* I intended to keep open till I could give you some account of my
☞ proceedings with Mrs. Townsend. It was some days before I saw her: And this intervenient space giving me time to re-peruse what I had written, I thought it proper to lay that aside, and to write in a stile a little less fervent; for you would have blamed me, I know, for the freedom of some of my expressions (*execrations*, if you please).[49]

---

[47] Christina Lupton, 'Creating the Writer of the Cleric's Words', *Journal for Eighteenth-Century Studies*, 34 (2011), 179.

[48] Keymer has called Sterne's use of the manicule in *Tristram Shandy* 'mock-Richardsonian' (*Sterne, the Moderns*, 74).

[49] Samuel Richardson, *Clarissa*, 7 vols. (London: Richardson, 1748), vol. 4, 328.

Here the manicule serves to 'mark the places devoted for vengeance', and indeed Lovelace undertakes a specifically textual revenge, using the manicule to indicate the extracts that he will appropriate and misrepresent after forging her handwriting.[50] His desire 'to gain a mastery' over Miss Howe's script through 'exact imitation' mimics that of the printer, who achieves mastery over the author's works by imitating the manuscript copy and who may infringe the author's copyright by editing the proof.[51] Richardson takes on all roles: author, designer and printer.

Flint has described Richardson's use of the manicule as signalling 'the degree to which the fiction is enmeshed in its mode of production' and, admittedly, in *Clarissa* the reader finds it difficult to forget that the text is a product of print despite Richardson promoting its handwritten origins in the preface.[52] Although Lovelace describes drawing each manicule himself by hand, the number of identical hands in the margin of one letter strains belief that we are reading a manuscript; as Flint remarks, this would be a laborious task for the writer.[53] But because Richardson pooled various collections of type to raise the 106 manicules required for the margin of the letter, these pieces of type are not, in fact, identical. Sterne's compositors also use more than one typeface for the six manicules in *Tristram Shandy*, and despite the fact that identical manicules were certainly available, two different manicules appear on page 164 of volume 4, with one visibly longer than the other. Rather than aim for a uniformity of design, the compositor of this page, perhaps under Sterne's guidance, emphasises the difference between the icons. Though this might appear innovative in the novel, this was by no means a new practice. The deliberate use of differently designed pieces of type recalls Gutenberg's creation of several different 'e' pieces, for example, to replicate the idiosyncrasies of manuscript and to meet the practical requirements of line justification.[54]

Both Richardson and Sterne employ the manicule to remind the reader of the novel's mode of production and the choices that print-conscious authors make when representing the handwritten through print. But whereas Richardson as a printer displays self-consciousness of his practice safe in the knowledge that he holds the copyright to his work, Sterne resorts to further experimentation in order to make his mark on his literary property. His innovation lies in the placement of the pointing hand device.

---

[50] Ibid., vol. 4, 327–8.   [51] Ibid., vol. 4, 348, 345.   [52] Flint, 'In Other Words', 650.
[53] Ibid., 658.
[54] Lotte Hellinga, 'Printing', in Hellinga and J.B. Trapp (eds.), *The Cambridge History of the Book in Britain, Vol. 3: 1400–1557* (Cambridge University Press, 1999), 76.

As we have seen, manicules before Sterne are most often located in advertisements, errata or title pages, paratextual locations traditionally associated with the authority of the printer rather than the author.[55] For example, printers of later editions of *Tristram Shandy* used a manicule to alert the bookbinder to his responsibility regarding the marbled page: '☞ The BOOKBINDER is desired to cover both sides of this leaf with the best marbled paper, taking care to keep the folio lines clear, and to preserve the proper margins.'[56] As Sherman suggests, the manicule is most often a secondary addition to the text, after it has left the hands of the author. However, in *Tristram Shandy* Sterne does not use the manicule as a marginal marker but invariably inserts it in the text within the line of type. This is perhaps an attempt to prove the author's control over all spheres of textual production, in that we may assume that such manicules have been produced simultaneously with the text and represent an intrinsic device of their repertoire. Whereas Richardson employs the manicule as a traditionally paratextual device, restricting it to the margin of one letter (a lengthy but ultimately isolated section of his novel), Sterne embeds the device as a feature of his creative practice. In employing it in the line of type, a domain traditionally associated with authorial control, he blurs the boundaries between author and printer, text and paratext, claiming power over the tools of the typesetter.

Sterne's mid-line use of an unstable print device – one difficult to ascribe to either author or printer – becomes doubly unstable in the case of Yorick's sermon. Lupton has noted that during the eighteenth century, sermons more than any other text are positioned on the boundary between the handwritten and the printed, with handwriting wearing the 'appearance of authenticity against the backdrop of print'.[57] Identifying a parson's

---

[55] The device appears in John Ozell's 1734–35 translation of *The Adventures of Telemachus*, where he points an accusatory manicule to the worst errors of a previous translator in a hypercritical paratext, 'Errors and Omissions in Mr. Boyer's TELEMACHUS, last Edition'. François de Salignac de La Mothe-Fénelon, *The Adventures of Telemachus, the Son of Ulysses*, John Ozell (ed.), 2 vols. (London: Innys, 1734–35), vol. 1, [n.p.].

[56] Sterne, *Tristram Shandy*, in *The Works of Laurence Sterne*, 7 vols. (London: Printed for the Proprietors, 1783), vol. 1, 269–70; Sterne, *Tristram Shandy*, in *The Works of Laurence Sterne*, 8 vols. (London: Printed for the Proprietors, 1790), vol. 1, 327–8; Sterne, *Tristram Shandy*, in *The Works of Laurence Sterne*, 8 vols. (London: Mozley, 1795), vol. 1, 266; Sterne, *Tristram Shandy*, in *The Works of Laurence Sterne*, 8 vols. (Edinburgh: Turnbull, 1803), vol. 1, 267–8. This paratext does not appear in the first edition, in which the marbled page was created by folding the margins of the page and dipping it in marbled ink. The marbled page is, of course, another example of Sterne's desire for idiosyncrasy: due to the method of hand-marbling, each copy of the first edition is unique. See Chapter 4, on the marbled page.

[57] Lupton, 'Creating the Writer', 178.

sermon with his own handwriting counted as evidence that he had composed it himself at a time when many parsons were known to have their sermons ghostwritten.[58] We learn from Tristram that Yorick annotates the margins of his sermons by hand, inscribing them with evaluative statements pointing out the strengths and weaknesses of his composition. In accordance with contemporary convention, Sterne represents this script with an italic typeface, mimicking a cursive hand:[59]

> ——*For this sermon I shall be hanged,—for I have stolen the greatest part of it.* *Doctor* Paidagunes *found me out.* ☞ *Set a thief to catch a thief.*——
> (6.11.48)

Yorick admits in his annotation that he has plagiarised most of his sermon, citing the proverb, '*Set a thief to catch a thief*', implying that only a plagiarist can know a plagiarist. The manicule, in its challenging gesture, literally points the finger, but to whom? The culprit is difficult to identify due to Yorick's use of a recycled expression which implicates both accused and accuser in the act of plagiarism. Moreover, who is responsible for this manicule: Yorick, Tristram or Sterne? In a printed text it is often difficult to attribute the manicule device to any one authority. The manicule's position mid-line, amid a paragraph set in italics to mimic Yorick's handwriting, might tempt us to believe that it was also handwritten by Yorick.

Within the same chapter, however, we soon witness a meddling instance of textual mediation, in a passage which takes the problem of identifying authorial property after print as its subject. Here, the manicule highlights an episode which reminds us of the (mis)representational power of the print medium. The piece of handwriting in question is described in meticulous detail.

> he had wrote——
>
> Bravo!
> ——Though not very offensively,——for it is at two inches, at least, and a half's distance from, and below the concluding line of the sermon, at the very extremity of the page, and in that right hand corner of it, which, you know, is generally covered with your thumb; [. . .] I am aware, that in publishing this, I do no service to *Yorick*'s character as a modest man;—but

---

[58] Sterne also ghostwrote sermons: Lupton, 'Creating the Writer', 172.
[59] For a discussion of the italic register and textual ownership with specific reference to the signature, see Goldberg, *Writing Matter*, 237–40. For Richardson's use of italics, see Joe Bray, '"Attending to the Minute": Richardson's Revisions of Italics in *Pamela*', in Bray, Miriam Handley and Anne C. Henry (eds.), *Ma(r)king the Text: The Presentation of Meaning on the Literary Page* (Aldershot: Ashgate, 2000), 105–19.

all men have their failings! and what lessens this still farther, and almost
wipes it away, is this; that the word was struck through sometime afterwards
(as appears from a different tint of the ink) with a line quite across it in this
manner, BRAVO——as if he had retracted, or was ashamed of the opinion
he had once entertained of it. (6.11.52–3)

Like the recurrent scenes showing Tristram writing his autobiography, this
description of Yorick's marginalia and the different representations of
'Bravo' provide an insight into the various stages of manuscript composition, depicting drafts both before and after Yorick's commentary was
crossed out. Sterne uses the commentary, written in a 'fair hand', as a
vehicle for discussing the print-manuscript interface, as shown in the
reference to 'publishing' and the pun on 'character'. Tristram's minute
description of the visual appearance of Yorick's manuscript commentary
reveals Sterne's play with the politics of typographic representation and
reminds us of his very particular requests regarding his printed page in his
letter to Caesar Ward. In line with Sterne's fear that his text may be
disfigured through print, Tristram's publication of Yorick's sermon results
in several distortions of the handwritten text. Tristram's detailed account of
the manuscript contrasts strongly with the appearance of the actual printed
page. For example, he describes the location of the word 'Bravo!' as 'at the
very extremity of the page', in the 'right hand corner', whereas the *mise en
page* of the novel sets it squarely in the middle of the line. Here Tristram
deliberately misinterprets Yorick's handwritten text, perhaps for emphasis,
highlighting his editorial authority over Yorick's manuscript. Furthermore,
the first representation of 'Bravo!' (sentence case with an exclamation mark)
is radically different from the second 'BRAVO' (upper case strikethrough;
see Figure 1.2). Tristram removes the exclamation mark in the second
instance, perhaps because he believes that Yorick was 'ashamed of the
opinion he had once entertained of it'. In accordance with the attitudes
towards printing at mid-century exemplified by Smith's manual, Sterne
believes that the typographer should simply reproduce the punctuation of
the author's original manuscript. Therefore, by providing us with two
different typographic representations of the same word, Sterne casts
Tristram as an unruly compositor freely interpreting Yorick's final authorial
intentions. In amending Yorick's manuscript, Tristram unwittingly reveals
the extent to which such a minute change can completely alter the tone of a
text, reflecting what Sterne worries may happen to his own work when it
leaves his hands for those of the printer. The manicule here functions as an
ambiguous marker of authenticity, representing the difficulty of deciding to
whom the final printed product really belongs.

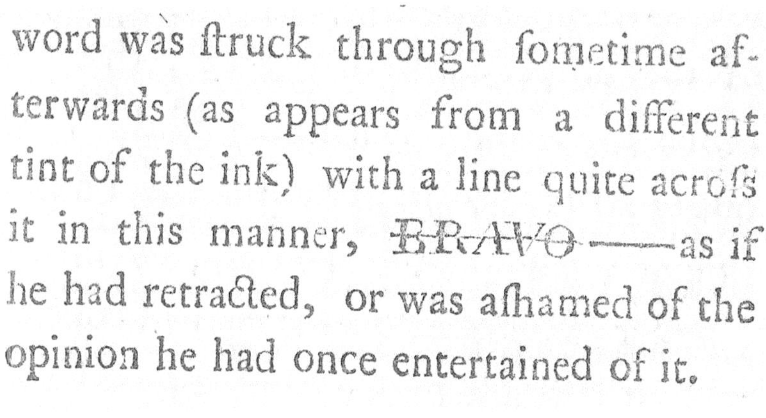

word was ftruck through fometime afterwards (as appears from a different tint of the ink) with a line quite acrofs it in this manner, ~~BRAVO~~ ——as if he had retracted, or was afhamed of the opinion he had once entertained of it.

Figure 1.2 'Handwritten' strikethrough '~~BRAVO~~' in *Tristram Shandy* (6.11.53). Image courtesy of Cambridge University Library

The manicule, in this instance, also heralds the appearance of a hitherto unnoticed experiment of Sterne's in representing the handwritten text. The first edition of *Tristram Shandy* includes a typographic oddity invisible in most modern editions: the second instance of '~~BRAVO~~' (the strikethrough version) appears to be handwritten (Figure 1.2).

The strikethrough slopes precariously downwards across shakily formed letters. However, we know that this 'handwritten' word is actually printed because it appears exactly the same in each copy of the first edition. It has been deliberately, and probably not without some difficulty, made to represent the handwritten. It seems impossible for '~~BRAVO~~' to have been formed by regular moveable type and overprinted with a long dash: the letters are packed too closely together for even a modified type (consider the serifs of the 'A' and 'V') and the line is unusually wobbly. It cannot have been copperplate technology, either, which leaves a tell-tale border impression, requires the use of a different kind of printing press and therefore, on a page like this which also includes text, would also require overprinting. This experimental device must have been created by a woodcut commissioned to fit within the leadings of the forme, so that it rests flush with the line of type.[60] This, of course, causes problems for subsequent editors; most modern editions represent '~~BRAVO~~' using

---

[60] My belief that the word was printed from a woodcut has grown out of discussion and correspondence with W.G. Day. Sterne playfully parodied the use of woodcut illustration in the novel elsewhere in *Tristram Shandy*: see Chapter 6 on engraved lines.

regular upper case type overruled with a straight line, but the editors of the Florida Edition motion towards the handwritten feel of the first edition ~~BRAVO~~ by using a pen-like, dipping strikethrough.[61] Unfortunately, there is no corresponding note in this edition to explain this visual effect, and no other modern edition tries to recreate the 'handwritten' letters.[62] With '~~BRAVO~~' Sterne refers to both the manuscript origins of the book and the process of printing. Woodcut technology, entailing hand-drawn designs transferred in mirror image to printing blocks before hand-engraving and printing, reproduces handwriting in a much more personal manner than could be effected using the Caslon typeface. Whose hand is represented here we do not know, but by extending a 'handwritten' element to the final printed product, Sterne pushes his claim for owner-ship – and his novelistic experimentation – to unprecedented lengths.

'~~BRAVO~~', perhaps the earliest instance of strikethrough in print history, is an innovation seemingly unnoticed by commentators, but it is not entirely unprecedented. Richardson anticipates Sterne's printed experimentation, this time in Clarissa's mad tenth paper, where fragments are skewed at diverse angles in order to imitate the twisted writing caused by her mental state. As W.G. Day has noted, many of the earlier novelist's visual devices seek to represent the handwritten.[63] Day has described the difficulty of setting up the forme in this way, almost certainly requiring the author's presence in the print shop to oversee the production of the desired effect.[64] But a closer link to Sterne's '~~BRAVO~~' can be drawn from Richardson's use of Grover's Scriptorial typeface to mimic Clarissa's signature at the end of one of her letters and of her will.[65] The typeface was commissioned for *Dawks's News Letter* (1696–1716), another text deliberately printed to imitate handwriting, in this case to remind the reader of handwritten journals that would appear during periods of print censorship.[66] Unfortunately, in the third edition of *Clarissa* Richardson omits the scriptorial typeface, which, as Keymer points out, suppresses

---

[61] Sterne, *The Life and Opinions of Tristram Shandy, Gentleman*, Joan New and Melvyn New (eds.), The Florida Edition of the Works of Laurence Sterne (Gainesville, FL: University Press of Florida, 1978), vol. 6, ch. 11, 516.

[62] Some early nineteenth-century editions use italics.

[63] W.G. Day, *From Fiction to the Novel* (London: Routledge, 1987), 92–4.

[64] Ibid., 97. See also the funeral processions in chapter 3.

[65] Richardson, *Clarissa*, vol. 7, 198; 309.

[66] Keymer, 'Jane Collier, Reader of Richardson, and the Fire Scene in *Clarissa*', in Albert J. Rivero (ed.), *New Essays on Samuel Richardson* (Basingstoke: Palgrave, 1996), 155. Grover's Scriptorial is not the only eighteenth-century typeface to imitate the handwritten. In 1796 John Trusler would print his *Twelve Sermons* in a typeface he created specifically to mimic handwriting. See Lupton, 'Creating the Writer', 167.

nostalgia in the earlier editions for the initial, controlled manuscript circulation of his work.[67]

Sterne's use of the manicule and his treatment of the handwritten reveal him to be particularly conversant with Richardson's innovations. But whereas Richardson experiments with handwriting to heighten the appearance of authenticity in his epistolary works, Sterne's innovations seek to inscribe a self-consciously printed product with the process of manuscript drafting, leaving a lasting appearance of the copy or holograph. There are also differences in terms of tools. Whereas Richardson employed a typeface, Sterne's innovation with representing the handwritten draws from a tradition of engraving manuscript. Examples of texts entirely engraved from handwriting include John Pine's luxurious edition of Horace (1733–37) and George Bickham's *Universal Penman* (1733–41), engraved from handwritten pages by eminent penmen. The latter text goes full circle, as not only do the engravings resemble manuscript but the penmen themselves also create scripts in imitation of contemporary print replicating blackletter, roman and italic typefaces.[68] Sterne draws on a basic and widespread use of italic to represent script, already developed by Richardson through his creative use of type in *Clarissa*, and takes it a step further. He considers tools from outside the typesetter's case, such as the engraving, creating in 'BRAVO' a word that is visually unique. Sterne's use of the strikethrough is undeniably innovative, and the shaky letters have yet to be re-represented in any subsequent edition. In Yorick's manuscript, or any manuscript, a crossed-out word would not strike the reader as unusual; writers have always scored through their work. Sterne couches this innovation in terms of appropriation (set a thief to catch a thief) while referring to the old technology of pen and ink. But in the process of transmitting the handwritten strikethrough word into printed artefact, the technique becomes surprising and original, exemplified by the fact that no strikethrough typeface existed until centuries later. In this sense, ~~BRAVO~~ is representative of many of Sterne's experiments. He hints that his experiments may not be wholly original and makes clear that any appropriations he does make may be as silent as Tristram's emendation of Yorick's text, and from sources as different from novels as sermons.

---

[67] Keymer, 'Jane Collier', 155.
[68] See, for example, the page designed by Peter Norman and engraved by Bickham: George Bickham, *The Universal Penman* (London: Printed for the author, 1733–1741), plate 20, 61. A later-century experimental text, *The End of Lusorium* (1798) openly imitates Sterne and is printed from engraved handwriting of a particularly irregular appearance. See René Bosch, *Labyrinth of Digressions* (Amsterdam: Rodopi, 2007), 275–9.

Through the extraordinary effort he takes to imprint his novel with signs of handwriting, he hints at some of the source material for his graphic pages: a manuscript culture which enabled literary property to be much more easily identified. 'BRAVO', in particular, functions as a hallmark of Sterne's authorship and his presence in the print shop, at which point subsequent editions, unable to recreate the complexities of the *mise en page* of the first edition, inevitably fail.

This analysis of hands, and specifically of the six printed manicules, in *Tristram Shandy* reveals the extent of Sterne's experimentation with the novel form during a period of change in which concepts of literary property and textual ownership become fraught with notions of authorial genius. Sterne explores those issues through the physicality of print, deploying typed manicules and a woodcut engraving to show the process of novelistic production as inherently dependent upon the technological representation and mediation of handwriting. Sterne's treatment of hands in *Tristram Shandy* provides just one case study of his practice as a visual novel writer, but in many ways it is exemplary. With the manicule and 'BRAVO' Sterne makes his mark as a unique fictional innovator engaging with historic book design practices, incorporating visual devices from existing and diverse written and printed genres into the novel, where they appear original. In their new context, Sterne uses manicules and images of handwriting to claim both the content and design of *Tristram Shandy* as his literary property alone, his invention. The range of print and manuscript source material considered here as inspiration for *Tristram Shandy*'s distinctive visual pages is only one step towards appreciating the scope of intertexts which feed into that novel's design. The rest of this book follows suit, exploring Sterne's graphic design of the eighteenth-century novel by placing his visual effects in their immediate book-historical contexts.

CHAPTER 2

The Black Page

In Chapter 1, we saw Sterne creating visually unique fiction hallmarked as his own through creative use of moveable type, a unique woodcut and his handwriting. Sterne's control over the appearance of his text and his concerns over the ownership of his copyright, symbolised in Chapter 1 by the print icon of the hand, appear again and again throughout this study. I have already identified some of the wide range of sources from which Sterne drew in creating *The Life and Opinions of Tristram Shandy, Gentleman* (1759–67): manuscript conventions, newspaper advertisements, Samuel Richardson's *Clarissa* (1747–48) and the copperplates of handwriting manuals. In this chapter, I interrogate the origins of his most recognised visual device, the black page, revealing its similarly eclectic pedigree. Positioning Sterne's iconic black page alongside age-old mourning iconography as well as emerging trends in typographic commemoration of real people and fictional characters, this chapter argues that Sterne simultaneously sought tradition and innovation when engaging with the trite print conventions of death. The result is the visual commemoration of a fictional character which is startlingly innovative while remaining well within the bounds of what Sterne's earliest readers would instantly have recognised as funereal iconography.

I Alas, Poor Yorick!

The death of Parson Yorick is one of the best remembered moments of *Tristram Shandy*, owing mainly to the visual markers of mourning that accompany Sterne's detailed description of the grave:

> He lies buried in a corner of his church-yard, in the parish of————, under a plain marble slabb, which his friend *Eugenius*, by leave of his executors, laid upon his grave, with no more than these three words of inscription serving both for his epitaph and elegy.
>
> | Alas, poor YORICK! | (1.12.71)

Sterne bordered the parson's epitaph with black leadings and offset the inscription from the rest of the text (Figure 2.1).

He printed Yorick's epitaph twice in *Tristram Shandy*, first as an illustration of the monumental inscription bound with black, and second – without the leadings – as that same inscription read aloud by passers-by. Sterne's first iteration of 'Alas, poor YORICK!' is printed to resemble a physical inscription through white space and centralised text while also illustrating the tombstone or grave through its surrounding black border. In addition to this typographic artistry, Sterne made directions for an entire leaf of *Tristram Shandy* to be printed on each side with a solid rectangular wood block (Figure 2.2).

By producing this image with a plain wooden printing block, Sterne refers to the basic tools of the book trade. The margins of the black page correspond exactly in size with the margins on the text-filled pages while the moveable type is replaced with a woodcut. He retains the page number in its usual place in the top margin in order to mimic the format of the rest of the pages in the novel. With the plain black rectangular shape Sterne encourages the reader to consider the blackness of the ink, the typesetting of the page, and the novel as a physical object. This device, the 'black page', soon came to epitomise Sterne's innovative approach to the novel form.

The black page has long been cited as the pre-eminent symbol of Sterne's literary experimentation. The narrator of Charles Jenner's 1770 novel, *The Placid Man; or, Memoirs of Sir Charles Beville*, records laughing at the black page, calling Sterne an 'inimitable ... eccentric genius'.[1] Joseph Hunter, an apprentice in a Sheffield warehouse, wrote in his journal for 1798 that, despite 'the fashion to cry down Sterne as the greatest plagarist [sic]', one of his favourite parts of *Tristram Shandy* was 'Yorick's death'.[2] By the end of the century, readers were indeed pondering the origins of this seemingly innovative device. In 1791, John Ferriar raised concerns which would escalate in their severity about the potentially plagiarised status of the black page and many of Sterne's passages. He noted that 'every one knows the black pages in Tristram Shandy', before going on to argue that the seemingly original device had been inspired by the black woodcut in Robert Fludd's *Utriusque cosmi maioris scilicet et*

---

[1] Charles Jenner, *The Placid Man; or, Memoirs of Sir Charles Beville* (London: Wilkie, 1770), 1:75.
[2] Joseph Hunter, *Journal*, British Library, Add. MSS 24, 879.

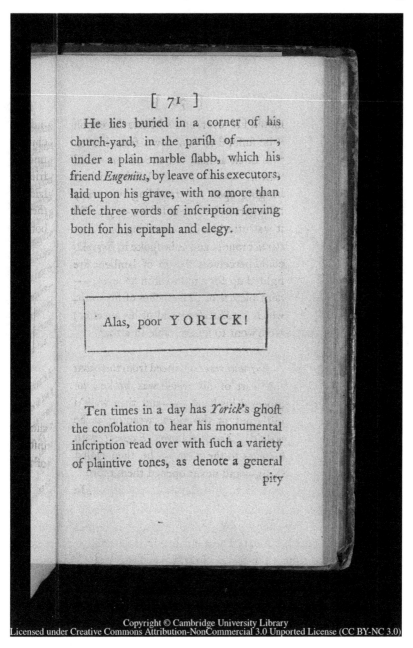

Figure 2.1   Yorick's epitaph with mourning borders (1759). Image courtesy of
Cambridge University Library

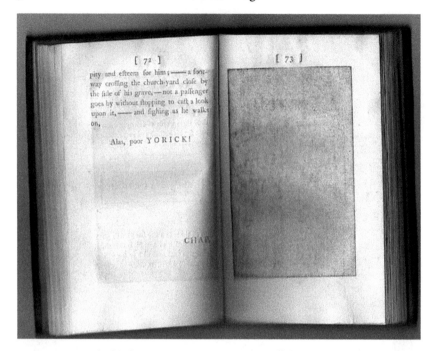

Figure 2.2   The black page (1759). Image courtesy of The Laurence Sterne Trust

minoris metaphysica, physica atque technica historia (1617).[3] Sterne's earliest biographer, Percy Hetherington Fitzgerald, revisited potential sources for Sterne's visual commemoration of Yorick and agreed with Ferriar in 1864 that Sterne's sources were probably esoteric seventeenth-century publications.[4]

While Richard Terry has investigated the plagiarism accusation against Sterne more broadly and Melvyn New's Florida Edition of the novel glosses the sources of the many textual echoes in *Tristram Shandy*, little scholarly attention has been paid to the origins of Sterne's visual commemoration of Yorick.[5] Alexis Tadié, in line with Ferriar and Fitzgerald, suggests in a footnote that Sterne may have been aware of innovative

[3] John Ferriar, 'Comments on Sterne', *Memoirs of the Literary and Philosophical Society of Manchester*, 4 (1793), part 1, 77. Ferriar's use of the plural term 'pages' correctly identifies the device as being double-sided.
[4] Percy Hetherington Fitzgerald, *The Life of Laurence Sterne* (London: Chapman, 1864), vol. 2, 419.
[5] Richard Terry, *The Plagiarism Allegation in English Literature from Butler to Sterne* (Basingstoke: Palgrave, 2010).

typesetting in seventeenth-century mourning publications, but scholars rarely compare the black page and Yorick's epitaph to publications contemporary with Sterne's.[6] One exception is Martha F. Bowden, who recognises that Sterne may have drawn from longstanding iconographic traditions of commemoration still in practice at the time he was writing *Tristram Shandy*. She calls the black page 'an intensification of the black border that often framed the title-page of funeral sermons', though the page itself could also be seen as the negative image of a bordered page.[7] Scholars have also been slow to align Sterne's treatment of death and commemoration with that of his fellow novelists. Thomas Keymer's study, *Sterne, the Moderns and the Novel* (2002), rectifies this gap in the scholarship by situating *Tristram Shandy* firmly in Sterne's immediate literary context, and in the process aligning the black page with the textual conventions of mourning evident in the anonymous *Ephraim Tristram Bates* and William Toldervy's *Two Orphans* (both 1756).[8]

This chapter considers Sterne's engagement with both contemporary literature and the traditional print culture of his profession as parson. Drawing together and developing suggestions by Tadié, Bowden and Keymer, I begin by considering the conventions and innovations of mourning iconography from 1612 to the mid-eighteenth century before exploring typographic epitaphs in novels from Richardson to Sterne. I demonstrate that Sterne's innovation in commemorating death lies in his deployment of a contemporary typesetting trend while simultaneously referencing a longstanding tradition of funereal iconography. Sterne dealt with the difficulties of innovation when representing death and grief by innovatively employing the tools of a stale and clichéd tradition of commemorative writing. He engaged with both contemporary and traditional forms of commemoration, proving that, even when creating something truly innovative, it remains impossible to escape convention entirely.

II Experiments and Conventions

By the 1750s, the golden age of funereal iconography had long since passed. Mourning literature was decorated with old and tired memento

---

[6] Alexis Tadié, *Sterne's Whimsical Theatres of Language: Orality, Gesture, Literacy*, Studies in Early Modern English Literature (Aldershot: Ashgate, 2003), 134, n. 28.
[7] Martha F. Bowden, *Yorick's Congregation: The Church of England in the Time of Laurence Sterne* (Cranbury, NJ: Associated University Presses, 2007), 145. I am grateful to one of the anonymous readers of this book manuscript for the latter suggestion.
[8] Thomas Keymer, *Sterne, the Moderns, and the Novel* (Oxford University Press, 2002), 69.

mori images and leadings. The fashion of mourning literature had reached
its peak in the early seventeenth century, when whole books, sermons, and
commemorative anthologies were printed with ever more elaborate
memento mori designs, reminding readers of their mortality so that they
might more effectively prepare for the Christian afterlife.[9] In 1612, the
death of the eighteen-year-old Henry, Prince of Wales, sparked a flood of
such publications. As prospective heir to his father's throne, his death by
typhoid fever caused widespread public mourning and inspired numerous
commemorative works. This tragedy caused a commemorative publishing
phenomenon unparalleled in its creative combination of ink and paper,
with printers attempting to distinguish their works from the mass of
available material through innovative and extravagant visuals.

Some such experiments share startling similarities with Sterne's black
page. Joshua Sylvester printed the title page of his *Lachrimæ Lachrimarvm*
(1612) entirely black, from edge to edge, with the text left white, as did
Cyril Tourneur, John Webster and Thomas Heywood in their *Three
Elegies on the Most Lamented Death of Prince Henrie* (1613). Using
woodcuts, these authors produced expanses of black ink resembling modern photographic negatives. John Taylor's *Great Britaine, All in Blacke*
(1612) bears similarities to Sylvester's text, with a title page depicting a
marble tomb and obelisks along with an inscription that symbolically
identifies the deceased through the letters 'H P' and three feathers marking
him as Prince of Wales. The pamphlet pages are printed with solid
rectangular blocks of black ink, each surmounted by a black arc. Despite
the absence of any evidence that Sterne saw these works, the resemblance
of some of their designs to the black page is striking. Yorick's black page, as
well as some of the black expanses visible in *Great Britaine, All in Blacke*,
have either been printed using blank blocks or with the reverse of ones
already engraved. With the blackness of the black page, then, Sterne
references the production process of traditional funereal iconography while
also referencing the reuse of woodcut technology in the popular press.
Sylvester's *Lachrimæ Lachrimarvm* perhaps holds the closest resemblance
to Sterne's black page, with his black rectangular woodcuts anticipating
those Sterne used for the black page in *Tristram Shandy* (Figure 2.3).
Sylvester printed the versos of this text with an emblem denoting the
Prince of Wales and the rectos with a white textbox framed with skulls,
skeletons and mummies. Sterne's fine black leadings framing Yorick's
epitaph echo Sylvester's bordering of the Prince's epitaph with thicker

---

[9] Such anthologies were sometimes presented in mourning wrappers. Scott L. Newstok, *Quoting
Death in Early Modern England: The Poetics of Epitaphs beyond the Tomb* (Basingstoke: Palgrave,
2009), 83.

rectangular blocks and skeleton ornaments. Compared with the woodcut images of Sterne's black page, images in commemorative pamphlets from 1612–13 are much darker, and lack the fine border of Sterne's lighter ink blocks. They also differ in that the seventeenth-century plates are uniformly black, while Yorick's black rectangle is darker along the edges. This intensification of blackness was probably produced through an uneven distribution of pressure in the printing press, with pressure naturally increased on the edges of the block; the solid colour of the seventeenth-century pages may have been produced by strategically packing the area over the image, behind the tympan, with extra packing sheets. The effect of the black page's fine, solid, darker edge is to call to mind the mourning borders of funeral publications while also referring us back to the leadings surrounding Yorick's epitaph, which also have their roots in that inky, earlier tradition.

The typographic extravagance of the commemorative publications for Prince Henry's death in 1612 may have been unmatched in the eighteenth century, but the deaths of royalty and nobility continued to test the ingenuity of printers in their attempts to convey accurately to readers the spectacles of large state funerals through moveable type. For those unable to attend grand state occasions such as coronations and funerals, ceremonial pamphlets not only described in detail the identities of participants in the procession, but also creatively typeset their pages to enable readers to imagine its order. The Dublin-printed pamphlet for the coronation of George II and Queen Caroline on 11 October 1727 typographically represented the procession through Westminster Hall. The printer experimented with the forme to indicate the order and position of each member of the procession, which was led by

Six-Clerks in *Chancery*.
Chaplains.
Aldermen and Sheriffs of *London*.[10]

Type is centred on the pages of this ceremonial pamphlet, its form resembling a long poem in which each line is allocated to a different rank of people parading through Westminster Hall. Eventually, almost fifty pages later, the procession culminates in the King's arrival:[11]

---

[10] *The Ceremonial of the Coronation of His Most Sacred Majesty Kind George II and of His Royal Consort Queen Caroline* (Dublin: Powell, 1727), 6.

[11] Ibid., 54. Paul Goring's work on the coronation of George III interrogates rhetorical journalistic conventions for conveying and mediating spectatorship. 'Newspapers, Spectatorship and the Coronation of George III'. Paper presented at After New Historicism: A Seminar Series Organised by Northumbria's Long-Eighteenth-Century Research Group, Northumbria University, 5 April 2017.

Figure 2.3   Joshua Sylvester's *Lachrimæ Lachrimarvm* (1612). Image courtesy of
Cambridge University Library

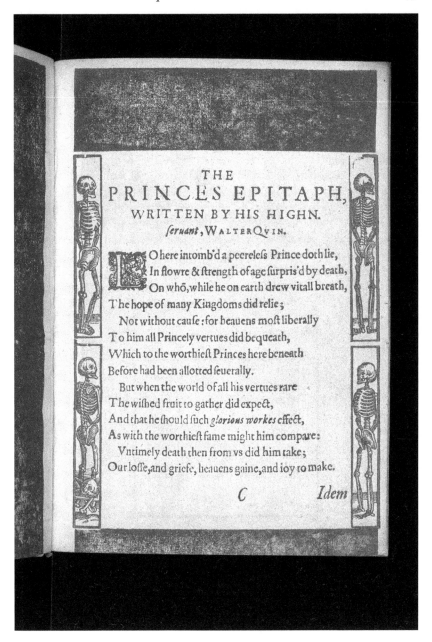

THE
PRINCES EPITAPH,
WRITTEN BY HIS HIGHN.
seruant, WALTER QVIN.

LO here intomb'd a peereless Prince doth lie,
In flowre & strength of age surpris'd by death,
On whō, while he on earth drew vitall breath,
The hope of many Kingdoms did relie;
   Not without cause: for heauens most liberally
To him all Princely vertues did bequeath,
Which to the worthiest Princes here beneath
Before had been allotted seuerally.
   But when the world of all his vertues rare
The wished fruit to gather did expect,
And that he should such *glorious workes* effect,
As with the worthiest fame might him compare:
   Vntimely death then from vs did him take;
Our losse, and griefe, heauens gaine, and ioy to make.

C   *Idem*

Figure 2.3 (*cont.*)

Gent. Pensioners.

The KING
In his Robes of Purple Velvet furr'd
with Ermin, the Crown of State
upon His Head, bearing the
Sceptre with the Cross in His
Right Hand, and the Orb in His
Left, supported and His Train
borne as before.

Gent. Pensioners.

Through typography, it is clear to see that the King was flanked by Gentlemen Pensioners, or the Honourable Corps of Gentlemen at Arms, who were professional bodyguards. When it came to major funerals, printers used similar techniques of typographic representation to indicate the order of processions but additionally used black leadings to indicate that the deceased was carried in a coffin. Whereas the description of the monarch in pamphlets of coronations described their dress (as in the King's 'Robes of Purple Velvet'), that of a deceased king or queen described the coffin: usually draped in a black velvet pall decorated with escutcheons, or coats of arms. Such was the case for the coffin of Queen Caroline in 1737:[12]

Lord Chamblerlain to the Queen.

Ten Gentlemen Pensioners, with their Axes revers'd.

The Canopy, borne by Gentlemen of the King's Privy Chamber.

Supporters of the Pall Dukes.

> The R O Y A L B O D Y,
> Carried by Ten or Twelve
> Yeoman of the Guard Covered
> with a large Pall of black
> Velvet, and lined with black
> Silk, with a fine Holland Sheet,
> adorned with Ten large
> Escutcheons painted on Sattin,
> under a Canopy of black
> Velvet.

Supporters of the Pall Dukes.

The Canopy, borne by Gentlemen of the King's Privy Chamber.

Ten Gentlemen Pensioners, with their Axes revers'd.

A Gentleman Usher
of the King's.

Garter Principal King of Arms.

Gentleman Usher of the black
Rod, the Rod to be revers'd.

Supporter to the
Chief Mourner a
Duke.

The Chief Mourner, supported by
Two Dukes, her Train borne by
Two Duchesses, assisted by the
Queen's Vice Chamberlain.

Supporter to the Chief
Mourner a Duke.

[12] *The Ceremonial Proceeding to a Private Interrment of Her Late Most Excellent Majesty Queen Caroline* (London: Stagg, 1737), 4.

The bodyguards of the 1727 pamphlet have been replaced in this one with a black box. The black leadings surrounding the description of the Queen's body not only draw the eye to her placement in the procession, the climax of the publication, but also symbolically represent the black box of her coffin. Nobility in the eighteenth century tended to be buried in sealed lead coffins, to help preserve their bodies. There is an inherent pun here, then, as the black box indicating the monarch's coffin is printed using moveable type also cast from lead. Black typographic boxes in pamphlets and newspaper articles literally impress upon the printed page the very material within which these monarchs are escorted to the grave. While many of the typographically inventive pages of ceremonial publications function as both text and illustration, those with mourning borders additionally play upon the capacity of print to memorialise and, literally, to preserve the dead. Printers of the *London Gazette* and the *Gentleman's Magazine* replicated the text of the official ceremonial pamphlet,[13] but they did not recreate the mourning borders around the queen's body. However, newspaper printers in the 1750s seemed to go further with iconographic typesetting, when black mourning borders were perhaps more widely available in compositors' type cases, as in the use of the black box device in representations of the coffins of Frederick, Prince of Wales in the *London Evening Post* of 1751 and Princess Caroline in *Lloyd's Evening Post* of 1758 (see Figure 2.4).[14] By the 1750s, then, typographic coffins were no longer confined to specialist pamphlets. Though black boxes would have interrupted the regularity of the eighteenth-century newspaper column, where they undoubtedly appeared novel, the fact that funereal typography had landed on the breakfast tables of readers across the nation meant that mourning iconography – and particularly mourning typography – was becoming mainstream.

The ceremonial typography of state funerals precedes Sterne's use of leadings to surround the phrase 'Alas, poor YORICK!' in *Tristram Shandy*. This context of court pomp plays into Yorick's intertextual origins as Hamlet's court jester which Sterne exploits in the novel to comic effect, but in paying respect to the humble parson Yorick through a typographic

---

[13] Queen Caroline's ceremonial was reprinted with creative typesetting but without black leadings in the *London Gazette* (20–4 December 1737) and the *Gentleman's Magazine* (vol. 7, December 1737, 765). For a full overview of Caroline's relatively private funeral, see Matthias Range, *British Royal Funerals: Music and Ceremonial since Elizabeth I* (Woodbridge: Boydell, 2016), esp. 155–61. The lavish funeral processions of Caroline, Lady Tyrconnel in 1730 and the Duke of Cumberland in 1787 were typographically represented as lists in newspapers of the time: *Daily Journal* (1 October 1730); *Fog's Weekly Journal* (3 October 1730); *World* (22 September 1790).
[14] *London Evening Post* (13–16 April 1751); *Lloyd's Evening Post* (4–6 January 1758).

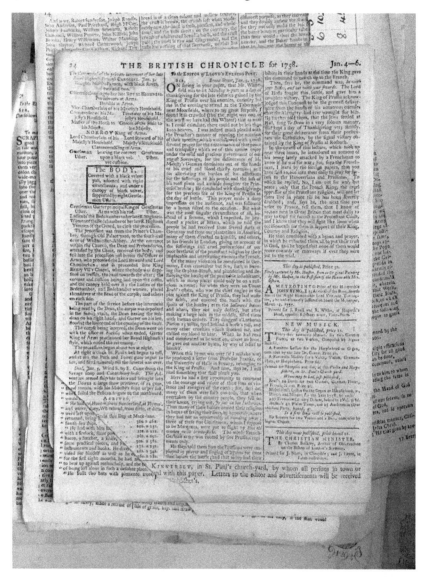

Figure 2.4 Princess Caroline's funeral as represented in *Lloyd's Evening Post* (1758).
Image courtesy of The Laurence Sterne Trust

device usually associated with the monarchy, Sterne also demonstrates how far readers were beginning to expect any printed description of a funeral to be accompanied by appropriate visual iconography. Readers familiar with the typographic coffin would expect the deceased's body to be inscribed (or described) within it, but Sterne's readers were presented with a quotation from *Hamlet*. What is preserved within the sealed lead box in *Tristram Shandy* is not Yorick's body but rather Literature with a capital 'L'. With this visual device Sterne indicates the capacity of print to perpetuate posthumous literary reputation by borrowing from ceremonials the performative act of impressing lead upon the novelistic page. The quotation within typographic leadings simultaneously indicates literary fame while encouraging readers to reflect on that very process of printed memorialisation. Sterne borrows from ceremonials and newspaper accounts of state funerals the typographic leadings which literally impress the printed page in a performative act of memento mori, reminding us of the flimsiness of human existence through the immortalising power of print.

Rather than becoming increasingly innovative, by the early eighteenth century the iconography of mourning in funeral literature had settled into a routine of unimaginative borrowings, and by mid-century more of this material was circulating than ever before. According to Ralph Houlbrooke, the 1750s and 1759 in particular, the year of Sterne's composition and publication of those volumes of *Tristram Shandy* in which Yorick is commemorated, witnessed the production of vast quantities of popular memento mori publications.[15] Many of these texts display thick, black mourning borders that frame the information on the title page, with some of those borders measuring seven millimetres wide. The most popular volumes of 1759 included William Sherlock's *A Practical Discourse Concerning Death* (1689), which Joseph Addison considered the most read book in English; it went through thirty-two editions by 1750 and eleven reprints in the 1750s alone. Elizabeth Singer Rowe's *Friendship in Death* (1728), was also popular in that decade, going through seven editions in the 1750s, and William Romaine's *Knowledge of Salvation Precious in the Hour of Death* (1759), a sermon published on the death of devotional writer James Hervey in January of that year, went through twelve London

---

[15] Ralph Houlbrooke, 'The Age of Decency: 1660–1760', in Peter C. Jupp and Clare Gittings (eds.), *Death in England: An Illustrated History* (Manchester University Press, 1999), 178–9.

editions alone before the year was out.[16] Every edition of Rowe and
Romaine's texts, and most of the London editions of Sherlock's, were
printed with mourning borders on their title pages. As the early seventeenth century marks the peak of experimental book design for the
commemoration of death, we can see that in the mid-eighteenth century
mourning literature remained extremely popular while continuing to
employ the same memento mori visuals, particularly the mourning
borders that Bowden sees Sterne exaggerating into the black page
woodcut. Houlbrooke calls this moment 'the age of the epitaph'.[17]

Bookseller T.N. Longman thought this moment fit to launch a new,
fifth edition of Josiah Woodward's *Fair Warnings to a Careless World, or,
the Serious Practice of Religion Recommended by the Admonitions of Dying
Men* (1707). From its initial appearance in 1707, the book had been
advertised as a text including 'suitable cuts', and in 1757 and 1758 notices
of the similarly visual fifth edition were a mainstay of the advertising pages
of major London newspapers.[18] Even those who had not read or purchased
a copy would have likely known about the existence of this text and its
visual accompaniments. Through the adjective 'suitable', the advert reveals
the bookseller's expectation that mid-century readers could accurately
imagine the kind of visuals that such a text might carry. The cuts referred
to *Fair Warnings'* copperplate illustrations of famous memento mori scenes
from history. The volume opens with the Earl of Rochester's death-bed
repentance as frontispiece and includes, for example, a full-page image of a
skeleton holding 'THE MIRROVR which Flatters not'.[19] Its marketable
properties comprise these images and the fact that it saved readers money
in associated funeral costs. On the title page, and in the appended
'Proposal for the Giving away at Funerals some Practical Books of
Divinity, instead of Rings and other the usual Presents', Woodward
encouraged readers to bulk buy his book (or other works of divinity)

[16] For a publication history of these items, see ibid., 179.
[17] Houlbrooke, *Death, Religion, and the Family in England, 1480–1750* (Oxford University Press, 2000), 357.
[18] See, for example, the *London Gazette*, 5–8 May 1707 and *Country Journal or The Craftsman*, 26 February 1737. Between 1757 and 1758, the fifth edition of the work appeared in many columns of classified advertisements, as in its announcement in the *Public Advertiser* of 16 December 1757; its constant presence in the *London Evening Post* 7–16 January 1758; and its appearance in the 6–8 April and 27–30 May issues of the *London Chronicle* of 1758.
[19] Josiah Woodward, *Fair Warnings to a Careless World, or, the Serious Practice of Religion Recommended by the Admonitions of Dying Men [...] To which is added, Serious Advice to a Sick Person by Archbishop Tillotson. As also, A Prospect of Death: A Pindarique Essay. With suitable cuts. Recommended as proper to be given at Funerals* (London: Aylmer, 1707). The Rochester image is usually the frontispiece and the skeleton precedes the Pindaric ode.

and distribute it at their funerals instead of the usual expensive souvenirs of mourning rings (dead investment, as Woodward saw them) and ill-fitting gloves.[20] Such gift books, Woodward argued, 'may be bound in Black with a Cypher of Mortality on the Cover',[21] and given away in remembrance of the deceased, complete with a personalised printed notice, for which the author provides some template text:

> In Remembrance of   the Daughter of   who Departed this Life the   of
> in the Year of our Lord   Being but   Years old. Interred in   Church.

> *Epitaph.*
> She's gone to Rest, just as She did Begin
> Sorrow to know, before she had known Sin;
> Death that doth Sin and Sorrow thus prevent,
> Is the next Blessing to a Life well spent.[22]

With this memento mori invitation to the reader to coproduce funeral text, Woodward's content and illustrations not only hammer home the prospect of impending death but also invite readers to complete their funeral arrangements on the printed page. Readers find themselves personalising this generic memorial text automatically, and cannot help but participate in the kind of future-planning that Woodward promotes. But his template text signifies that memorialisation is limited by convention; our names might differ, but the message remains the same.

This appetite for funerary publications at mid-century coincided with and contributed to a 'mania for graveyard literature',[23] accounting in part for the popularity of Thomas Gray's *Elegy Wrote in a Country Churchyard* (1751), which went through fourteen editions before 1759.[24] The *Elegy*'s half title page was printed with skulls within heavy black leadings, which the printer probably used in order to exploit the mid-century cult of mourning and the selling power of texts stamped with its iconography. Memento mori woodcut images and print ornaments were fashionable in mid-century literary works, where they were often divorced from their original contexts of grief and mourning. Such images decoratively (and arbitrarily) punctuated eighteenth-century novels, including Richardson's *Pamela* (1740) and John Cleland's *Memoirs of a Woman of Pleasure*

---

[20] Ibid., title page.   [21] Ibid., 227.   [22] Ibid., 232.
[23] Kelly McGuire, 'Mourning and Material Culture in Eliza Haywood's *The History of Miss Betsy Thoughtless*', *Eighteenth-Century Fiction*, 18 (2006), 284.
[24] Ibid., 281, n. 2.

(1748–49), ornamenting section breaks and filling white space between chapters.[25] In a 1754 issue of his magazine *The Connoisseur*, George Colman responded to a recent outburst of illustrated elegies printed to commemorate the death of Prime Minister Henry Pelham by criticising the use of woodcut images for the purpose of spinning out literary texts:

> They are encompassed with dismal black lines, and all the sable emblems of death …. These little embellishments were originally designed to please the eye of the reader, as we tempt children to learn their letters by disposing the alphabet into pictures. But in our modern compositions, they are not only ornamental but useful. An angel or a flowerpot, at the beginning and end of every chapter or section, enables the bookseller to spin out a novel, without plot or incident, to a great number of volumes; and by the help of these decorations properly disposed I have known a little piece swell into a duodecimo, which had scarce matter enough for a six-penny pamphlet.[26]

Colman prints this piece under the epigram '*O quanta species cerebrum non habet!* PHÆDR. A beauteous head, but oh! devoid of Brains',[27] implying that Grub Street productions set greater store by a work's appearance than by its content. As Colman complained, stock images such as urns and flowerpots were everywhere, not only because they made literary works appear longer but also because repurposing woodcut images was cheaper than commissioning fresh artwork. It was not just mourning publications that continued to use the same iconography as had been employed during the previous century, but novels too.[28] The comic potential of recycled images can be seen in early eighteenth-century broadside mock-elegies employing much-recycled memento mori designs, such as *Mr. P-----dg's Elegy on the Death of Mr. John Gadbury* (1704), which featured mourning borders, skulls, cross-bones and hourglasses; the heavily bordered *Elegy on the Lamented Death of Poor Truth and Honesty; Who Departed this Life, with the Renowned Paper Call'd the London-Post* (1705); and a similarly decorated punning elegy upon the death of Matthew Buckinger (1722), 'the famous little-man (without arms or legs)', sometimes attributed

---

[25] Such devices can be explored in Hazel Wilkinson's database, Compositor (formerly Fleuron), available at https://compositor.bham.ac.uk/, last accessed 5 June 2020.

[26] Mr. Town [George Colman], *The Connoisseur*, 8 (Thursday 21 March 1754) 45.   [27] Ibid., 43.

[28] Alexandra Franklin, 'The Art of Illustration in Bodleian Broadside Ballads before 1820', *Bodleian Library Record*, 17 (2002), 327–52; Hazel Wilkinson, 'Printers' Flowers as Evidence in the Identification of Unknown Printers: Two Examples From 1715', *The Library*, 14 (2013), 70–9; Janine Barchas, *Graphic Design, Print Culture, and the Eighteenth-Century Novel* (Cambridge University Press, 2003).

to Swift.[29] The printers of these mock-epitaphs and satiric elegies created humour and satire out of old leadings and memento mori designs in ways which anticipate Sterne's own experimentation in *Tristram Shandy*.

Sterne was an active participant in the print culture of his profession as parson, having published *The Case of Elijah and the Widow of Zerephath, Consider'd*, his *Abuses of Conscience* sermons in 1747 and 1750 and, later, *The Sermons of Mr. Yorick* in 1760 and 1766. The title of Sterne's collected sermons reminds us that his profession was also Yorick's, and Yorick, too, would have been aware of the literature of mourning. After all, Yorick composes Le Fever's funeral sermon, considers it his best work, and bequeaths it to the Shandy family for Tristram to edit and publish. Whether or not this sermon would feature mourning borders, Tristram never tells us, but Yorick (and Sterne) would certainly have been aware of the visual conventions by which Le Fever would be commemorated should the manuscript reach the printing house. Sterne would have been aware of the wealth of memento mori literature available in the years leading up to his publication of *Tristram Shandy*. After all, he had targeted the Dodsley brothers with his manuscript for these volumes, and the book-sellers' success with Gray's *Elegy* – replete with memento mori iconography on the half-title – and the wider cult of mourning in the book trade in this period may have coloured his innovative bordering of Yorick's epitaph and his use of the black page woodcut.

Unlike Robert Dodsley, however, who marketed Gray's *Elegy* with conventional funereal icons on the halftitle page where it could be seen by would-be purchasers, Sterne decorated pages 73 and 74 of *Tristram Shandy*, hiding his device as a surprise within the text, and using an image that self-consciously drew attention to the tools perpetuating those conventions. With the black page device, Sterne creatively hints at hackwork, or the kind of literary production that cannot afford new designs and uses available materials such as leadings and a blank printing block. Yet he also nods towards the ongoing debate over the visual appearance and production costs of the novel with his extravagant use of ink and paper. The black page represents the raw material of book design – the wood block on which designers would trace and then engrave their images – in a way that

---

[29] *An Elegy on the Lamented Death of Poor Truth and Honesty; Who Departed this Life, with the Renowned Paper Call'd the London-Post* (London, 1705), National Library of Scotland, Crawford. EB.346; *An Elegy on the Much Lamented Death of Matthew Buckinger, the Famous Little-Man (without Arms or Legs) who Departed this Life at Cork, Sept 28, 1722* (n.d.), Cambridge University Library, Hib.3.730.1.

shows how print conventions are simultaneously insufficient (in responding to death) and excessive (in their inkiness). With a black page that is in
one sense blank, Sterne hints at the difficulties of coming up with an
appropriate manner of commemorating a character at a moment when the
print market was saturated with memento mori iconography and
symbolism.

III   The Clichés of Commemoration

By the time Sterne was writing *Tristram Shandy* in 1759, commemorative
writing had long been predictable. In 1713, a century after the experiments
commemorating Henry, Prince of Wales, Addison mocked the ubiquity of
mourning iconography in the *Spectator*, in a letter responding to the death
of the fictional Sir Roger de Coverly. The correspondent specifically
demands that Addison use the requisite print conventions to commemorate his best-loved character:

> It is with inexpressible Sorrow that I hear of the Death of good Sir *Roger*,
> and do heartily condole with you upon so melancholy an Occasion. I think
> you ought to have blacken'd the Edges of a Paper which brought us so ill
> News, and to have had it stamped likewise in Black. It is expected of you
> that you should write his Epitaph, and, if possible, fill his Place in the Club
> with as worthy and diverting a Member.[30]

The letter argues that de Coverly deserves commemoration with the
traditional methods of marking death through print. Here, Addison pokes
fun in particular at the mourning borders and black woodcut stamps that
were 'expected' of the printer at such a pivotal moment. The letter-writer's
very specific requests regarding the writing of an epitaph, and a page
stamped in black, its edges printed with mourning borders, describe with
remarkable accuracy the very conventions Sterne would later use to commemorate the death of his own much-loved character Yorick.

Sterne was self-aware about commemoration in print. His concerns
about the insincerity of mourning iconography are most evident when
he addresses death and grief in his writing. When his friend Anne James
fell seriously ill in 1768 (but would recover, dying much later in 1798),
he wrote an epitaph for her that avoided contrived or 'labour'd'
imagery:

[30] Joseph Addison and Richard Steele, Letter to *The Spectator*, 518 (Friday 24 October 1713), 251.

Columns, and labour'd urns but vainly shew,
An idle scene of decorated woe.
The sweet companion, and the friend sincere,
Need no mechanic help to force the tear.[31]

In this epitaph, penned in the year that the final instalment of *Tristram Shandy* was published, Sterne disdains 'decorated woe', by which we may infer printed or engraved memento mori designs. Sterne's epitaph for his friend also reveals how far he invested in literature as a means of commemorating the dead, despite attempting in *Tristram Shandy* to distance his work from trite memento mori conventions.

Sterne provides both Walter and Tristram with literary opportunities to overcome these trite conventions. When grieving over the sudden death of his young son, Bobby, Walter finds some comfort in philosophy, which, as Tristram puts it, 'has a fine saying for every thing.—For *Death* it has an entire set' (5.3.27). Like Tristram with Yorick's epitaph, Walter romanticises the concept of mortality through invoking ruined tombs and monuments:

> '—*To die*, is the great debt and tribute due unto nature: tombs and monuments, which should perpetuate our memories, pay it themselves; and the proudest pyramid of them all, which wealth and science have erected, has lost its apex, and stands obtruncated in the traveller's horizon' (5.3.28).

The trope of literature outlasting monuments appeals to Walter, who, like Sterne, is particularly concerned with his posthumous reputation. Before long, through extensive philosophising, 'he had absolutely forgot my brother Bobby' (5.3.35). After recollecting the situation, however, his first thought is 'to sit down coolly, after the example of *Xenophon*, and write a TRISTRA-*pædia*, or system of education for me; collecting first for that purpose his own scattered thoughts, counsels, and notions; and binding them together, so as to form an INSTITUTE for the government of my childhood and adolescence' (5.16.70–1). While philosophy might have provided consolation in the immediate term, only book production can satisfy Walter over the next three years. Tristram takes on his father's work, completing the book by composing a chapter on sash windows, and then plans to publish it. Moreover, he certainly seems to have inherited his father's response to death, and resorts to the technology of the book to commemorate the generation of Shandys before him.

---

[31] Sterne, 'To Lydia Sterne' (9 April 1767), in *The Letters, Part 2, 1765–1768*, Melvyn New and Peter de Voogd (eds.), The Florida Edition of the Works of Laurence Sterne (Gainesville, FL: University Press of Florida, 2009), vol. 8, letter 204, 573. Unfortunately no manuscript exists for this letter.

After Yorick's early death and commemoration in the first 1759 instalment of the novel, Sterne's anxieties regarding the 'labour'd' imagery of death continue to surface in later volumes as Tristram realises he must eventually record the demise of the previous generation of Shandys. By the sixth volume, published in 1762, Tristram begins to imagine reaching that 'dreaded' point in his autobiography, the death of his uncle Toby:

> ——But what——what is this, to that future and dreaded page, where I look towards the velvet pall, decorated with the military ensigns of thy master—the first—the foremost of created beings;——where, I shall see thee, faithful servant! laying his sword and scabbard with a trembling hand across his coffin, and then returning pale as ashes to the door, to take his mourning horse by the bridle, to follow his hearse, as he directed thee;—— where—all my father's systems shall be baffled by his sorrows; and, in spite of his philosophy, I shall behold him, as he inspects the lackered plate, twice taking his spectacles from off his nose, to wipe away the dew which nature has shed upon them——When I see him cast in the rosemary with an air of disconsolation, which cries through my ears,——O Toby! in what corner of the world shall I seek thy fellow? (6.25.109)

This long, disconnected double question is symptomatic of Tristram's distress at the prospect of commemorating his uncle Toby. The 'velvet pall', 'rosemary' and 'lackered plate', which might elsewhere for Sterne prove inadequate to the task of commemoration (becoming what he might call the decorations of 'idle woe'), are here inflected with his distinctive sentimental tone. The detail with which Tristram anticipates describing the future scene evokes engravings of funeral parlours, such as *The Funeral*, Plate 6 of Hogarth's *A Harlot's Progress* (1732), and yet this is simultaneously a non-description. Sterne presents clichéd images – coffin, hearse, drapes – as components of an uncertain future narrative, a point at which Tristram might never and, in fact, does not, arrive due to his own failing health:

> '——Gracious powers! which erst have opened the lips of the dumb in his distress, and made the tongue of the stammerer speak plain——when I shall arrive at this dreaded page, deal not with me, then, with a stinted hand' (6.25.110).

Tristram appeals for inspiration to enable him to rise above the stale verbal and visual terminology of funereal discourse. Sterne suggests that assistance from the muses is most urgently required at the moments in which he is writing about death. Yet he seems to answer Tristram's plea in implying that the solution to the problem lies not in the wielding of the pen, but in the creative use of the page. In having Tristram look ahead to the 'dreaded page' (a phrase he repeats) upon which he must inscribe the details of

Toby's funeral, Sterne reminds us of the black page and his iconographic commemoration of Yorick, implying that the most lasting and most successful commemoration is bestowed not by the words nor images but by the page itself.[32]

Sterne suggests that an author's powers of inspiration were most on trial when writing about death. Despite *Tristram Shandy*'s references to the stale and clichéd conventions of commemorative works (including the 'coffin', 'ashes' and 'rosemary' of Toby's funeral, and the black inky woodcut commemorating Yorick), Sterne avoids such conventions as 'Here lies', 'ever to be lamented' and images of urns and scythes; Tristram, after all, undertakes a non-rendering of the funeral, and the woodcut for Yorick depicts no icon. Sterne uses the very tools of a tradition fraught with insincerity and unoriginality as a point of departure for his own iconographic contribution, showing his consciousness of the fact that print commemoration is often far from innovative. At the same time, he produces a leaf of remarkable, and now renowned, originality. Through the concurrent presence and absence of recognisable funereal signposts, the black page indicates to readers that the figure of the skull, the memento mori icon par excellence, lies beneath an unfathomable double-sided page of black ink.

IV   Typographic Epitaphs

With the black page and Yorick's epitaph, Sterne followed the woodcut images typical of seventeenth-century commemorative volumes with typographic epitaphs emerging in a corpus of mid-century novels, many of them comic. Novels such as Richardson's *Clarissa*, Henry Fielding's *Tom Jones* (1749), Thomas Amory's *Life of John Buncle* (1756), Tobias Smollett's *Peregrine Pickle* (1751) and Edward Kimber's *The Juvenile Adventures of David Ranger* (1757) typographically commemorate characters' deaths while calling attention to the conventions of commemorative engravings.[33]

Master printer Richardson established the trend for typographic epitaphs in *Clarissa*. Belford records seeing Clarissa's self-devised coffin

---

[32] Sterne highlights this fact in *A Sentimental Journey* (London: Becket, 1768), when Yorick meets a French officer and it reminds him of Toby: Yorick's travel journal is rescued 'from violation' by writing Captain Tobias Shandy's name on one of its pages: 1.179 in the first edition.

[33] Thomas Amory, *The Life of John Buncle, Esq* (London: Noon, 1756), 455–6, n. 1; Edward Kimber, *The Juvenile 55 Adventures of David Ranger, Esq*, 2 vols. (London: Stevens, 1757), vol. 1, 64–5; vol. 2, 267–78.

inscription, which Richardson offset from the rest of the text and centred on the page:

> The principle device, neatly etched on a plate of white metal, is a crowned serpent, with its tail in its mouth, forming a ring, the emblem of Eternity, and in the circle made by it is this inscription:
>
>
>
> *CLARISSA HARLOWE.*
>
> APRIL X.
>
> [Then the year]
>
> ÆTAT. XIX.
>
>
>
> For ornaments: At top, an hour-glass winged. At bottom, an urn.[34]

Richardson exploits his capacity as a printer to make moveable type signify inscription, through spacing and capitalisation of the text which Clarissa imagines – designs – as engraved. He presents this design within a series of letters from Belford to Lovelace, where simply the anticipation of viewing the 'devices and inscriptions' has Belford frightened.[35] Before viewing the design, Belford dreams of flying hourglasses, spades, mattocks, skulls ('deaths-heads') and 'Eternity'.[36] Lovelace upbraids him:

> But, faith, Jack, thou art such a tragi-comical mortal, with thy leaden aspirations at one time, and thy flying hour-glasses and dreaming terrors at another, that, as Prior says, *What serious is, thou turn'st to farce*; and it is impossible to keep within the bounds of decorum or gravity, when one reads what thou writest.[37]

Richardson's description of Belford being terrified by the memento mori imagery turns what had been apparently sincere concerns about mortality into subtle comedy. The reader is encouraged to laugh at Belford as Richardson subverts the melancholic tone of his letter with Lovelace's sneering response. Like Sterne, Richardson undercuts a potentially hackneyed scene with dark humour.

Through the exchange between Lovelace and Belford, Richardson, like Sterne, reflects in his novel the ubiquity of memento mori iconography in this period. Richardson hints that some icons are more common than others. He spells out to the reader that a circular crowned serpent represents eternity, but the relative brevity with which he describes the hourglass and urn ('For ornaments: At top, an hour-glass winged. At bottom, an urn') points to their widespread use by mid-century. Unlike the anxious

---

[34] Samuel Richardson, *Clarissa*, 7 vols. (London: Richardson, [1748]), Belford to Lovelace, letter 32, vol. 7, 130.

[35] Ibid., Belford to Lovelace, letter 31, vol. 7, 129.

[36] Ibid., Belford to Lovelace, letter 32, vol. 7, 129.

[37] Ibid., Lovelace to Belford, letter 34, vol. 7, 136.

Belford, Lovelace emerges as a reader upon whom memento mori iconography cannot take effect. For Lovelace, these symbols are simply 'flying' abstractions. Richardson thereby highlights the futility of memento mori iconography as a device to work on the attitude of a villain who has been little concerned with the Christian afterlife. The virtuous and innocent Clarissa, on the other hand, appears still to accept their effectiveness and to consider them appropriate decorations for her coffin plate. Unlike Sterne, Richardson's purpose is not to query the effectiveness of memento mori iconography and funereal inscription more generally. Rather, Lovelace's immunity to this iconography functions as yet another reminder of that character's distasteful inclination to laugh at Clarissa's impending fate.

In Belford's letter, the white page of the novel resembles the 'plate of white metal' upon which the iconography is 'neatly etched'. Just two years later, in the first edition of *Tom Jones*, Fielding takes Richardson's representation of inscription a step further, allocating Captain John Blifil's epitaph a page of its own:

> Here lies,
> In Expectation of a joyful Rising,
> The Body of
> Captain JOHN BLIFIL.
> LONDON
> had the Honour of his Birth,
> OXFORD
> of his Education.
> His Parts
> were an Honour to his Profession
> And to his Country:
> His Life to his Religion
> and human Nature.
> He was a dutiful Son,
> a tender Husband,
> an affectionate Father,
> a sincere Friend,
> a devout Christian,
> and a good Man.
> His inconsolable Widow
> hath erected this Stone,
> The Monument of
> His Virtues,
> and of Her Affection.[38]

---

[38] Henry Fielding, *The History of Tom Jones, A Foundling*, 4 vols. (London: Millar, 1749), vol. 1, 106.

Fielding makes the epitaph self-conscious of its status as a typographic representation of a monument to the dead by playing upon the epitaph's connection with both materiality and content ('*this* Stone, / The Monument of / [Blifil's] Virtues') and encouraging us to consider the novel, too, on both planes. The reader suddenly becomes aware of the novel not only as a narrative but also a physical codex subjected to authorial decisions concerning book design.

Fielding's epitaph for Blifil highlights the problem of maintaining epitaphic conventions when the deceased conducted a life little deserving of commemoration. This was an issue that had been under debate for some time, as Thomas Fuller had complained in 1642: 'In some monuments . . . the red veins in the marble may seem to blush at the falshoods [*sic*] written on it. He was a witty man that first taught a stone to speak, but he was a wicked man that taught it first to lie.'[39] In 1712 the *Spectator* also raised the issue of the difference between truth and fable in the construction of epitaphs, and Alexander Pope, like Fuller, invoked a pun on 'vein' in his oft-quoted epitaph for Elijah Fenton (1729): 'This modest stone, what few vain marbles can, / May truly say, Here lies an honest man.'[40] In 1756 Samuel Johnson cited this verse in his 'Dissertation on the Epitaphs written by Pope' to emphasise the need for epitaphic veracity. Johnson complained that the epitaphic form at this time was notorious for exaggerating the qualities of the deceased, or even outright fiction-making, while conceding that 'the poet is not to be blamed for the defects of his subject'.[41] Fielding's epitaph for Blifil in *Tom Jones*, described as 'an Epitaph in the true Stile',[42] satirises this ongoing concern about commemorative verse. Fielding puns on the 'here lies' convention, having the epitaph both identify the location of Blifil's body and counterfeit his qualities: 'a dutiful Son, | a tender Husband, | an affectionate Father, | a sincere Friend, | a devout Christian, | and a good Man'.[43] He suggests that a true or representative epitaph falsifies the merits of the deceased, rendering Blifil's epitaph a comic example of the inability of commemorative writing to escape its own conventions.

Like Richardson and Fielding, Smollett employed typography in *Peregrine Pickle* – typeface, layout, white space, page break, the centring of the text – to represent the gravestone of Commodore Trunnion:

[39] Thomas Fuller, *The Holy State* (Cambridge: 1642), 188–9 BL, Add. MSS 694.i.2.

[40] Addison and Steele, *Spectator*, 551 (Tuesday 2 December 1712), 442–52; [Samuel Johnson], 'A Dissertation on the Epitaphs written by Pope', *The Universal Visiter* [*sic*], *and Monthly Memorialist* (5 May 1756), 216.

[41] Ibid., 210.   [42] Fielding, *Tom Jones*, vol. 1, 100.   [43] Ibid., 106.

Here lies,
Foundered in a fathom and an half,
The Shell
Of
HAWSER TRUNNION, Esq;
Formerly commander of a squadron
In his Majesty's service,
Who broach'd to, at five P.M. Octr. X^r.
In the year of his age
Threescore and nineteen.

He kept his guns always loaded,
And his tackle ready manned,
And never shewed his poop to the enemy,
Except when he took her in tow;
But, his shot being expended,
His match burnt out,
And his upper works decayed,
He was sunk
By death's superior weight of metal.
Nevertheless,
He will be weighed again
At the Great Day,
His rigging refitted,
And his timbers repaired,
And, with one broad-side,
Make his adversary
Strike in his turn.[44]

As did Fielding in *Tom Jones*, Smollett had the inscription printed on a single page to signify the marble or stone surface,[45] manipulating page breaks and typesetting to print the epitaph on a single page of the novel. With these pages blurring the distinction between text and image, they marked the novel as a material medium rather like the gravestone depicted. But whereas Fielding's epitaph interrogates the tendency of epitaphs to speak well of the dead, Smollett's deals with an altogether different convention, focusing instead on Trunnion's unexceptional qualities in order to exploit an extended metaphor on the deceased's career in (and preoccupation with) the navy.

Epitaphs have long metaphorised their subjects and their occupations, but with the typographic placement of text, Smollett refers to a subgenre of

---

[44] Tobias Smollett, *The Adventures of Peregrine Pickle*, 4 vols. (London: Wilson, 1751), vol. 3, 50.
[45] See Chapter 4 for an analysis of the origins and meaning of Sterne's coloured leaf.

metaphorical epitaphs occasioned by the death of printers.[46] Most cast the deceased printer as a book happily stripped of its errata, to be resurrected in a new edition on judgement day. The most famous of this type is the self-composed epitaph of Benjamin Franklin, written in 1727, some decades before his actual death in 1790:

The Body
of
Benjamin Franklin, Printer
Like the Cover of an old Book
Its Contents worn out
And Stript of its Lettering + Gilding
Lies here food for the worms.
Yet the work shall not be lost
For it will (as he believed) appear once more
In a new + most beautiful Edition
Corrected + amended
By
The Author
Born June 6. 1706.[47]

Franklin's is representative of the genre of printer's epitaphs, figuring the codex as the perishable body and print as resurrection through the publication of a new edition. Representing his Christian faith in parentheses, Franklin shows his awareness of these epitaphs to favour creative metaphor over listing the piety or virtues of the deceased. Jacob Tonson's epitaph, printed in the *Gentleman's Magazine* in 1736, likens the deceased's gravestone to a paratext, calling it a 'marble index' indicating the location of his body, while invoking the discourse of Grub Street: 'And he who many a scribbling elf | Abridged, is now abridged himself.'[48] This line, aside from its appropriate use of line breaks to represent typographic alteration, is doubly comic in that the epitaph is itself 'paraphras'd',[49] with the parallel Latin text considerably shorter and therefore an abridgement of its English counterpart. Many similar printers' epitaphs appear in C.H. Timperley's *Dictionary of Printers and Printing* (1839), where occasionally the metaphor changes to a different sector of the book trade. The epitaph for Peter Gedge (1818), printer of the *Bury and Norwich Post*, compares the deceased to a font of type and God to a type-founder: 'Like a worn out

---

[46] C.H. Timperley, *A Dictionary of Printers and Printing* (London: Johnson, 1839).
[47] Benjamin Franklin, epistolary 'epitaph' (1727), published as figure 2.3 in Newstok, *Quoting Death*, 70.
[48] *Gentleman's Magazine*, Edward Cave (ed.), 6 (1736), 106.   [49] Ibid.

type, he is returned to the founder, in the hope of being recast in a better and more perfect mould.'[50] While entertaining, such printers' epitaphs betray a certain vanity about the trade in that they co-opt God into the deceased's occupation as printer or bookseller.

The printer's epitaph shares with the emerging novelistic epitaph a self-conscious emphasis on the materiality of the printed book. Perhaps the most self-aware novelist to employ typographic epitaphs in this period was William Toldervy. His expertise in the field of epitaphic inscription had been demonstrated by his publication of *Select Epitaphs* (1755), the first major English collection of funerary inscriptions, which preceded by eighteen months his novel, *The History of Two Orphans*.[51] Three of the four volumes of *Two Orphans* included at least one epitaph offset from the rest of the text, calling attention to the very material in which he specialised.[52] His own death notice, for example, reads: 'on Wednesday last died at his Lodgings in Cheapside aged 41, Mr. William Toldervy, the Editor of a Valuable collection of Epitaphs.'[53] One contributor to the *Critical Review* could not forget Toldervy's last editorial project while reading his novel:

> It is not long since Mr. *Toldervy* ... disobliged the World with a collection of old epitaphs, and inscriptions upon tomb-stones; this is a point of learning in which he is deeply skilled, as he has shewn in the *Orphans*; where, by way of novelty, we find many monumental inscriptions; together with several songs, lugged in without rhime or reason.[54]

This review offers a brief insight into a reader's response to a typographic epitaph. For all that Toldervy's novelistic epitaphs are much briefer than those by Fielding and Smollett, and share the page with blocks of text, the reviewer nonetheless recognises the novelty of such a device. Yet by mentioning Toldervy's editorial project in the same breath as *Two Orphans*, the reviewer subtly hints at the source of this seeming novelty on the page. For the reviewer, at least, this does not appear to detract from the novelty of the device appearing within the format of the novel despite the fact that Toldervy's incorporation of epitaphs lacks artistic finesse (they are 'lugged in'). A reader encountering the black page and Yorick's epitaph in *Tristram Shandy* would have had a similar experience reading *Two Orphans*: one of

[50] Timperley, *Dictionary of Printers*, 866.
[51] Keymer, 'William Toldervy and the Origins of Smart's *A Translation of the Psalms of David*', *Review of English Studies*, 54 (2003), 62.
[52] William Toldervy, *The History of Two Orphans*, 4 vols. (London: Owen, 1756), vol. 1, 6–8; vol. 2, 98; vol. 2, 201–3; vol. 3, 39.
[53] *Daily Advertiser* (5 January 1763), quoted in Keymer, 'William Toldervy', 60.
[54] *Critical Review*, 2 (1756) 342–3.

simultaneous surprise and recognition at the inclusion of print practices from a different genre within a volume of fictional prose. Sterne's experiments in *Tristram Shandy* were original within the novel while having an identifiable pedigree from elsewhere in contemporary publishing.

In evoking the materiality of the tombstone, Fielding and Smollett – and to a lesser extent Richardson and Toldervy – create self-reflexive pages. Through capitalised roman type and white space, these authors encourage their readers to view the book as a material object like the tombstone the page purports to depict. The deployment of the page as a commemorative monument, graven like the tomb, materially invokes the belief promoted in printers' epitaphs that literary works have one obvious advantage over tombs and monuments: their ability to be renewed with each subsequent printed edition. But Sterne and the mid-century novelists' employment of typographic epitaphs problematises such a straightforward formula for lasting fame by playing upon the flimsiness of the paper.[55] Each typographic epitaph paradoxically mimics physical monuments while simultaneously mimicking broadside elegies and other popular but ephemeral works. Printed epitaphs, as self-reflexive pages, encourage onlookers to consider their own mortality and that of the literary form in which these epitaphs are printed. Yorick's epitaph, therefore, has a clear pedigree, from Shakespearean allusion, to seventeenth- and eighteenth-century mourning borders, through to its *mise en page* reminiscent of other mid-century novels. As such, Sterne was able to reference historic literary and recent print innovations in commemoration before surpassing them with his double-sided black page.

V   Imitation and Innovation

The ambiguous and comic resemblance of the poor-quality visuals printed in ephemeral publications to Sterne's own visual page was recognised by George Stayley, an early Shandean imitator. He created his own exaggerated black page device in his work *The Life and Opinions of an Actor* (1762), consisting of six consecutive visual pages: two filled with black, rectangular woodcuts depicting the night sky and the other four featuring smaller woodcut images on an expanse of white space representing the sun rising and setting.[56] The black-printed pages in particular resemble

[55] Keymer argues that the marbled page is paradoxical in its evocation of material endurance by means of flimsy paper. *Sterne, the Moderns*, 79.
[56] George Stayley, *The Life and Opinions of an Actor*, 2 vols. (Dublin: Printed for the Author, 1762), vol. 1, 206–11, esp. 208–9.

Sterne's, but Stayley added to his own design a scattering of white stars and a moon. They differ from Sterne's device in being printed across a double-page spread, rather than on the front and reverse sides of one leaf. On one level, Stayley's pages showing night and day reflect the passing of time (his text at this point records the narrator's nap), but they also function on a satirical level. Stayley mocked Sterne's black page by claiming within the narrative that such devices were merely filler: 'This [. . .] is the new way of writing: A species of composition which will produce you a volume a day, and licence to sleep half the time.'[57] In other words, visual pages provided much-needed respite for exhausted authors and enabled them to fill pages – at a time when hack writers were known to be paid per page – without having to exert too much effort. Nevertheless, in exploring Sterne's innovations while also satirising them, and in redirecting the visual page's context of mourning to one of sleep, Stayley suggested that Sterne's black page assists the development of the narrative while being cost- and time-efficient.

A later imitator of *Tristram Shandy* focused on the typographic rather than the woodcut element of Sterne's commemoration of Parson Yorick's death, joining in the tradition of representing death through moveable type in the mid-century novel. While Stayley presented his work as an imitation of Sterne's, this anonymous admirer sought to pass off his volume as the next instalment of *Tristram Shandy*. The spurious ninth volume (1766) therefore aimed to imitate as closely as possible Sterne's idiosyncratic mode of expression, employing asterisks, dashes and unfinished sentences in order to present the text as authentic. To this list of typographic and stylistic characteristics of Shandean writing the author contributed a typographic epitaph as a quintessentially Sternean literary technique. In this volume, it is Corporal Trim who dies and is typographically commemorated:

> Here lyes
> The body of corporal Trim.
> His virtues are recorded in the immortal works of
> Tristram Shandy.
> His vices, if he had any,
> lye buried with him.
> Mr. Toby Shandy dedicates this monument to his Memory.
> 1730.[58]

[57] Ibid., 212.

[58] *The Life and Opinions of Tristram Shandy, Gentleman: Vol. IX* (London: Durham, 1766), 142. Two spurious ninth volumes were published in 1766. This is the anonymous volume; the other was written by John Carr.

This epitaph is a simplified version of Sterne's typographic commemoration of Yorick, without leadings or a self-reflexive page. It resembles more closely Richardson and Toldervy's epitaphs than those by Fielding and Smollett because it covers half a page, rather than using a whole page to evoke the gravestone. It shares with Smollett's epitaph for Trunnion the reference to printers' epitaphs through its claim that *Tristram Shandy* is immortal, though its proposed reverence for Sterne's text is undermined by the author's seeming ignorance of Tristram's proposed funereal scene in volume 6, which has Trim outlive Toby to rest his sword and scabbard on his master's coffin. Nevertheless, the imitator situates Sterne, as does this chapter, in a circle of contemporary authors producing novels that seek to represent death and the complexities of commemoration through creative typesetting.

Sterne's offsetting of the epitaph 'Alas, poor YORICK!' follows the contemporary fashion in mid-century fiction for typesetting inscriptions as if they were graven in stone rather than printed on paper. His innovation in *Tristram Shandy* lies in his pushing the typographic epitaph's problematic textual/visual status to its limit through printing the epitaph with a black page, which, in its double-sidedness, becomes both text (epitaph, ink) and paratext (illustration, paper). Because the black page is identical on both recto and verso, Sterne emphasises more than any of his contemporaries the materiality of the novel medium. The black page might better be termed the 'black leaf', in that the term 'page' technically refers to the surface of the leaf, of which there are two. Unlike the gravestone pages in *Tom Jones* and *Peregrine Pickle*, typographic illusions quickly shattered with the turn of the page, Sterne's black page is three-dimensional, emphasising more than any other mid-century novel its material substance. While Fielding and Smollett simply remind the reader of the surface of the page with their seemingly engraved text, with the black page Sterne forces a reconsideration of the entire process of book production: writing, printing and binding. In making the black page reminiscent of the rest of the pages in the volume through identical margin width and page numbering, Sterne subverts the reader's expectations of what should appear within the margins of a page dealing with a beloved character's death. In keeping with his evasion of the clichés of commemorative discourse, as in his rhetorical non-treatment of Toby's death, the result is a symbolic lack of text or image; the page is devoid even of catchwords. With Yorick's epitaph, Sterne develops a typographic device (a speaking or narrating page) to a more abstract level of self-consciousness, taking earlier authors' experiments with typeface and layout and their use of a self-reflexive page to a level that – in his distinctive comic tone – questions the ability of ink and paper to sensitively represent death and mourning.

The novelistic epitaph as employed by Richardson, Fielding, Smollett and Toldervy, which has been hitherto underplayed and underexplored in relation to Sterne's print experiments, emerges here as a precursor to Yorick's commemoration.[59] Sterne accompanied this recent novelistic technique with the iconography of an easily recognisable memento mori tradition through the borders that frame Yorick's epitaph and the wood-cuts of the black page. Viewing the histories of these techniques in tandem – typographic placement with woodcut decoration – reveals the full context of Sterne's innovative tribute to Yorick. Through this combi-nation of old and new print traditions, he participated in a widespread cult of mourning at mid-century while commenting on the formulaic staleness of its associated iconography.

Together, the black page and Yorick's epitaph interrogate iconographic traditions such as mourning borders, creative typesetting and black memento mori woodcut images. Sterne's distinctive combination of avail-able print techniques provokes in the reader a sense of recognition while simultaneously generating surprise over his exploitation of the staid conven-tions of commemorative writing. They demonstrate Sterne's experimenta-tion with and departure from the prose works of his contemporaries while also revealing how far this experimentation was couched within a long tradition of funeral literature. In his renowned commemoration of Parson Yorick's death, often taken to epitomise his originality, Sterne shook up tired imagery, all the while reminding the reader of the clichés of commemora-tion. He satirised the staleness of print by stripping back the act of meaning-making to its most basic components (woodcut, ink, margins and page number) to create a profoundly experimental and arresting device. In thereby representing the creative act, he undertook at once to commemorate and to send into posterity the artist's work and its characters, while self-reflexively commenting on that very process of textual memorialisation. This process can only transcend cliché, and therefore have the capacity to be memorable, when it reworks existing traditions through the creative manip-ulation of widespread tools and techniques.

---

[59] Louis Lüthi posits Sterne's black page as the very first of many self-conscious pages in the novel form, implying a lack of precursors. Lüthi, *On the Self-Reflexive Page* (Amsterdam: Roma, 2010).

CHAPTER 3

The Sermon

Perhaps the most sustained example of Sterne's creative use of moveable type to produce a single visual effect is the sermon scene in *Tristram Shandy*. Responding to the first instalment of Sterne's novel, Horace Walpole thought the sermon was 'the best thing' in it,[1] and an anonymous correspondent of 1760 praised Yorick and Trim's reading of his sermon as the parts of the novel 'I was most pleased with myself'.[2] Readers lauded Sterne's incorporation of a religious text into the novel, partly because it seemed to be a didactic device, but also because it prompted reflections on literary form. In 1759 William Kenrick called Sterne 'masterly' in 'The address with which he has introduced an excellent moral sermon, into a work of this nature (by which expedient, it will probably be read by many who would peruse a sermon in no other form)'.[3] Poet Robert Buchanan argued that with the 'Abuses of Conscience' in *Tristram Shandy* Sterne reached those who would not usually read sermons, and left them keen to read more:

> Tristram Shandy gave a spread
> To Trim's sermon, that allured
> Mony a ane the same to read.
> Yea, and mony a ane wha never
> Read a sermon o'er before,
> By his Shandean method clever,
> Read it a' an' wish'd for more.[4]

[1] Horace Walpole, 'Extract from a letter to Sir David Dalrymple', 4 April 1760, in Alan B. Howes (ed.), *Laurence Sterne: The Critical Heritage* (London: Routledge, 1974), 55.

[2] 'Letter, 15 April 1760 supposedly from an (unidentified) acquaintance of Sterne to a friend, first published in *St James Chronicle* in April 1788 and reprinted here from the *European Magazine*, xxi (March 1792), 169–70', in Howes, *Critical Heritage*, 58.

[3] William Kenrick, 'Extract from William Kenrick's unsigned review in the *Monthly Review*, Appendix to xxi (July–December 1759), 561–71', in Howes, *Critical Heritage*, 47.

[4] Robert Buchanan, Preface, *Poems on Several Occasions* (Edinburgh: Moir, 1797), 6.

The responses of Kenrick and Buchanan might suggest that with the sermon scene Sterne had converted some of his less devout readers to sermon reading. But the way in which Sterne's texts were packaged in subsequent years shows that it was not the sermon proper which editors and booksellers perceived as being of lasting interest to readers. It was the version of the 'Abuses of Conscience' with interruptions from Shandean characters that continued to be reprinted after Sterne's death, in all editions of the *Beauties of Laurence Sterne* as well as in *Gleanings from the Works of Laurence Sterne: Comprising Tales, Humorous and Descriptive, Sermons, Letters &c.* (1796). 'Trim's sermon', as Buchanan pointedly notes, rather than Sterne's sermon, was the great success.

The sermon scene begins with Dr Slop turning up at Shandy Hall quicker than expected, which reminds Toby of Stevinus's celebrated sailing chariot, purported to be as fast as the wind. Toby sends Trim for a copy of Stevinus's works. When asked if he can find a sailing chariot in the book, Trim turns the book upside down and shakes it. Surprisingly, some 'thing' falls out: a text he instantly identifies as a sermon:

> taking hold of the two covers of the book, one in each hand, and letting the leaves fall down, as he bent the covers back, he gave the book a good sound shake.
>
> There is something fallen out, however, said *Trim*, an' please your Honour; but it is not a chariot, or any thing like one:—Pri'thee, Corporal, said my father, smiling, what is it then?—I think, answered *Trim*, stooping to take it up,—'tis more like a sermon,—for it begins, with a text of scripture, and the chapter and verse;—and then goes on, not as a chariot,—but like a sermon directly. (2.15.93–4)

Martha Bowden has commented that 'Trim's recognition of the genre of the piece is not surprising, as sermons then as now were formulaic and instantly recognizable'.[5] Nor is it surprising that Sterne's readers, then as now, instantly identified the text as a sermon, when it was not only described by Trim but also appeared in the text, printed in the pages of *Tristram Shandy*. The sermon scene relies on readers recognising the conventions Trim notices: the 'chapter and verse' (centred on the page in upper case type with roman and Arabic figures), 'a text of scripture' (in italics), and the first line ('like a sermon directly') (2.17.102) (Figure 3.1). Both of Sterne's surviving manuscript sermons

---

[5] Martha F. Bowden, *Yorick's Congregation: The Church of England in the Time of Laurence Sterne* (Cranbury, NJ: Associated University Presses, 2007), 104.

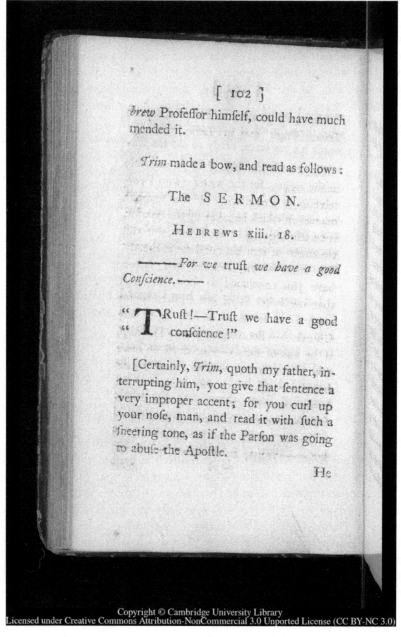

[102]

brew Profeſſor himſelf, could have much
mended it.

Trim made a bow, and read as follows :

The S E R M O N.

HEBREWS xiii. 18.

————*For we* truſt *we have a good*
Conſcience.————

" TRuſt !—Truſt we have a good
" conſcience !"

[Certainly, *Trim*, quoth my father, interrupting him, you give that ſentence a
very improper accent; for you curl up
your noſe, man, and read it with ſuch a
ſneering tone, as if the Parſon was going
to abuſe the Apoſtle.

He

Figure 3.1   'The Abuses of Conscience' in *Tristram Shandy* (1759). Image courtesy of
Cambridge University Library

are laid out in this way, with the first page beginning with the chapter and verse, and a text of scripture before the sermon proceeds immediately below. Using moveable type, Sterne creates an image in *Tristram Shandy* of a manuscript sermon which is in the process of being read aloud by Trim, incorporating the formal elements of that genre within his novel as a design feature.[6]

Like Trim, we recognise the 'Abuses of Conscience' in *Tristram Shandy* as a sermon, thanks to Sterne's careful deployment of typographic data. When Buchanan wrote that 'Tristram Shandy gave a spread' to the sermon, he indicated both rhetorical room and the space of the book: the sermon goes on to sprawl across several double-paged spreads in volume 2: forty-eight pages in total. Sterne frequently interrupts the sermon – by both puncturing the printed image of the sermon and disrupting Trim's oratory – to continue the conversation between the Shandean company. At those points, he introduces a print character from the visual conventions of play texts, so that readers can distinguish between sermon text and Shandean plot: square brackets. In drama, as they do here, square brackets codify and therefore clarify two different forms of discourse. In this textual image, the square brackets also divide the page into sermon and fiction. The manuscript status of the text read aloud by Trim also provides a context for interpreting the square brackets as markers enclosing material which an editor has inserted into a manuscript, which highlights Tristram's role as editor and curator of these pages. The constructedness of the sermon scene is inescapable.

This chapter begins by documenting square brackets in sermons known to have shaped Sterne's liturgical writing and exploring sermons in fiction before *Tristram Shandy*. It then compares the bracket-laden pages of the sermon in *Tristram Shandy* with similarly printed works of closet drama and dramatic fiction, generically ambiguous publications emerging at mid-century. Sterne relies on his readers recognising the typographic codes of sermons, drama and edited texts, and being able to apply them to his fiction. As in each instance of a printed manicule and in the surprising black page, with the sermon scene in *Tristram Shandy* Sterne pushes his readers to reflect on the printedness of the book. The sermon confronts readers with the mark-up and typographic packaging of their reading material, and more obviously than any of the other visual effects created in the novel, references the sermon as another print cultural genre

---

[6] See, for example, Sterne, 'Penancies', Pierpont Morgan, New York, MS MA 418; 'Temporal Advantages of Religion', Huntington Library, California, MS HM 2100.

informing Sterne's novel design. Throughout the 'Abuses of Conscience', Sterne makes us cognisant of his work's cross-generic heritage by forcing us to draw upon reading skills usually flexed in genres other than the novel, deciphering punctuation and page layout more often found in plays and scholarly editions while encouraging us to question the determinacy of the printed word and the status of manuscripts in print.

I   Sermons in Print

Sermons rely on delivery for effect, and scholars have studied them for clues regarding their preachers' rhythm, pause and tone.[7] Madeleine Descargues-Grant notes that the 'performative' intention of Sterne's sermons is visible in rhetorical strategies such as his regular use of subjective inflections ('let us'; 'I beseech you') and his frequent use of imperative and exclamatory forms, which allow us in some way to analyse the immediacy of these texts as oral discourse.[8] Sermons are oral genres, Christopher Fanning notes, which require the print medium to 'convey the rhetorical impact of the preacher's presence'.[9] Print was a tool by which preachers could take care to indicate as closely as possible a sermon's intended delivery – which, in some cases, became prioritised over its content – in a movement responding to *An Essay on the Action Proper for the Pulpit* (1753), in which James Fordyce helped to establish affect as a priority in mid-century sermon delivery.[10] Preachers from Anglican, Puritan and Methodist traditions had long used punctuation in their written sermons to direct inflection and pause in delivery. James Downey describes (rounded, rather than square) parentheses – with commas – as forming part of Joseph Butler's endlessly qualifying prose, expressive of his thoughts which 'came thick and fast, clamouring for expression'.[11] Each of the works of Bishop Lancelot Andrewes, Roger Pooley argues, is 'a script for an oral performance'; Andrewes uses italics and punctuation – colons, semicolons and parentheses – as 'notation for

[7] Phyllis M. Jones and Nicholas R. Jones (eds.), Preface, *Salvation in New England: Selections from the Sermons of the First Preachers* (Austin, TX: University of Texas Press, 1977), n.p. [Google Books].
[8] Madeleine Descargues-Grant, 'Sterne's Dramatic Persuasion', in W.B. Gerard (ed.), *Divine Rhetoric: Essays on the Sermons of Laurence Sterne* (Newark, NJ: University of Delaware Press, 2010), 218.
[9] Christopher Fanning, 'On Sterne's Page: Spatial Layout, Spatial Form, and Social Spaces in *Tristram Shandy*', *Eighteenth-Century Fiction*, 10 (1998), 429–50, 434.
[10] Paul Goring, *The Rhetoric of Sensibility in Eighteenth-Century Culture* (Cambridge University Press, 2005), 53.
[11] James Downey, *The Eighteenth-Century Pulpit: A Study of the Sermons of Butler, Berkeley, Secker, Sterne, Whitefield and Wesley* (Oxford: Clarendon, 1969), 41.

the spoken voice'.[12] Phyllis M. Jones and Nicholas R. Jones demonstrate that early Puritan preachers in New England used 'rapid and unsystematic punctuation, probably based on the speech rhythms of the preacher's voice rather than on syntactical considerations (except when the two coincided)'.[13]

Much of the scholarship on brackets as typography focuses on parentheses rather than square brackets or 'crooks', as Sterne called them. Parentheses work, as John Lennard has shown, as a literary rhetorical device to facilitate digression.[14] They were also used by eighteenth-century authors to aid expression, where, as Anne Toner has argued, 'They mark a departure from words that in some way is performed or can be understood as performable'.[15] Both of these functions can be said to be undertaken by square brackets, too, and they will be familiar to twenty-first-century readers. Square brackets can be digressive by enclosing extra-textual information, as in a textual editor's interventions, and can indicate performance through distinguishing descriptive action from speech, as in play scripts. But they are distinct from parentheses in that they mark a harder boundary between text and bracketed content, one which enables a text to be read in two ways simultaneously: both with and without the bracketed passage. They also differ from parentheses in that they indicate a change in voice or origin. In play scripts, we interpret the material within square brackets as to be read silently, whereas the dialogue that surrounds it is to be imagined as spoken aloud. In edited texts, square-bracketed content usually indicates material generated by an editor rather than an author. It is usually text which is intended to be read and interpreted as different from, or extraneous to, its surrounding content.

But this is not the case in sermons. In sermons by authors Sterne is known to have consulted, square brackets are used to highlight and make more visible to the reader a specific printed word and its apparently fixed meaning. The presence of square brackets within a sermon would not itself have raised the eyebrows of Sterne's earliest readers, who would have been familiar with the conventions of printed sermons, though their frequency

[12] Roger Pooley, *English Prose of the Seventeenth Century, 1590–1700* (London: Routledge, 2014), 106.

[13] Jones and Jones, *Salvation in New England*.

[14] John Lennard, *But I Digress: The Exploitation of Parentheses in English Printed Verse* (Oxford: Clarendon, 1991).

[15] Anne Toner, *Ellipsis in English Literature: Signs of Omission* (Cambridge University Press, 2015), 7.

and use in the context of *Tristram Shandy* would have been, no doubt, surprising.[16] And though they are the authors from whom Sterne most often borrowed, William Wollaston, Samuel Clarke, Joseph Hall and John Tillotson were not alone in using square brackets to fine-tune meaning in their sermons. Clarke and Wollaston are the only two theologians cited by Sterne in his sermons. Melvyn New has identified that Sterne borrows passages from Wollaston in eight of his sermons. Wollaston tends to use italics for emphasis, but some words are further highlighted through square brackets, as in the following: '*By the general idea of good and evil the one* [pleasure] *is in it self desirable, the other* [pain] *to be avoided.*'[17] Wollaston's brackets fix meaning. They make very clear what he means by the terms 'one' (pleasure) and the 'other' (pain) while also flagging those words, 'pleasure' and 'pain', as representing concepts which he will go on to systematically interrogate in a bid to ascertain the correlation between happiness and truth. The capacity of square brackets to frame words was also recognised by Samuel Clarke, who used them in *A Discourse Concerning the Being and Attributes of God* (1705) to highlight 'the Word, [God]' as representing 'the Idea of God including Self-Existence'.[18] In *Contemplations on the History of the New Testament* (1614), passages from which Sterne quoted verbatim in *The Case of Hezekiah and the Messengers* (1763), Joseph Hall closely interrogates the meaning of words and how they should be delivered: 'Neither is this [*If*] a note of doubt', he writes, 'but of assertion.'[19] Italics and square brackets work together here, as Hall ponders the 'note' of a word, and how it can have a different meaning depending upon its delivery. In these passages

---

[16] Publishing statistics seem to support the common statement that sermons were the most popular genre throughout the century. Jack Lynch has shown that 5.3 per cent of the 4,255 works catalogued in the English Short Title Catalogue as published in 1750 had titles identifying them as sermons, with only 3.4 per cent of titles indicating dramatic works, 2.9 per cent poetry, and 1.2 per cent novels or stories. Jack Lynch, 'Reading and Misreading the Genres of Sterne's Sermons', in *Divine Rhetoric*, 84.

[17] William Wollaston, 'Of Happiness', *The Religion of Nature Delineated*, 6th ed. (London: Knapton, 1738), 35. I have selected this edition as the one most likely to have been consulted by Sterne, given its place in the library catalogue (p. 26, item 640). On the (un)reliability of the catalogue as a source indicating Sterne's reading see *The Life and Opinions of Tristram Shandy, Gentleman: The Notes*, Melvyn New, Richard A. Davies and W.G. Day (eds.), The Florida Edition of the Works of Laurence Sterne (Gainesville, FL: University Press of Florida, 1984), vol. 3.

[18] Samuel Clarke, *A Demonstration of the Being and Attributes of God, the Obligations of Natural Religion*, 2nd ed. (London: Knapton, 1706), 31, n. 1, 97. This edition appears in the auction catalogue.

[19] New, Introduction, *Sermons*, 11. Joseph Hall, 'Zacheus', *Contemplations on the History of the New Testament*, William Dodd (ed.), 2 vols. (London: Davis, 1759), vol. 1, 215–35, 234.

deploying square brackets, Sterne's forebears examine and attempt to work against the ambiguity of the printed word, in a bid to render it fixed.

Because speakers have the power to radically change a text's meaning through gesture, movement and facial expression,[20] and readers to read against the grain, one sentence can therefore hold radically different meanings, and in sermons and religious writing this could be controversial or even blasphemous. Tillotson, whose works have been widely recognised as influencing Sterne's sermons and theology,[21] used punctuation to confront an instance of misreading. In the preface to his 1671 *Sermons*, Tillotson defended himself against a charge of misquoting William Rushworth, '*cogging in the word* [all], *making his Principle run thus*, that the greatest hopes and fears are applyed to the minds of [all] Christians'.[22] Tillotson uses square brackets in the first instance for emphasis (like Clarke), to typographically frame a word, and in the second as an editorial device, to demarcate an unwanted intervention in his original writings. Square brackets here (as in the works of Clarke, Hall and Wollaston) draw attention to the exact words of Tillotson's text and their intended meaning. More specifically, Tillotson was engaging in a much wider seventeenth-century argument around Scripture as a rule of faith which, as Marcus Walsh highlights, in 'very large part concerned itself, inevitably, with fundamental problems about the nature, determinacy, stability, and comprehensibility of the printed book'.[23] Sterne uses square brackets to explore the concerns of his Anglican forebears, using the markers in *Tristram Shandy* to interrupt his sermon and demonstrate in comic fashion how a text – despite its apparent fixity through print – can be interpreted in wildly different ways according to the hobby horses of its individual auditors. By using square brackets to interweave sermon with fiction, Sterne exemplifies some of the repurposing of religious text that can be undertaken when it is shared with readers through print.

Though his antecedents strove against it, Sterne took advantage of the indeterminacy of words in his sermons, where, as Downey has shown, he

---

[20] Marcus Walsh, 'Text, "Text", and Swift's *A Tale of a Tub*', *Modern Language Review*, 85 (1990), 290–303, 293.

[21] Lansing Van der Heyden Hammond, *Laurence Sterne's* Sermons of Mr. Yorick (New Haven, CT: Yale University Press, 1948); Arthur H. Cash, *Laurence Sterne: The Later Years* (London: Methuen, 1986); John Stedmond, *The Comic Art of Laurence Sterne* (University of Toronto Press, 1967), 141.

[22] John Tillotson, Preface, *Sermons Preach'd upon Several Occasions* (London: Gellibrand, 1671), n.p. Tillotson was here defending himself from charges by John Sergeant, in *Sure-Footing in Christianity* (London: 1665). For a full discussion of this debate see Henry G. Leeuwen, *The Problem of Certainty in English Thought 1630–1690* (London: Springer, 2013), 32–45.

[23] Walsh, 'Text', 290.

regularly played upon the emotions of his congregation by 'first offending their moral sensibilities by a seemingly blasphemous statement, then, by means of some adroit dialectical framework, eluding blame himself while leaving his congregation to puzzle the reason for its outrage'.[24] New has argued that this was not a new or innovative device.[25] While outrage would usually be suppressed in a church setting, print and publication gives it freedom to vent. 'The Abuses of Conscience' opens in the way Downey describes. Sterne begins by typographically emphasising the word 'trust' when citing the line from the scripture '*For we* trust *we have a good conscience*'. Through interweaving the sermon in *Tristram Shandy* with the response of a 'congregation', Sterne explores the differing effects of this emphasis on his audience:

> ——*For we* trust *we have a good Conscience*.——
> "Trust!—Trust we have a good conscience!"

> [Certainly, Trim, quoth my father, interrupting him, you give that sentence a very improper accent; for you curl up your nose, man, and read it with such a sneering tone, as if the Parson was going to abuse the Apostle.
>   He is, an' please your Honour, replied Trim. Pugh! said my father, smiling.
>   Sir, quoth Dr. Slop, Trim is certainly in the right for the writer, (who I perceive is a Protestant) by the snappish manner in which he takes up the Apostle, is certainly going to abuse him,—if this treatment of him has not done it already. [...]] (2.15.102–3)

Because of the secular environment in which the sermon is delivered, in the Shandy parlour, Walter and Slop are able to air their views. Anglican Walter believes that the first line of the sermon means one thing, interpreting the word 'trust' in a conventional manner, while Catholic Slop believes it to mean another, interpreting 'trust' as inflected with a note of query or ambiguity. Walter questions Trim's delivery of the line, while Slop sees the 'improper accent' as arising from the preacher's text. The problem is that both the roman emphasis of the initial instance of the word and the exclamation mark and dash after the second 'Trust' indicates a delivery which makes us reconsider, or question, the text, potentially altering its meaning. In this example, we witness how punctuation in the sermon facilitates a delivery replicating as closely as possible the oratorical effects indicated by the sermon's writer, demarcated through typography: it becomes clear that the preacher, Sterne/Yorick, intends to convey his

[24] Downey, *Eighteenth-Century Pulpit*, 147.   [25] New, Preface, *Sermons*, viii.

words with such an ambiguous tone. Sterne's square brackets, rather than rendering meaning more fixed, as in the work of his predecessors, provide space for it to be interrogated and explored at length. What he shares with Clarke, Hall and Wollaston, however, is the use of square brackets as an amplifying or highlighting device to explore the radical possibilities of print circulation.

As the sermon goes on, the square brackets provide a space in which Slop and Walter respond to and argue over its meaning. The beginning of the sermon hangs on the 'correct' way to read that one word, 'trust', the ambiguity of which Slop blames on the freedom of the press:

> [Then the Apostle is altogether in the wrong, I suppose, quoth Dr. *Slop*, and the Protestant divine is in the right. Sir, have patience, replied my father, for I think it will presently appear that St. *Paul* and the Protestant divine are both of an opinion.—As nearly so, quoth Dr *Slop*, as East is to West; —but this, continued he, lifting both hands, comes from the liberty of the press.

> It is no more, at the worst, replied my uncle *Toby*, than the liberty of the pulpit; for it does not appear that the sermon is printed, or ever likely to be.

> Go on, Trim, quoth my father.] (2.17.110)

The joke here is that the text we are reading is, of course, printed, but there is humour, too, in the fact that the sermon was both preached and printed by Sterne before its appearance in *Tristram Shandy*. This is underlined when, after yet another interruption, Walter urges Trim to 'go on with the rest of thy characters, *Trim*' (2.17.118). Sterne lays bare to readers the printedness of this episode through its white space and typography, especially square brackets. By the end of the sermon, Tristram reveals that the 'manuscript' we have been reading was indeed, later, printed: 'Can the reader believe, that this sermon of Yorick's was preach'd at an assize, in the cathedral of York, before a thousand witnesses, ready to give an oath of it, by a certain prebendary of that church, and actually printed by him when he had done' (2.17.154). With this clever play on chronology, we realise that though the text was a manuscript at the time that it was read aloud by Trim, it had been printed by the time Tristram was writing about it. The sermon episode, then, is one which both describes a manuscript text while recording Tristram's negotiation of printed matter within his narrative. It aligns the subjective 'editing' – a major tool of which is the square bracket – that Trim and the Shandean auditors have enacted on the manuscript with Tristram's own editing of the sermon in his autobiography, as well as with Sterne's self-editing of a near-decade-old text. With the sermon scene in *Tristram Shandy*, Sterne casts doubt on the square bracket's seeming ability in textual editing and sermon printing to indicate objectivity and to direct interpretation.

Both Slop and Toby express suspicion of print in general. With appropriate print censorship, Slop seems to suggest, an author would not be permitted to disagree with St Paul. Toby does not disagree with this point, pacifying Slop by pointing out the sermon's manuscript status. Despite these differences in opinion, Toby and Slop both indicate the power of print to disseminate ideas beyond any single church congregation, where they may be taken out of context, just as they are doing to a sermon Sterne had already printed in York in 1750. Sterne also makes clear the reasons for Slop and the Shandys' difference of opinion over the opening of his sermon: each auditor of the sermon interprets that text (as well as the rest of it) as befits his own interests and religious persuasion. Through interrupting his sermon with these competing interpretations, Sterne demonstrates how far any efforts to fix meaning and to protect against polysemy might be thwarted, even if the delivery of a text is in keeping with its author's well-typeset intention, and it is always evident to Sterne's readers that this entertainment is a melange of forms.

II   Sermons in Fiction

Sterne's incorporation of a sermon into prose fiction caught the attention of his early readers, who noticed the formal experimentation of the episode in *Tristram Shandy*. The anonymous author of *A Supplement to the Life and Opinions of Tristram Shandy, Gent.: Serving to Elucidate that Work* (1760) uses the 'Abuses of Conscience' to justify its own unusual form:

> Hang method!—'tis only a restraint upon genius;—had the great *Shakespear* been tied down by its rules, he would never have been the man he was.
>
> I ended my last volume with a sermon, and I'll begin this with a simile.[26]

The author reminds readers of the sermon in the most recent volume of *Tristram Shandy* as a means of exploring the concept of innovative writing, aligning Shakespeare and Sterne as writers who similarly flouted rules.[27] The

---

[26] *A Supplement to the Life and Opinions of Tristram Shandy, Gent.: Serving to Elucidate that Work* (London: Printed for the Author, 1760), 1.

[27] The author of the *Supplement* combines sermon and simile in the above extract in a way which suggests that they are equivalent literary techniques. Clearly homiletic prose is far more unusual in fiction than figurative language, but the latter is the only resource which the anonymous author can muster. The joke, here, is that the book does not 'begin with a simile' at all, which is revealed pages

imagined society of clockmakers in *The Clockmakers Outcry Against the Author of the Life and Opinions of Tristram Shandy* (1760) wonder what to make of the sermon and the 'ludicrous manner' in which it is incorporated into the fiction. When one asks, 'what think you of the sermon in the second volume?' another opines, 'I think well enough, but wonder how the devil it came there'. Sermon writing is so distinct from novelistic prose that the clockmaker imagines the homily as a layabout pamphlet thoughtlessly left within its pages. This deliberate slippage of the moment that Trim finds the sermon in the pages of Stevinus with the reader encountering it within *Tristram Shandy* underlines the way in which the sermon's incorporation within a novel was perceived as innovative in 1760. It is Sterne's literary-typographic 'Method', the process which explains 'how the devil it came there' which both the *Supplement* and the *Outcry* identify as 'strange' in *Tristram Shandy*. The *Outcry* suggests that while the sermon itself might be unusual in a work of fiction, the way in which it is interwoven with comic writing produces a 'strange and unnatural succession of sense and ribaldry'.[28] Separating passages of sense and ribaldry only by means of square brackets was considered controversial by one early reviewer of *Tristram Shandy*:

> What do you think of his introducing a sermon in the midst of a smutty tale, and making the preacher curse and swear by way of parenthesis?— ('D—n them all, quoth Trim.') There's divinity for you.[29]

With that two-part question, the reviewer identifies the sermon scene as unprecedented in form (we might read 'introducing' in the sense of innovating as well as of incorporating) while also exemplifying the means by which Sterne's formal innovation was achieved: parentheses, or square brackets as they appeared in the original first edition.

Despite the surprised responses of Sterne's early reviewers and imitators, sermons had featured in fiction before *Tristram Shandy*, but without such visual cues for delivery. *The Pardoner's Tale* in Geoffrey Chaucer's *Canterbury Tales* is the most memorable example of this in the English tradition, but Boccaccio had also included a sermon in the *Decameron*. Before *Tristram Shandy*, Sterne had written a satire on the art of sermon

---

later (due to Shandean digression) to be a comparison between a painter's pallet and a placenta, serving to illustrate creation.

[28] *The Clockmakers Outcry Against the Author of the Life and Opinions of Tristram Shandy: Dedicated to the Most Humble of Christian Prelates* (London: Burd, 1760), 38.

[29] 'Grand Magazine, iii (April 1760), 194–8', in Howes, *Critical Heritage*, 64.

writing, the 'Rabelaisian Fragment', though it includes no actual sermon.[30] However, editor New silently amends Sterne's square brackets in the Fragment to round ones, despite there being six sets of square and only two round in the manuscript.[31] Samuel Richardson presents a precedent in *Pamela*, when Mr Williams delivers a sermon on Proverbs 24:25, 'an excellent Discourse on Liberality and Generosity, and the Blessing attending the right Use of Riches'. Richardson describes the sermon rather than transcribes it, though he deploys an italic typeface to help readers imagine printed sermons, which often italicised the Biblical text:

> *There is that scattereth, and yet increaseth; and there is that withholdeth more than is meet; but it tendeth to Poverty. The liberal Soul shall be made fat: and he that watereth, shall be watered also himself.* And he treated the Subject in so handsome a manner, that my Master's Delicacy, who, at first, was afraid of some personal Compliments, was not offended, he judiciously keeping to the Generals; and it was an elegant and sensible Discourse, as my father said.[32]

Reflecting on the day's psalms to his dinner guests, Mr B suggests that Pamela sing her own version of Psalm CXXVII. She had composed a version of it during her imprisonment by Mrs Jewkes, adapting the Israelites' sorrow at their exile into despair befitting her circumstances. Mr B presents her with an ultimatum, that he read it now or Pamela sing it later, and she opts for the former. According to Mr B's direction, Mr Williams and Mr B take turns reading a couple of stanzas from the original and from Pamela's version:

> Mr. *Williams* pulling out his little Pocket Common-prayer Book, read the first two Stanzas.

I.

WHEN we did sit in Babylon,
The Rivers round about:
Then in Remembrance of Sion,
The Tears for Grief burst out.

---

[30] But, as Paul Goring has noted, the fragment shares with the first two volumes of *Tristram Shandy* a concern about how words might be delivered overlaid with an 'ironic probing of elocutionary discourse'. Goring, *Rhetoric of Sensibility*, 190.

[31] Sterne, 'Fragment in the Manner of Rabelais: Autograph Manuscript, [1759 Jan–Feb]', Pierpont Morgan, MA1011.

[32] Samuel Richardson, *Pamela: Or, Virtue Rewarded*, 2nd ed. (London: Richardson, 1741), vol. 2, 134.

II.

We hang'd our Harps and Instruments
The Willow-trees upon:
For in that Place Men, for that Use,
Had planted many a one.

My Master then read:

I.

WHEN sad, I sat in B—n-hall,
All watched round about;
And thought of every absent Friend,
The Tears for Grief burst out.

II.

My Joys, and Hopes, all overthrown,
My Heart-strings almost broke:
Unfit my Mind for Melody,
Much more to bear a Joke.

The Ladies said, It was very pretty; and Miss *Darnford*, That somebody else had well observed, that I had need to be less concerned than themselves.

I knew, said my Master, I should get no Credit by shewing this. But let us read on, Mr. *Williams*. So Mr. *Williams* read;

III.

Then they, to whom we Pris'ners were,
Said to us tauntingly;
Now let us hear your Hebrew *Songs,*
And pleasant Melody.

Now this, said my Master, is very near: And read;

III.

Then she, to whom I Pris'ner was,
Said to me tauntingly;
Now chear your Heart, and sing a Song,
And tune your Mind to Joy.

Mighty sweet, said Mr. *Williams*. But let us see how the next Verse is turn'd.[33]

---

[33] Ibid., 137–8.

Richardson combines prose and verse in order to represent Mr Williams and Mr B reading aloud the different psalms, as well as the reception of those psalms by the female audience. Rather than an interpolated poem, the piece is presented as a performance, fragmented by indications of different speakers and responses. The prose text informs us who is speaking or reading aloud, inviting us to imagine the text delivered in a specific manner, just as in Trim's sermon in *Tristram Shandy*. But because of the different forms of prose and poetry, Richardson need not transgress existing typographic conventions to keep the different discourses visually distinct on the page and navigable by the reader. For the 'Abuses of Conscience' in *Tristram Shandy*, Sterne would need to use punctuation to separate sermon and novel text, creating a *mise en page* entirely unprecedented in the eighteenth-century novel.

While sermons may have been unusual in fiction before Sterne, elements of performance were not uncommon, with writers incorporating rhetorical conventions of drama into their prose. Rosalind Ballaster and Kristiaan P. Aercke have demonstrated the reciprocal relationship between drama and fiction in the period leading up to the publication of *Tristram Shandy*.[34] Seventeenth-century novelists such as Aphra Behn and William Congreve had also written for the stage, and seventeenth- and eighteenth-century prose writers often incorporated elements of drama in order to enhance the verisimilitude of their fictions. Aercke asserts that: 'In the course of the century novelists and narrators became increasingly interested in creating scenes of showing that turn the reader or the narratee into a spectator by means of a stream of detailed information: a subtext of performance, about who is doing what with whom and where and in what costume and against what background'.[35] Aercke could be describing the 'Abuses of Conscience' scene, but Sterne achieves his positioning of the reader as spectator not just through the use of detailed information – a 'subtext of performance' – but also in a visual manner, through square brackets, markers also used in printed drama. It was in this period that printed drama had begun to accrue some visual conventions and readers came to expect a certain visual uniformity in play books, including the

[34] Ros Ballaster, '"Bring(ing) Forth Alive the Conceptions of the Brain": From Stage to Page in the Transmission of French Fiction to the English Restoration Novel', in Jacqueline Glomski and Isabelle Moreau (eds.), *Seventeenth Century Fiction: Text and Transmission* (Oxford University Press, 2016), 183–97.

[35] Kristiaan P. Aercke, 'Congreve's *Incognita*: Romance, Novel, Drama?' *Eighteenth-Century Fiction*, 2 (1990), 293–308, 297.

appearance of square brackets.[36] The *mise en page* of these texts comprises dialogue labelled with speakers' names, white space to clarify changes in speaker and in scene/act, and parentheses to denote 'action' or stage directions.[37] When Ballaster claims that '[t]he new prose fiction of the novel sought to emulate that experience of being close to a real person, a body with powers of affect in voice and performance, enjoyed in the drama', we not only recognise the proximity of novels to plays, especially Ballaster's examples of Jane Collier and Sarah Fielding's *The Cry* (1754), Charlotte Lennox's *Female Quixote* (1752) and Eliza Haywood's *Adventures of Eovaii* (1736), but can also appreciate how far that experience in *Tristram Shandy* is one created through creative page design.[38]

Julie Stone Peters argues that stage directions at mid-century became increasingly used for the purpose of bringing 'the performance to the reader', as a vital sign denoting action at the point of inclusion.[39] In play texts, parentheses often indicate that two different discourses – that without brackets and that within – are to be read as happening at one and the same time.[40] More generally, they require that readers understand their basic function of inter-leaving a text with a double narrative: one which is to be understood as spoken, and the other which is intended to be left unsaid but read. At the time of the first appearance of *Tristram Shandy*, the mid-eighteenth-century novel in which dramatic print effects had been most visible was Richardson's *Sir Charles Grandison* (1753), a work which New has demonstrated that Sterne probably read and engaged with in his own novel.[41] Ira Konigsberg stresses that visually, *Grandison* 'resembles a long dramatic script'.[42] In *Grandison*, square brackets separate narrative and non-narrative content, to indicate time ('Wednesday.] He is just returned from a visit to Sir Hargrave'),[43] place

---

[36] Julie Stone Peters, *The Theatre of the Book, 1480–1880: Print, Text, and Performance in Europe* (Oxford University Press, 2003), 24.

[37] Jonathan P. Lamb, 'Parentheses and Privacy in Philip Sidney's *Arcadia*', *Studies in Philology*, 107.3 (2010), 317; Peters, *Theatre*, 56, 58; Claire M.L. Bourne, 'Dramatic Typography and the Restoration Quartos of *Hamlet*', in Emma Depledge and Peter Kirwan (eds.), *Canonising Shakespeare: Stationers and the Book Trade, 1640–1740* (Cambridge University Press, 2017), 145–52.

[38] Ballaster, 'Satire and Embodiment: Allegorical Romance on Stage and Page in Mid-Eighteenth-Century Britain', *Eighteenth-Century Fiction*, 27 (2015), 637.

[39] Peters, *Theatre*, 62.

[40] Bourne, *Typographies of Performance in Early Modern England* (Oxford University Press, 2020), 87.

[41] New, 'Richardson's *Sir Charles Grandison* and Sterne: A Study in Influence', *Modern Philology*, 115 (2017), 213–43.

[42] Ira Konigsberg, *Samuel Richardson and the Dramatic Novel* (Lexington, KY: University of Kentucky Press, 1968), 119.

[43] Richardson, *The History of Sir Charles Grandison*, Jocelyn Harris (ed.), 3 vols. (London: Oxford University Press, 1972), vol. 3, 7.4.266.

('*In Lady L's closet.*]'),[44] or that a letter has been enclosed in another ('[*Under Cover, directed as before*]').[45] Most often, Richardson uses print conventions from drama to present letters as dramatic dialogue.[46] Such an example might be seen in a letter to Lucy Selby, when Harriet Byron becomes acutely aware that her letter might be boring to read. She notes that she is 'fond of plays', so,

> it is come into my head, that, to avoid all *says-I*'s and *says-she*'s, I will henceforth, in all dialogues, write names in the margin: So fansy, my dear, that you are reading in one of your favourite volumes.
> *Harriet.* Do you know Lady D.?
> *Miss Gr.* Very well: But I did not know that you did, Harriet.[47]

The dialogue continues in the manner presented above, with names italicised and, in the case of Miss Grandison, abbreviated, as we might expect to find such paratexts in printed drama. But Harriet expresses concern that this *mise en page* is so much dependent upon performance that it might read awkwardly in a letter: 'those things that go off well in conversation, do not always *read* to equal advantage', a claim belied by the fact that Lucy's 'favourite volumes' to read are plays.[48] Later in the novel, Lucy and the recently married Harriet, now Lady G., take turns writing one shared letter:[49]

> For the humour's sake, as well as to forward each other, on the joyful occasion, we shall write by turns:
> Lucy; taking up the pen.] Dear Lady L. . . .
> Lady G.] Here, here, child! . . .[50]

As in a play script, the square brackets distinguish information from dialogue, separating the main text from directions which inform the reader how to interpret it. And as in closet drama, the page design aids readers to imagine a performance that never happened, not even within the world of the fiction. The letter writers simply rely on their readers' skilled negotiation of punctuation, a skill carried over from reading non-novelistic prose, to make their letters more interesting.

Square brackets appear rarely in *Tristram Shandy* outside the context of the 'Abuses of Conscience' sermon. One pair bracket Tristram's

[44] Ibid., 7.34.365.   [45] Ibid., vol. 2, 7.24.338.
[46] Konigsberg, *Dramatic Novel*, 119–20. See, for example, Richardson, *Grandison*, vol. 1, 2.7.300. Sylvia Kasey Marks points out that dialogue is the literary form which plays the largest role in this epistolary novel. Marks, Sir Charles Grandison: *The Compleat Conduct Book* (Lewisburg, PA: Bucknell University Press, 1986), 62.
[47] Richardson, *Grandison*, vol. 1, 2.5.273.   [48] Ibid.   [49] Ibid., vol. 3, 6.46.200.
[50] Ibid., 6.52.218, 229.

editorial intervention in Slawkenbergius's Tale, where he wishes to
note that his father always read a certain passage with triumph
(4.0.47–9). A whole series of square brackets serve a similar function
in Walter's edits of Toby's apologetical oration, or 'My Brother Toby's
Justification of His Own Principles and Conduct in Wishing to
Continue the War':

> I have had the good fortune to meet with it amongst my father's papers,
> with here and there an insertion of his own, betwixt two crooks, thus [ ],
> and is endorsed,
>
> My Brother Toby's Justification of His Own Principles and Conduct in
> Wishing to Continue the War.
>
> I may safely say, I have read over this apologetical oration of my uncle
> Toby's a hundred times, and think it so fine a model of defence,—and
> shews so sweet a temperament of gallantry and good principles in him, that
> I give it the world, word for word (interlineations and all), as I find it.
> (6.31.123–4)

Walter's interlineations of Toby's apologetical oration, however, are
after the fact. Like the *Grandison* letters, the text within square
brackets, or crooks, represents textual commentary rather than indicating delivery and reception. Tristram provides directions for reading
this mark-up, revealing his editorial practice of including the text and
its commentary through the typographically exaggerated 'crooks'.
Here, Sterne draws attention to codes that his readers, by this point,
were already adept at understanding. These brackets in particular are
funny because of their size. They loom large on the page, in a much
larger type than the surrounding and enclosed text, satirising by
exaggerating the typographic conventions of textual editing which are
usually intended to be discreet. In the 'Abuses of Conscience' sermon,
square brackets are similarly comic, because of their number and
frequency, and because each pair of markers enclose an amusing
vignette of the Shandy family listening to the sermon out of context.
The longer those vignettes are, the more effectively Sterne questions
the primacy of text and subtext, and the intended invisibility of
parenthetical commentary.

Another scene in *Tristram Shandy* featuring a text that is read aloud
carries brackets which seem to enclose stage directions, when Doctor Slop
wishes to damn Obadiah (for tying up his bag so tightly) using Walter's
copy of Ernulphus's Curse. Slop would rather read the text to himself, but
the threat of the alternative – Toby reading it aloud – means that he goes

through with the performance. As in the 'Abuses of Conscience' sermon, this performance is interrupted by comments from the Shandy family in square brackets:

> "May he (Obadiah) be damn'd wherever he be,—whether in the house or the stables, the garden or the field, or the highway, or in the path, or in the wood, or in the water, or in the church.—May he be cursed in living, in dying." [Here my uncle Toby taking the advantage of a minim in the second barr of his tune, kept whistling one continual note to the end of the sentence—Dr. Slop with his division of curses moving under him, like a running bass all the way.] (3.11.47)

Tristram's mediation of both Slawkenbergius's Tale and Ernulphus's Curse is in keeping with the use of brackets in edited texts, where bracketed content indicates editorial intervention, as in the apologetical oration. But readers are also encouraged to read brackets in the 'Abuses of Conscience' scene and Ernulphus's Curse as they would read them in drama. In the sermon scene in *Tristram Shandy*, the most sustained use of brackets in the novel, the major function of square brackets was not just to indicate non-verbal action but also to encourage readers to imagine that action – whether pause, tears or whistle – delivered by a fictional character. In *Tristram Shandy* Sterne highlights the centrality of what textual editors would consider to be 'accidentals' to the creation of meaning, requiring his readers to navigate punctuation as indicative of essential non-verbal aspects of literary performance.

The pages carrying Yorick's sermon in *Tristram Shandy* were certainly, as early reviewers recognised, unprecedented in form, despite the fact that sermons had appeared in fiction before 1759. But much of the amusement of the 'Abuses of Conscience' episode arises from issues of size and scale. Sterne sustains the comic interplay between sermon and Shandean fiction across forty-eight pages, innovatively deploying typographic markers in ways which emphasised to readers his formal innovation of including an entire sermon within a novel, while paying at least as much attention to commentary as to the manuscript. In this experiment of extraordinary scale, his novel on these pages becomes a script or closet drama indicating to the reader how the sermon was performed within the fiction. Like Richardson, Sterne imports into the novel brackets, printed markers most associated with play scripts in this period, to underpin his prose with a performative energy. Like the *Grandison* letters, and like closet drama, Sterne relies on readers recognising print conventions in order to give life to his prose.

III   Dramatic Sermons

Within three months of the appearance of the first instalment of *Tristram Shandy*, Sterne was advertising his collected sermons, drawing upon the fact that he had – through means of square brackets – turned the 'Abuses of Conscience' sermon by 'Yorick' into a performance. *The Sermons of Mr. Yorick* was first advertised as forthcoming in the York and London press on 4 March 1760 under the title of the *Dramatick Sermons of Mr. Yorick*, but Sterne later dropped the 'Dramatick' adjective before publication:[51]

> *To be printed in Two Volumes, Price 5s. and to be delivered to the Subscribers in May next,*
> The DRAMATICK SERMONS
> OF
> Mr. YORICK.
> Published by TRISTRAM SHANDY, Gentleman.
>
> Subscriptions for which are taken in by John Hinxman, (from Mr. Dodsley's, in Pall-Mall, London, Successor to the late Mr. Hildyard) Bookseller in Stonegate, York.[52]

By the time the volumes were advertised in the *Whitehall Evening Post* for 19 April 1760, the title had taken the form that we recognise today. Anne Bandry conjectures that Sterne pre-sold his sermons as *The Dramatick Sermons of Mr. Yorick*, and that it appeared as such on the subscription leaflets and receipts circulating in York and London at the time, none of which survive.[53] As Bandry and Tim Parnell point out, Sterne admired the dramatic style of sermonising. In France he praised sermons by the abbé Denis-Xavier Clément, describing them as 'more than theatrical, and greater, both in action and delivery, than Madame Clairon, who, you must know, is the Garrick of the stage here'.[54] To advertise sermons in this period as dramatic was unremarkable, and Sterne's sermons are indeed dramatic in the traditional sense of dramatising the speech of Biblical characters as dialogue. But it was particularly dangerous in Sterne's case, because of that other incendiary

---

[51] Tim Parnell, '*The Sermons of Mr. Yorick*: The Commonplace and the Rhetoric of the Heart', in Thomas Keymer (ed.), *The Cambridge Companion to Laurence Sterne* (Cambridge University Press, 2009), 64–78, 65; Anne Bandry, '*Tristram Shandy*, the *Public Ledger*, and William Dodd', *Eighteenth-Century Fiction*, 14 (2002), 321.

[52] The *York Courant*, 4 March 1760.   [53] Bandry, *Public Ledger*, 321.

[54] Sterne, 'To Elizabeth Sterne' (15 March 1762), in *The Letters, Part 1, 1739–1764*, New and Peter de Voogd (eds.), The Florida Edition of the Works of Laurence Sterne (Gainesville, FL: University Press of Florida, 2009), vol. 7, letter 83, 238.

word in the title for the collection: 'Yorick'.[55] Sterne was calling his
sermons dramatic while claiming them to be the work of a fictional
character whose name recalls both a bawdy novel and Hamlet's dead
jester. But it most deliberately invokes the context of the sermon scene
in *Tristram Shandy*, the very first 'sermon of Mr. Yorick'. The proposed
title plays upon the manner in which Sterne's earlier, and now his most
famous, sermon had reached a wide enough readership to make this
Sermons venture plausible. Walter had explicitly called the 'Abuses of
Conscience' dramatic – 'I like the sermon well, replied my father,—'tis
dramatic' (2.17.151) – and the sermon is dramatic in two senses: the
first according to the traditional definition, and the second in the sense
of being typographically presented as a performance, punctuated with
square brackets including supplementary information about the reception of the sermon by a cast of Shandean auditors.

'The Abuses of Conscience' sermon in *Tristram Shandy* is more obviously concerned with dramatic effect than the original, due to its new
context of being read aloud by Trim, but Sterne also presented the
1750 text as one to be imagined as a performance. The full title of
Sterne's 'Abuses of Conscience' in 1750 followed the title page
conventions of declaring the name of the preacher, the occasion of its
delivery and some members of its original audience:

> *The Abuses of Conscience: Set Forth in a Sermon, preached in the Cathedral
> Church of St. Peter's, York, at the Summer Assizes, Before the Hon. Mr. Baron
> Clive, and the Hon. Mr. Baron Smythe, on Sunday, July 29, 1750. By
> Laurence Sterne, A.M. Prebendary of the said Church. Published at the
> Request of the High Sheriff and Grand Jury.*

New has stressed that we must take into account the occasional nature of
sermons, and the fact that Sterne chose to preach about conscience at the
summer assizes, which dealt with criminal court cases, has an impact
upon how we should read the sermon.[56] Walter clearly adheres to this
view. When Trim reads this sermon aloud in *Tristram Shandy*, he quickly
infers by the text's detailing of the terrors of jails that 'this sermon has
been composed to be preach'd at the Temple,–or at some Assize'

---

[55] Judith Hawley has argued that this element of the sermons is underplayed in the modern scholarly
    edition. Hawley, Review, 'The Sermons of Laurence Sterne', *Essays in Criticism*, 48 (1998), 80–8.
[56] New, 'Reading the Occasion: Understanding Sterne's Sermons', in W.B. Gerard (ed.), *Divine
    Rhetoric: Essays on the Sermons of Laurence Sterne* (Newark, NJ: University of Delaware Press, 2010),
    101–19.

(2.15.130). But the occasion also has an impact on who was present in 1750: the High Sheriff and the Grand Jury. The 1750 edition opens with a dedication to

Sir WILLIAM PENNYMAN, Bart High Sheriff of the County of YORK,
AND TO

Sir Edmund Anderson, *of* Kildwick-Percy, *Bart*. Ralph Pennyman, *of* Beverly; Montagu Brook, *of* Skelton; Thomas Norcliffe, *of* Langton; John Hutton, *of* Marske; William Turner, *of* Clints; Thomas Fawkes, *of* Farnley; Richard Langley, *of* Wykeham-Abbey; George Montgomery Metham, *of* North-Cave; Tindal Thompson, *of* Setterington; Thomas Robinson, *of* Beckhouse; Edmund Charles Blomberg, *of* Kirkby-Misperton; Francis Best; *of* Beverly; Thomas Bradshaw, *of* Hemsworth; Roger Beckwith, *of* Handall-Abbey; William Sutton, *of* Carleton; Peter Conset, *of* Brawith; George Iveson, *of* Bilton; Richard Bawson, *of* Poppleton; William Meeke, *of* Wighill-Park; John Taylor, *of* Foulforth; Charles Cottrell, *of* Scarborough; and Ralph Lutton, *of* Knapton, *Esquires*.[57]

Sterne goes on to thank the men for their encouragement to print the sermon, which grants him the opportunity of 'doing Good' while declaring how much he honours and esteems them.[58] As well as marketing his sermon as a worthy text by association with this impressively long list of influential people who supported it into print, an additional effect of this dedication is to recreate its original congregation. Again, this was conventional. In print, this enables readers of sermons to imagine sermon texts as historically specific oratory. Given the local publication of the 'Abuses of Conscience' sermon in York, readers may have been able to imagine responses of people who they likely knew. 'The Abuses of Conscience' would, of course, have a much more dynamic fictional audience or 'congregation' in *Tristram Shandy*. In both the 1750 and the 1759 instances of this sermon, the text is offered to readers as one which, from the onset, is to be imagined as delivered in front of and received by individual auditors. Print presented Sterne with the possibility of this text being read in new contexts. This paratextual attempt to specify the original context of the oral sermon functions in a similar way to his square brackets in the sermon scene in *Tristram Shandy*, where they seek to limit or control the proliferation of different interpretations all the while also foregrounding the fact that print presents the opportunity for a dangerous proliferation of interpretation.

[57] Sterne, Dedication, *The Abuses of Conscience* (York: Hildyard, 1750), i–ii.   [58] Ibid., iii.

For Trim's reading of the sermon, Sterne borrows from the established protocols of printed drama and in particular its square brackets. If we read Trim's performance of the sermon as a monologue, the action within square brackets sometimes includes stage directions, indicating non-verbal action such as his gesturing towards the words on the page:

> "In how many kingdoms of the world," [Here Trim kept waving his right hand from the sermon to the extent of his arm, returning it backwards and forwards to the conclusion of the Paragraph.]

> "In how many kingdoms of the world has the crusading sword of this misguided saint-errant spared neither age, or merit, or sex, or condition?— and, as he fought under the banners of a religion which set him loose from justice and humanity, he shew'd none; mercilessly trampled upon both,——heard neither the cries of the unfortunate, nor pitied their distresses." (2.17.140)

The bracketed directions make clear that Trim spent an entire paragraph of Yorick's sermon gesticulating. Sterne begins that paragraph, interrupts it with the commentary, and then repeats its beginning in order to print it whole. He thereby creates an exercise in reading, ensuring that the reader, having understood the non-verbal commentary for best imagining this scene, can appreciate the text with an image of gesticulating Trim in mind throughout. Sterne's page layout here makes obvious the patterns of reading that bracketed directions encourage: square brackets enclose information which sometimes requires that we revisit text in order to read it in the correct manner. Through the repetition of the opening line of the paragraph ('In how many kingdoms of the world'), Sterne makes his parenthetical commentary, a discourse usually secondary to the main text and therefore optional, unavoidable.

Throughout the sermon, the primacy of the bracketed subtext is compounded by the typographic setting of these pages: bracketed commentary spans the full width of the text block, whereas the sermon is presented within quotation marks repeated before each line of the sermon (as is conventional in the period), which nudge the sermon text towards the right-hand margin. The bracketed narrative, therefore, has more space on the page than the sermon, indicating the sermon's relative secondary status. This is also clear from the fact that initially, the sermon is almost abandoned; the first line of the 'Abuses of Conscience' and the discussion that arises from it prompts Trim to begin to tell the story of his brother in the Inquisition, his emotional response to which shapes his delivery of the sermon when Walter encourages him to 'read on' (2.17.106). Rather than continue from that point, however,

Trim returns to the very beginning, with Sterne printing the headings over again. This repeated printing of the sermon heading and opening, like Trim's repetition of the line 'In how many kingdoms in the world', underlines the performance element of this scene, the humour of which relies on the idiosyncrasies of Trim's reading and delivery: this is a script for a performance rather than an interpolated text.

As the Shandean interjections become shorter and more frequent, the sermon appears even less like an interpolated text. Slop dozes through Trim's reading, until the preacher uses the example of the banker and the physician to explore the importance of religion being accompanied by morality, at which point he starts: 'I know the banker I deal with, or the physician I usually call in [there is no need, cried Dr. Slop, (waking) to call in any physician in this case] to be neither of them men of much religion' (2.17.135). In this short interruption of the text, the action of Slop waking adds humour to his comment, emphasising how far all of the Shandean auditors are prone to take parts of the sermon out of context according to their own biases. Similarly, Trim cannot hear the preacher's use of the example of the prisons of the Inquisition without calling to mind his brother's sad situation, which results in the fragmentation of the sermon and Walter stepping in to finish the reading:

> "To be convinced of this, go with me for a moment into the prisons of the inquisition." [God help my poor brother *Tom*.]—"Behold *Religion*, with *Mercy* and *Justice* chained down under her feet,——there sitting ghastly upon a black tribunal, propp'd up with racks and instruments of torment. Hark!— hark! what a piteous groan!" [Here *Trim*'s face turned as pale as ashes.] "See the melancholy wretch who utter'd it,"—[Here the tears began to trickle down] "just brought forth to undergo the anguish of a mock trial, and endure the utmost pains that a studied system of cruelty has been able to invent."—[D—n them all, quoth *Trim*, his colour returning into his face as red as blood.]—"Behold this helpless victim delivered up to his tormentors,—his body so wasted with sorrow and confinement."——[Oh! 'tis my brother, cried poor *Trim* in a most passionate exclamation, dropping the sermon upon the ground, and clapping his hands together [. . .] .] (2.17.142–4)

Within square brackets, Sterne zones in upon the minute details of the scene, especially Trim's bodily response to the reading material, as the colour drains from and returns to his face and he begins to cry. The typography of this passage maps emotional effects onto the text that caused them, marking precisely where each phrase, as in the groan described by the preacher, sparks an acute physiological reaction in the reader, as in Trim's turning pale.

By using square brackets in similar ways to those found in play scripts, Sterne creates two discrete discourses: the sermon itself, and the Shandy family comically revealing their characters in response to it. But while square-bracketed directions are often secondary to the action in play scripts, it quickly becomes clear in the sermon scene in *Tristram Shandy* that Sterne has subverted the conventions we thought we recognised. The space on the page allocated to the bracketed action is much larger, and the growing fragmentation of the sermon text as the bracketed action increases its frequency soon means that the responses of the Shandy household become our main focus of attention. Another effect of this growing fragmentation is that the printed page begins to become untidy, as sermon text and fiction vie for dominance. Sterne waits until the sermon reading is entirely over before revealing to us that the text we have been reading has had a print history of 'plunder', and that it is included here as a 'sample' of a bundle, which, if it is liked, 'will make a handsome volume, at the world's service' (2.17.154–5). Tristram's announcement of another potential publication – one which soon came to fruition in the octavo-formatted *Sermons of Mr. Yorick* – to complement and perhaps stand alongside the octavo format *Tristram Shandy* highlights the hybridity of fiction and sermon genres in the creation of the 'Abuses of Conscience' episode, itself produced using the print conventions of yet another genre: drama.

IV Dramatic Fictions

When Sterne (unsuccessfully) pitched to Robert Dodsley the first two volumes of *Tristram Shandy*, he was directing his work to the very man whose career had been built on writing and publishing texts by authors experimenting across the boundary between novels and plays. Dodsley's *The Toy-Shop* (1735) was one of the most high-profile plays more successful as a reading text than as one intended to be performed. In a letter to his friend William Wright, Dodsley remembered that 'tho' I design'd it for the stage, yet unless its novelty would recommend it, I was afraid it would not bear a publick representation, and therefore had not offered it to the actors'.[59] With these concerns in mind, Dodsley sent his manuscript to Alexander Pope for feedback in 1733. Pope agreed, concerned that it might not be the kind of play that would display its full potential in performance: 'I like it, as far as my

---

[59] Robert Dodsley, 'An Epistle to a Friend in the Country [to Mr Wright of Mansfield]' [1735–6], *The Correspondence of Robert Dodsley 1733–1764*, James E. Tierney (ed.) (Cambridge University Press, 1988), 68, n. 4.

particular judgment goes. Whether it has action enough to please the stage, I doubt: but the morality and satire ought to be relished by the reader'.[60] Pope nevertheless recommended Dodsley's play to John Rich, theatre manager of Lincoln's Inn Fields, who decided to stage it. *The Toy-Shop* was a hit. It was first performed on 3 February 1735 and was in print the following day. But its performance was eclipsed by the success of the book, which went through eleven editions over the next two years. The printed success of *The Toy-Shop*, along with a £100 loan from Pope, enabled Dodsley to set up his bookselling business soon afterwards, and was the well-known means of raising the poet from footman to successful London bookseller. Even years after its initial print run, theatrical historians and biographers continued to focus on *Toy-Shop* as printed text rather than performance. In his 1810 *Works of the English Poets*, Alexander Chalmers called it an 'excellent satire, for it scarcely deserves the name of drama'. He accounted its popularity in print to it 'being indeed much better calculated for the closet than the stage', indicating its closer proximity to closet drama intended for private reading.[61]

In *The Toy-Shop* Dodsley represents the visit of two ladies and a gentleman to a fashionable toy shop to watch the toy-man riff upon the follies of the age while selling his trinkets to gullible punters at inflated prices. The perceived readability of the play arises from its dependence upon the wit of its leading character, which results in a relative lack of quick-fire dialogue and substantial action; the shoppers are more like an audience than fellow characters. The few stage directions that accompany the text appear in three different modes: stage directions beneath the line; right-aligned stage directions in square brackets; and a footnote. The first two of these are visible in Figure 3.2.

Centred stage directions beneath the line and right-aligned stage directions in square brackets are common in drama of this period. They leave readers with little doubt about the timing of the accompanying action, generally indicating that the speaker completes that line before the action takes place (e.g. leaving the stage). But some of Dodsley's right-aligned stage directions jostle for space on the page with the main text, encouraging us to interpret the non-verbal action as happening at the same time as that piece of dialogue. The toy master's line 'Methinks I have had a

---

[60] Alexander Pope to Robert Dodsley, 5 February 1733, *Correspondence of Alexander Pope*, George Sherburn (ed.), 5 vols. (Oxford: Clarendon, 1956), 3.346.

[61] Alexander Chalmers, *The Works of the English Poets, from Chaucer to Cowper* (London: Johnson, 1810), 315. John Genest, in his *Account of the English Stage*, 10 vols. (Bath: Rodd, 1832), wrote that *The Toy-Shop* 'has great merit, but seems better calculated for perusal than representation': vol. 3, 460.

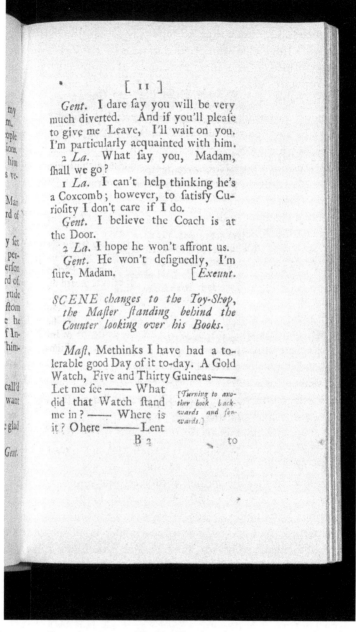

[11]

Gent. I dare ſay you will be very much diverted. And if you'll pleaſe to give me Leave, I'll wait on you. I'm particularly acquainted with him.

2 *La.* What ſay you, Madam, ſhall we go?

1 *La.* I can't help thinking he's a Coxcomb; however, to ſatisfy Curioſity I don't care if I do.

Gent. I believe the Coach is at the Door.

2 *La.* I hope he won't affront us.

Gent. He won't deſignedly, I'm ſure, Madam.   [*Exeunt.*

SCENE changes to the Toy-Shop, the Maſter ſtanding behind the Counter looking over his Books.

Maſt, Methinks I have had a tolerable good Day of it to-day. A Gold Watch, Five and Thirty Guineas—— Let me ſee —— What did that Watch ſtand me in? —— Where is it? O here ——Lent *[Turning to another book backwards and forwards.]*

B 2   to

Figure 3.2   Stage directions in *The Toy-Shop* (1735). Image courtesy of Cambridge University Library

tolerable good Day of it to-day–Let me see …' sits beside one such
indented direction which reveals that while delivering that line he is
consulting his account book (Figure 3.2): '[*Turning to another book backwards and forwards.*]' These coterminous directions, emphasised with
italics, inflect our comprehension and encourage us to return to the text
in order to modify our understanding of its delivery. The emphasis on
reading over performance in *The Toy-Shop* is underlined by the footnote
stage direction. In this case, the maid's line, and the manner in which she
is to deliver it, does not appear in the script proper but is described,
narrative-like, in the note on the bottom of the page:

> *Here her Maid enters and delivers a Box, from which the Lady pulls out a dead
> Dog, kissing it, and weeping.* Lucy *too pretends great sorrow, but turning aside
> bursts out a Laughing, and cries, "She little thinks I poison'd it."*

Dodsley's page, in his placement of the line '*She little thinks I poison'd it*'
enacts on a typographical level the dramatic technique of the aside. On
stage, an aside functions as a form of digression from the main action, in
that information is presented to an audience without the other characters
hearing it or knowing about it. It briefly draws the audience's attention
away from the action, just as Dodsley's footnote draws the reader to the
foot of the page and away from the dialogue. His *mise en page* in some
sense parallels his *mise en scene*, requiring the reader to glance down at the
note just as the audience would have to direct their attention away from
the main action in order to catch the maid's contribution to the performance. And perhaps the maid's line does not appear in the script proper
because it is so much determined by the non-verbal: her line is secondary
to her pretend sorrow and then laughter, and dependent upon such action
for its satiric bite. Asides in Dodsley's play and plays known to have been
read by Sterne, such as Susanna Centlivre's *The Busy Body* (1709), and
John Vanbrugh and Colley Cibber's *The Provok'd Husband: Or, a Journey
to London* (1728), are usually brief.[62] Whereas Dodsley borrows the
footnote – a printed technique which facilitates reading – in a one-off
move which gives life to his drama, Sterne borrows square brackets to
bring drama to his novel in a much more sustained way. Centlivre and
Vanbrugh tend to use the conventional '[Aside]' device, enclosed in square

---

[62] Sterne, 'To Robert Foley' (17 December 1762), *The Letters, Part 1*, vol. 7, letter 104, 302. No MS
survives.

brackets, which indicates that a line or snippet of dialogue is to be delivered in that way.[63] In eighteenth-century printed drama, square brackets surround the label rather than the dialogue itself, whereas in *Tristram Shandy* and the 'Abuses of Conscience' sermon, the material within square brackets is the main dialogue. Pages of printed drama, where square brackets commonly feature, anticipate the pages of Sterne's sermon scene, in demanding of readers that they combine modes of reading in order for the work to have maximum impact. In interweaving sermon and novel using techniques borrowed from drama, *Tristram Shandy*, from its first instalment, was a hybrid text.

Despite Dodsley's initial intentions and the origins of his piece in performance, *The Toy-Shop* was also a curious amalgam of genres. Its hybrid status was prominent even on the title page, through the subtitle, 'A Dramatick Satire'. Dramatic satire had existed for centuries, though Dodsley was the first dramatist to explicitly define his work using that phrase. As a genre label, 'dramatic satire' tends to be used synonymously with 'critical burlesque',[64] and it was particularly popular during the first part of the eighteenth century, especially given the success of John Gay's *Beggar's Opera* (1728). Jean Marsden defines it as 'designed to be staged rather than read'.[65] There were exceptions, though, as in the *Humours of Whist: A Dramatic Satire, as Acted Every Day at White's and Other Coffee-Houses and Assemblies* (London: Roberts, 1743). Its author, an unidentified S.F. esq., seemed to perceive that dramatic satire was a fitting vehicle for representing the hysteria Edmund Hoyle had been perceived to perform

---

[63] As when Miranda tells the audience, '*Miran.* [*Aside.*] Oh! that I durst speak—', or when Manly undermines John Moody's words to the audience in a series of comic asides while appearing to humour him. Susanna Centlivre, *The Busy Body* (1709), in *The Works of the Celebrated Mrs. Centlivre* (London: Knapton, 1760), vol. 2, act 2, 79; John Vanbrugh and Colley Cibber, *The Provok'd Husband: Or, a Journey to London* (London: Watts, 1728), 1.1.32.

[64] Esp. on the model of George Villier's *The Rehearsal* (1671, published in 1672). See Kimball King, *Western Drama through the Ages* (Westport, CT: Greenwood, 2007), 98. Matthew J. Kinservik sees the difference between satiric comedy and dramatic satire as depending upon the degree to which a play is referential and therefore satiric rather than abstractly comedic; ultimately we must consider the play's theatrical context. He sees Fielding deploying the form to attack the political opposition in *Pasquin: A Dramatic Satire on the Times: Being the Rehearsal of Two Plays, Viz. a Comedy, Call'd the Election; and a Tragedy, Call'd the Life and Death of Common-Sense* (London: Watts, 1736): Kinservik, *Disciplining Satire: The Censorship of Satiric Comedy on the Eighteenth-Century London Stage* (Lewisburg, PA: Bucknell University Press, 2002), 20–3, 82–3. See also Deborah Payne, 'Comedy, Satire, or Farce? Or the Generic Difficulties of Restoration Dramatic Satire', in James E. Gill (ed.), *Cutting Edges: Postmodern Critical Essays on Eighteenth-Century Satire* (Knoxville, TS: University of Tennessee Press, 1995), 1–22, and J. Douglas Canfield, *Tricksters and Estates: On the Ideology of Restoration Comedy* (Lexington, KY: University Press of Kentucky, 1997).

[65] Jean I. Marsden, 'Dramatic Satire in the Restoration and Eighteenth Century' in Ruben Quintero (ed.), *A Companion to Satire: Ancient and Modern* (Oxford: Blackwell, 2008), 161.

on the public stage about the invasion of his copyright for his *Gamester* textbook (1742). This closet drama, only ever intended to be read, plays on the term 'dramatick' to emphasise the rowdiness of the coffee houses where gambling was rife. In this, the author was drawing upon hybrid forms never intended for performance, like the 'dramatic history' pioneered by John (or James)[66] Baillie's *The Patriot: Being a Dramatick History of the Life and Death of William the First Prince of Orange* (1736), which promoted printed drama as the best format for presenting history to young people as entertainment. A Sternean imitator would also adopt this genre for their anonymous fiction, *The Dramatic History of Master Edward, Miss Ann, Mrs. LLwhuddwhydd, and Others* (1763), where the term 'history' is used in the Fielding-esque sense. The imitator's choice of form is clearly informed by what was considered to be outlandish or experimental at that moment.

Dodsley seems to have held that the hybrid style of his drama was desirable to audiences and readers. When he set up his bookselling business, he marketed his follow-up play, *The King and the Miller of Mansfield* (1737), with the subtitle, 'a dramatic tale' and, as a performance, it was more successful than *The Toy-Shop*.[67] He and his brother published Jane Collier and Sarah Fielding's *The Cry: A Dramatic Fable* (1754), an experimental text in this tradition. Collier and Fielding's text was never intended to be performed, and its subtitle, 'a dramatic fable', drew upon the printed heritage of drama in order to push the boundaries of novel writing; as the authors claimed in the Introduction:

> stories and novels have flowed in such abundance for these last ten years, that we would wish, if possible, to strike a little out of a road already so much beaten. There are two obvious reasons for such a deviation. One is the real excellence of some of those writings, both as to humour, character, moral, and every other proper requisite, which (without an affected humility) we by no means promise fully to equal, much less to surpass; and the other reason is, that we may not be thrown aside as increasing the number

---

[66] Terence Tobin, 'A List of Plays and Entertainments by Scottish Dramatists 1660–1800', *Studies in Bibliography*, 23 (1970), 105.

[67] It opened on 29 January 1737 with Theophilus Cibber in the leading role, had a run of thirty-seven performances in its opening season, became the most popular play of the year and was performed every year thereafter. On 7 January Dodsley entered his play in the stationer's register. Harry M. Solomon, *The Rise of Robert Dodsley: Creating the New Age of Print* (Carbondale, IL: Southern Illinois University Press, 1996), 55.

of that set of trifling performances, whose names we presume are most of
them already devoted to oblivion.[68]

They give two reasons for their experimentation. First, they modestly
claim to be unable to equal recent novels of 'excellence', alluding to the
works of Richardson, Collier's friend, and Henry Fielding, Fielding's
brother. Second, they decide that experimentation will catch the attention
of their readers, set it above 'trifling performances', and prevent their work
from being cast aside. A contributor to the *Monthly Review* felt that this
format was indeed eye-catching: 'The odd title of this performance arises
from the plan our author has struck out, which is entirely different from
that of any modern novelist'.[69] Ultimately, however, it was felt to be too
esoteric: 'the plan, we fear, [is] too abstracted from the present taste, to
procure the work as many readers as it deserves'.[70] Such a response provides an indication of how readers may have felt when encountering play-
script conventions within a work otherwise deemed to be a novel. The
'Abuses of Conscience' in *Tristram Shandy*, as a sermon cum performance,
must have seemed similarly unusual.

Through orchestrating a courtroom format with characters relating their
histories to the cry, an allegorical audience or jury before whom the principle
characters in the otherwise typical romance story are brought, Collier and
Fielding place the characters' thoughts and motivations under the spotlight.
The text most takes on the appearance of a script on the first page of each
'scene', especially through rubrication ('Part the First | Scene I.') and the
names of all characters who will appear in the scene capitalised and centred on
the page ('PORTIA. UNA. THE CRY.').[71] Portia is then reintroduced as
speaker through the capitalisation and centring of her name above her speech.

Because the pages rarely represent quick-fire dialogue, due to the fact
that the text comprises Portia's relation of a lengthy account of her life to
Una and the cry, the scene changes create similar effects to many of
Sterne's visual pages, lurching readers out of the comfort of prose reading
in order to remind them of its printed packaging and the cues by which
they have learned to interpret information. *The Cry* retains, on the vast
majority of its pages, the printed appearance of a novel. There are two
exceptions. The first is a dialogue between lovers which the authors use to
illustrate that jealousy, rather than demonstrating affection, is merely a

---

[68] Jane Collier and Sarah Fielding, Introduction, *The Cry: A New Dramatic Fable* (London: Dodsley,
1754), vol. 1, 7–8.
[69] *Monthly Review*, 10 (1754), 280.   [70] Ibid., 282.   [71] Collier and Fielding, *The Cry*, 1.17.

form of derision.[72] Its short responses and square brackets around stage directions indicating tone of delivery highlight by default the degree to which play-script conventions in *The Cry* have hitherto been quite subtle. The dialogue is so visually different from the surrounding text that these pages appear as a tipped in script when compared with the surrounding prose.[73] Here, the dialogue between the jealous lovers is rendered more readable because of its typography. Later in *The Cry*, Collier and Fielding again deploy quick-fire dialogue to enable Portia more accurately and more entertainingly to represent the views of her friend and love rival, Melantha. Portia assumes Melantha's character in a sort of roleplay for the entertainment of Una and the cry:

> *Portia.* Now then suppose me to be *Melantha*, and speaking thus.
> *Portia*, [*in the assumed character of Melantha.*] I danced in company with *Demetrius* at a ball.[74]

Collier and Fielding make use of square brackets to supplement the identification of Portia as playing the role of Melantha. This device borrows from play scripts the custom of printing the speaker's true identity rather than their assumed identity so that actors can easily locate their lines in the text. But such a practice requires readers to be familiar with negotiating and synthesising parenthetical information. Here, Collier and Fielding were drawing upon the growing ability of readers to recognise in prose works elements of dramatic typography and to apply their principles to other genres. Like Collier, Fielding and Richardson, Sterne depends on his readers' ability to recognise, navigate and synthesise typographic directions for how his narrative should be received.

As texts, play scripts require readers to negotiate spoken word and non-verbal action. Sterne requires much more of his readers, insisting that they fluently navigate very different kinds of literary texts. In his interpolation of the 'Abuses of Conscience' sermon, Sterne was literally transcribing into *Tristram Shandy* text which had already circulated in print. That text's reception by its Shandean audience as 'dramatick' highlights the origins of his idiosyncratic use of the bracket as simultaneously dramatic and sermonic. Sterne also draws from the 'dramatic fable' pioneered by Collier and Fielding, and the dramatic satires of both performed and closet drama, experimental forms depending on reading practices learned elsewhere. He creates a comic scene in Trim's reading aloud of the sermon which highlights that sermon's textuality, where the

---

[72] Ibid., 1.95. [73] Ibid., 1.97–100. [74] Ibid., 2.143.

humour of the performance and reception of that text is directly and self-consciously generated by unusual-in-this-context but widely known and navigated typographic conventions. Reading this episode in *Tristram Shandy* against Sterne's influences in terms of sermons and hybrid literary fiction reveals him reflecting on the capacity of typography to animate his work. Its success depends on the reader recognising the typographic templates of sermons and drama, and being able to bring different reading skills to the novel. We are thereby able to see his tendency to keep abreast of contemporary publishing trends and his comic manner of assimilating them within his novel, while taking these techniques further to experiment with his own signature mode of visual self-reflexivity.

CHAPTER 4

The Marbled Page

I A Natural Philosophy of Noses

(Broken) noses cast a long shadow in *Tristram Shandy*, especially in the second instalment (volumes 3 and 4) which carries the marbled page. It opens with Elizabeth's prolonged labour and Tristram's eventual arrival into the Shandy family, when his nose is crushed during a bungled forceps delivery. Walter is left reeling, and throws himself prostrate on the bed in an exasperated fury, as Tristram explains:

> No doubt, the breaking down of the bridge of a child's nose, by the edge of a pair of forceps,—however scientifically applied,—would vex any man in the world, who was at so much pains in begetting a child, as my father was,—yet it will not account for the extravagance of his affliction, nor will it justify the unchristian manner he abandoned and surrender'd himself up to.

> To explain this, I must leave him upon the bed for half an hour,—and my uncle Toby in his old fringed chair sitting beside him. (3.30.144–5)

Tristram goes on to account for Walter's vexation by explaining that his father had dedicated much of his life to collecting books on the history and natural philosophy of noses. He departs from this scene of woe to explain that many generations of Shandys have suffered from anxieties around noses. Tristram begins with his great-grandmother, who had insisted upon a marriage article which allowed her a large jointure due to her fiancé having little or no nose. This long-running family concern with the facial member goes some way towards explaining Walter's staying in bed for the rest of the volume, and his peculiar bibliographical bent.

Walter's book collecting is passionate but it has been a challenge: despite the 'many millions of books in all languages, and in all possible types and bindings' which have been 'fabricated upon points not half so much tending to the unity and peacemaking of the world' (3.34.161), he can

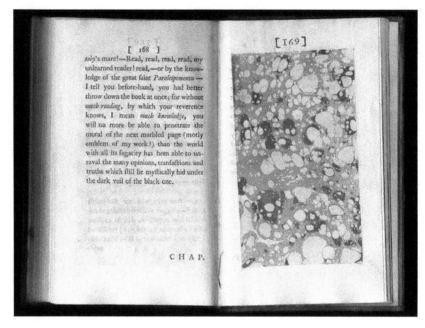

Figure 4.1   Marbled leaf in the first edition of *Tristram Shandy*, vol. 3 (1760). Image
courtesy of The Laurence Sterne Trust

find very few written on the subject of noses. Those he finds are contradictory, like the works of Prignitz and Scroderus, the first of which suggests
that the fancy begat the nose (3.38.180), and the other vice versa.[1] It is
here, in the third volume of *Tristram Shandy*, which Sterne devotes almost
entirely to medical books about noses, that he inserts his most startling
innovation, the marbled page (Figure 4.1).

It is introduced as follows:

> —Read, read, read, read, my unlearned reader! read—or by the knowledge
> of the great saint Paraleipomenon—I tell you before-hand, you had better
> throw down the book at once; for without much reading, by which your
> reverence knows I mean much knowledge, you will no more be able to
> penetrate the moral of the next marbled page (motley emblem of my work!)

[1] W.G. Day has shown that Sterne drew his references to Bouchet, Panocrates and Grangousier from
John Ozell's footnotes to the nose passage in Rabelais's *Gargantua and Pantagruel*. Day, 'Sterne and
Ozell', *English Studies*, 53 (1972), 434–6.

than the world with all its sagacity has been able to unravel the many opinions, transactions, and truths which still lie mystically hid under the dark veil of the black one. (3.36.168)

Reading, Tristram suggests, will enable his readers to understand the remarkable coloured leaf. His repetition of the imperative 'Read, read, read, read' perhaps indicates that it is a certain kind of reading – extensive, compulsive, (ac)cumulative – that will provide the key: reading like Walter Shandy.

Readers have long been fascinated by the marbled page. Walter Scott was one of the earliest to publish his interpretation of the leaf, in his introduction to *Tristram Shandy* for Ballantyne's Novelist's Library (1821–24). He read the leaf as an instance of Sterne playing the harlequin, with the black and marbled pages functioning as affected performances by the author.[2] More recently, diverse and entertaining interpretations of the page have emerged. The most frequent is that the marbled page, like other visual devices in Sterne's works, expresses what text cannot accurately capture. Everett Zimmerman states that the black and marbled pages are a comment on the book as a human body, whose 'very bodily status allies it with the grave'.[3] And nowhere are bodies more bookish than in volume 3 of *Tristram Shandy*. J. Paul Hunter sees the marbled leaf as an allusion to the intertextual relationship between fictional texts and graphic illustrations.[4] Despite these diverse interpretations of Sterne's marbled page, scholars do seem to be unanimous on its status as a self-reflexive, bookish device. In fact, the most frequent reading of the marbled page is as a joke on marbled endpapers, with Sterne comically accelerating the reader's sense of closure by bringing forward an image of completion.[5] As Peter de Voogd has shown, marbled endpapers were not popular in England before 1770, though Sterne is very likely to have had

[2] Walter Scott, 'Preface to Sterne', *The Novels of Sterne, Goldsmith, Dr. Johnson, Mackenzie, Horace Walpole, and Clara Reeve* (London: Hurst, 1823), vol. 5, xvii.
[3] Everett Zimmerman, '*Tristram Shandy* and Narrative Representation', *The Eighteenth Century*, 28.2 (1987), 140.
[4] J. Paul Hunter, 'From Typology to Type: Agents of Change in Eighteenth-Century English Texts', in Margaret J.M. Ezell and Katherine O'Brien (eds.), *Cultural Artifacts and the Production of Meaning: The Page, the Image, and the Body* (Ann Arbor, MI: University of Michigan Press, 1994), 53.
[5] James Swearingen, *Reflexivity in* Tristram Shandy*: An Essay in Phenomenological Criticism* (New Haven, CT: Yale University Press, 1977). This interpretation is also offered by Diana Alexandra Patterson, '"The Moral of the Next Marbled Page" in Sterne's *Tristram Shandy*', PhD thesis, University of Toronto (1989), 90. Peter de Voogd disputes this interpretation in 'Laurence Sterne, the Marbled Page, and the "Use of Accidents"', *Word and Image*, 1 (1985), 285.

access to editions from continental Europe, which had commonly used marbled endpapers long before this time.[6]

W.G. Day, Peter de Voogd and Diana Patterson have undertaken the most thorough bibliographical and interpretative studies of Sterne's marbled leaf, foregrounding the device as a highly significant moment in this novel and in the history of book design more broadly. Day's bibliographical study of the page will be further explored below. In a reading of the page which situates Sterne's page within a context of painting, de Voogd argues that the marbled leaf illustrates *Tristram Shandy*, the whole work, in its full complexity, which 'like the marbled page, is seemingly haphazard, the child of contingency, accidental, utterly dependent on the whims of chance and circumstance'.[7] Diana Patterson's articles and PhD thesis provide a comprehensive overview of the history of paper marbling and three ideas for what Sterne's page might represent: a series of puns; an anti-counterfeiting device; and, in line with de Voogd, a symbol of the book as a whole.[8] What is not disputed in these studies of Sterne's device is that Sterne was probably drawing upon the frequent appearance of marbling in the bookbinding process (if not as endpapers).

Contributing to scholarly consensus on the marbled page as a binding joke, this chapter for the first time historicises the marbled page metaphor as a satiric device in literature before *Tristram Shandy*. It situates Sterne's remarkable visual device within a history of colour book illustration dominated by scientific works of the kind treasured by Walter Shandy. It also recounts the history of marbled paper, commonly recognised as bookbinding material but lesser known as medical packaging for nostrums prescribed to treat wounds and ailments. As a colour illustration in the instalment of *Tristram Shandy* addressing a wounded nose, the colour and dimensions of the marbled leaf hold parallels with colour-illustrated medical books and distinctively packaged branded remedies. Sterne's marbled page, therefore, references a wide range of paper materials seeking to theorise, diagnose and treat malfunctioning bodies.

II   Coloured Book Illustration

The most startling element of the marbled page to the eighteenth-century reader would have been the fact that it is coloured. At mid-century, readers

---

[6] Patterson, 'The Moral of the Next Marbled Page', 31; De Voogd, 'Use of Accidents', 285.
[7] Ibid., 285.   [8] Patterson, 'The Moral of the Next Marbled Page'.

and would-be purchasers were most likely to encounter colour on title pages, and that colour was almost always red. Red ink was reserved for the title pages of prestige volumes, printed in smart red characters in a claim for status, as in the first editions of Chambers' *Cyclopaedia* (1728) and Thomas Shaw's *Travels in Barbary and the Levant* (1738), and the title pages of such classic literary volumes as Pope's *Works of Shakespeare* (1723–5), John Baskerville's 1762 edition of Horace and many of Jacob Tonson's editions of Dryden's works. As Janine Barchas has argued, aside from the 1724 and 1738 editions of Daniel Defoe's *Colonel Jack*, coloured (red) ink was rarely applied to unknown fictional texts,[9] though it was more familiar on publishers' rubric posts, where one copy of a title page might have been printed in red to arrest the attention of passers-by. In *Epistle to Arbuthnot* (1735), Pope explores the red typography of advertising as a poetic signifier for literary fame:

> What though my name stood rubric on the walls,
> Or plaster'd posts, with claps, in capitals?
> [...]
> I sought no homage from the race that write;
> I kept, like Asian monarchs, from their sight.[10]

Despite the posters, or 'claps', highlighting his name in red capitals, Pope seeks no fame, 'no homage from the race that write'. In the *Dunciad*, he singles out publisher Bernard Lintot's rubric post as a masthead for disposable fiction:

> Hence springs each weekly Muse, the living boast
> Of Curl's chaste press, and Lintot's rubric post,
> Hence hymning Tyburn's elegiac lay,
> Hence the soft sing-song on Cecilia's day,
> Sepulchral lies, our holy walls to grace,
> And New-year Odes, and all the Grubstreet race.[11]

In his notes to these lines in the second edition of the *Dunciad Variorum* (1729), Pope reminds us that Lintot 'usually adorn'd his shop with Titles in red letters'.[12] However, this satire of rubrication as a cheapening device is context-specific, with Pope deriding rubric posts all the while that the title pages of his *Rape of the Lock* (Lintot, 1714) were printed in

[9] Janine Barchas, *Graphic Design, Print Culture, and the Eighteenth-Century Novel* (Cambridge University Press, 2003), 60.
[10] Alexander Pope, 'Epistle to Arbuthnot', *The Major Works*, Pat Rogers (ed.), Oxford World's Classics (Oxford University Press, 2008), 343, l. 215–16 and 219–20.
[11] Pope, *Dunciad Variorum*, 2nd ed. (London, 1729), 57, l. 37–42.   [12] Ibid., 57, l. 38.

red ink. Through disparaging red typography Pope simultaneously called attention to his own canonical status. The title pages of the *Rape of the Lock* were not just red on the rubric post, but in every copy, highlighting Pope's name, the title of his poem, 'London' and Lintot's name, and undoubtedly catching the eye. In a move which perhaps echoes Pope's disdain for rubrication in the *Dunciad*, Sterne tucks away the marbled page in the middle of the third volume of *Tristram Shandy*; in its location the leaf is altogether more demure than existing practices of printing coloured ink in literature. Lintot used red ink to catch the eye of the reader and to indicate literary value. Sterne's earliest purchasers would not have known that the work included an expensively produced colour image, suggesting that elaborate advertising strategies were unnecessary given Sterne's sudden and meteoric rise to fame.[13] His lavish investment in four coloured inks for the marbled page is therefore a defiant statement about the value of his work. The marbled page in *Tristram Shandy* rewards sustained attention at the same time as it demonstrates his capacity to continue innovating and surprising his audiences within a work which had been experimental from its very beginning.

While Sterne was not the first author to include coloured ink within his work, books sold with colour illustrations in this period were luxury collectables.[14] Novels were rarely illustrated at all in their first editions, and mass-produced colour illustrations of literary works were a much later invention.[15] The two genres in which colour illustrations would be most commonly found were books of science and fine art. Readers would know from the newspaper advertisements of a title, and sometimes its title page, whether to expect colour within the pages of such a work, and the inclusion of colour added to the price of the book at the point of purchase. This is mainly because coloured images required extra effort and financial investment on the part of the book's publisher or designer. Elizabeth Blackwell's *A Curious Herbal* (1737–39), for example, boasted beautiful

[13] Siv Gøril Brandtzaeg, M-C. Newbould and Helen Williams, 'Advertising Sterne's Novels in Eighteenth-Century Newspapers', *The Shandean*, 27 (2016), 27–58.

[14] Sarah Lowengard, 'Colour Printed Illustrations in Eighteenth-Century Periodicals', in Christina Ionescu (ed.), *Book Illustration in the Long Eighteenth Century: Reconfiguring the Visual Periphery of the Text* (Newcastle: Cambridge Scholars, 2011), 58.

[15] The earliest known printed colour images in books emerged in the 1460s and were made from one colour ink only. Elizabeth L. Eisenstein, *The Printing Press as an Agent of Change: Communications and Cultural Transformations in Early Modern Europe* (Cambridge University Press, 1979), 567.

illustrations of medicinal plants and was sold at two prices, one price for the plain text and another to have it hand-coloured by Blackwell herself. This book was unusual in that it was coloured from original specimens in the Chelsea Physic Garden, instead of from artworks. The text was stamped with the approval of the Society of Apothecaries and advertised as 'useful' by the Royal College of Physicians, who provided a testimonial for the publication. According to the college, it was colour that made the *Herbal* particularly useful, better enabling readers to identify the plants depicted in the volume. Coloured images were never a surprise in eighteenth-century books. To include coloured ink and not advertise the fact was a lavish act of book design which necessitated additional financial risk if the volumes did not sell.

With almost all colour book illustrations from incunabula to the eighteenth century, colour was added after the fact. The most common means of producing coloured pages in books in this period was the post-printing technique of hand-colouring, freehand or with stencils, undertaken by a range of people including professional colourists, printers, binders, purchasers and owners.[16] It was mostly an optional extra, but three remarkable scientific works from the first half of the eighteenth century were distributed solely in coloured form. These were Eleazar Albin's *A Natural History of Birds* (1731–38), Mark Catesby's *Natural History of Carolina, Florida and the Bahama Islands* (1731–43) and James Smith's *Flower Garden Display'd [...] and Coloured to the Life* (1732), the text for which was written by Richard Bradley. Catesby was the first to use folio-sized hand-coloured engravings, and he is celebrated now for innovatively placing animals and plants within elaborate backgrounds of native flora.[17] A regular contributor to the Royal Society, Catesby was loaned the capital to produce the book by one its members, and in 1733 Catesby himself was elected a fellow. This reflected not only his skill in ornithology but also his mastery of coloured ink, through which Catesby was better able to express and disseminate specialist knowledge of the natural world; colour afforded scientific works higher value in terms of their utility. The title page of Timothy Sheldrake's *Botanicum Medicinale* (1759) highlighted the efficacy of colour, proclaiming that 'The colours of every Part are minutely described; for Utility it must be esteemed preferably to any HORTUS

[16] Lowengard, 'Colour Printed Illustrations', 57, 60.
[17] Amy R.W. Meyers et al. (eds.), *Empire's Nature: Mark Catesby's New World Vision* (Chapel Hill, NC: University of North Carolina Press, 1998).

SICCUS extant'. They should buy the *Botanicum*, he hints, in its coloured rather than plain state.[18] It was 'Designed to promote Botanical Knowledge, prevent Mistakes in the Use of Simples in compounding and preparing Medicines, to illustrate, and render such Herbals as want the just Representation in their proper Colours more Useful'.[19]

In these rare editions of texts intended to be sold ready-coloured in every copy, standardisation was more easily achieved. Producers of botanical works, for example, could make sure that any hand-coloured image was checked against the original painting for consistency. But differences remained in all coloured images due to subjective interpretations of the surrounding text and different levels of skill and access to inks, despite scientific works loudly claiming that standardised shades of ink meant more accurate scientific knowledge. Scientific authors longed for a uniform means of producing colour images. But at mid-century, it was difficult, time-consuming and expensive to machine-print images with multiple colours. The earliest polychrome techniques were initially developed not for book illustration but to create prints of famous artworks. They required overprinting to create a single coloured image, and they were inspired by new understandings of colour production arising from the growing popularity of Isaac Newton's *Opticks: or, A Treatise of the Reflexions, Refractions, Inflexions and Colours of Light* (1704), which argued for the primacy of the colours red, yellow and blue.

After Newton, artists and printers began to believe that every colour could be represented using a foundation of just those three colours. Jacob

---

[18] According to the title page, the prices (unbound) were as follows: royal coloured 6-0-0, plain 3-0-0; small coloured 3-0-0, plain 2-2-0. Timothy Sheldrake, *Botanicum Medicinale* (London: Millan, 1759).

[19] Sheldrake appealed to consumers to buy the more expensive version of his text by arguing for improved understanding through colour and pointing out what he felt to be an inadequacy in Linnaeus's system, his omission of colour. Linnaeus had not dealt with colour partly because the specific shades and tones of plants were dependent upon the place in which they grew but also because of the difficulty in reproducing identical tints of ink. See Kärin Nickelsen, *Draughtsmen, Botanists and Nature: The Construction of Eighteenth-Century Botanical Illustrations*, New Studies in the History and Philosophy of Science and Technology (Dordrecht, Netherlands: Springer, 2006), 15. Sterne and his contemporaries had no choice but to deal with the instability of coloured inks. Only after his death would colour become more standardised. In 1769 German botanist Jacob Christian Schaeffer devised his *Plan for a Universal Relationship of Colours; Or Research and Model for Determining and Naming Colours in a Way that is Useful to the General Public*. Schaeffer proposed his own taxonomy for systematically naming and identifying colour in order to aid natural science in identifying the colour properties of plants or insects. He designed hand-coloured charts with accompanying recipes for the accurate production of specific shades of ink in a method anticipating today's Pantone system. Jacob Christian Schaeffer, *Entwurf einer allgemeinen Farbenverein; oder Versuch und Muster einer gemeinn⟨utzlichen Bestimmung und Benennung der Farben* (Regensburg: Weiß, 1769). See Nickelsen, *Draughtsmen*, 18.

Christoff Le Blon pioneered his trichromatic printing process in Amsterdam in around 1710, which involved overprinting different copper mezzotint plates inked by hand in blue, yellow and red (in that order) to create one multicolour print of a famous painting,[20] democratising access to unique pieces of art and supplying the growing demands of print collectors on the continent. This was essentially an early form of today's CMYK printing process, the invention of which Le Blon announced in his 1722 dual-language publication, *Coloritto*, in English and French. Likewise, English printer John Baptist Jackson also experimented with colour printing to satisfy the eighteenth-century demand for reproductions of classic oil paintings. Jackson also overprinted blocks but used wood instead of copper, and instead of three plates used four or more.[21] His single-sheet reproduction of Rembrandt's *Descent from the Cross* (1738), for example, is printed from four blocks in yellow, grey and two shades of brown.[22] Despite his innovation, Jackson remained unpopular, and his manifesto did not endear him to the art community; it criticised his rivals and ignored the experiments of practitioners such as Le Blon, who had initiated the incorporation of colour-printed images into books and received a patent for colour printing.[23]

The earliest known colour mezzotint image is one of Le Blon's anatomy images, a 'Dissected human testicles and penis showing the symptoms of

[20] Bamber Gascoigne, *Milestones in Colour Printing 1457–1859: With a Bibliography of Nelson Prints* (Cambridge University Press, 1997), 8.

[21] John Baptist Jackson, *An Essay on the Invention of Engraving and Printing in Chiaro Oscuro* (London: Millar, 1754), 8. For examples, see the twenty-four celebrated Venetian paintings reproduced in Jackson's *Titiani Vecelii, Pauli Caliarii, Jacobi Robusti, et Jacobi de Ponte, opera selectiora a Joanne Baptista Jackson Anglo, ligno cœlata, et coloribus adumbrata* (Venice: Batista, 1745).

[22] Metadata from John Baptist Jackson, after Rembrandt van Rijn, 'Descent from the Cross' (1738), National Gallery of Art, Washington DC, accession number Kainen 1962, no. 13, 2012.92.523. Jackson, *Essay*, 5. In his *Essay*, which included eight polychrome plates, Jackson staked his claim as the first English colour printer. He saw himself as recovering the Renaissance practice of chiaroscuro, boasting that 'an Art recovered is little less than an Art invented', and at the same time advertising his services as a producer of expensive colour wallpaper. Emerging in the first decade of the 1500s, chiaroscuro woodcuts had indeed gone some way towards creating multiple colours. Until Jackson's book, eighteenth-century connoisseurs found that though examples of these artworks survived, clear instructions for the chiaroscuro practice did not. Chiaroscuro engravings (in wood and, later, copper) used the colour of the paper as a highlight and printed it with blocks inked in increasingly darker shades of the same or similar hues to create depth. Examples of Jackson's wallpaper survive in the British Museum (1918,0713.59, 1731–45) and the Victoria and Albert Museum (E.2696-1920, 1744).

[23] During his time in London, Le Blon been granted a royal patent for his three-colour process before relocating to Paris, where he was granted the privilege of colour printing by the French Crown in 1739. 'A New Method of Multiplying of Pictures and Draughts by a Natural Colleris with Impression,' English Patent no. 423 issued to James Christopher Le Blon (5 February 1719).

an infection with gonorrhoea pinned to a board'.[24] It was printed to be bound with a popular pamphlet on venereal disease composed by Jonathan Swift's physician, William Cockburn. *The Symptoms, Nature and Cure of Gonorrhoea* (1713) went through four editions and was translated into French, with some early editions including a similar black and white engraving of a dissection.[25] Le Blon's image would have increased sales of Cockburn's text, making it highly collectable, and he was commissioned by Nathaniel St André to produce a full series of colour anatomy prints but the project collapsed.[26] When Le Blon died, his former student, Jacques Fabien Gautier (later Gautier d'Agoty), successfully fought off other students and rivals to have the privilege of colour printing transferred to him.[27] Gautier continues to hold a sensationalised reputation for his titillating colour-printed anatomies, which show corpses as if they were living, depicted in sexually suggestive poses with their skin peeled back and organs showing.[28] But he innovated in the book trade, too, when in the 1750s he launched the first tricolour-printed periodical, *Observations sur L'Histoire naturelle, sur la Physique et la Peinture* (1752–55), making ownership of colour-printed literature more freely available to a wide, if specialised, readership.[29] Around this time, producers of botanical books slowly began to experiment with colour mezzotints, but these were produced in a much more basic fashion. As Wilfrid Blunt and William Thomas Stearn point out, these 'colour prints' were most often simply printed in green ink rather than black and touched up by hand afterwards. A few plates were printed in two or three colours.[30]

---

[24] British Museum (1928,0310.101). Peter Krivatsy argues for another image of an anatomised shoulder to be the first colour print (also by Le Blon), in Arent Cant's *Dissertatio anatomico-theoretica inaugural* (1719), but I cannot locate the item at the National Library of Medicine where Krivatsy identifies it. Both probably appeared in the same year. Krivatsy, 'Le Blon's Anatomical Color Engravings', *Journal of the History of Medicine and Allied Sciences*, 23.2 (1968), 153–8. Le Blon's image is available at: http://peccadille.net/2013/01/17/815/, last accessed 5 June 2020. Le Blon and Gautier produced many anatomical illustrations, though only three of Le Blon's anatomical images survive. His works in general are very rare.

[25] The first edition was published by Graves in London in 1713. The 'third edition with additions' published in 1719 by Strahan includes a black and white engraving of the penis, and the 'fourth edition with additions' (1728, also Strahan) includes that and a second cross-section of the penis.

[26] Dániel Margócsy, *Commercial Visions: Science, Trade, and Visual Culture in the Dutch Golden Age* (University of Chicago Press, 2014), 186.

[27] Gascoigne, *Milestones*, 63.

[28] Lowengard, 'Colour Printed Illustrations', 63. See, for example, d'Agoty's coloured mezzotints: 'Muscles of the back in a Female', after dissections by J.F. Duverney (1746); 'Two Dissected Heads, on Sacking', after dissections by Tarin, *Anatomie de la tete* (1748).

[29] Margócsy, *Commercial Visions*, 195.

[30] Society of Gardeners, *Catalogus Plantarum. A Catalogue of Trees, Shrubs, Plants, and Flowers, Both Exotic and Domestic, Which are propagated for Sale in the Gardens near London* (London: Society of

Meanwhile, the world of literary illustrations was monochrome. As in the case of Henry Fielding's *Tom Jones*, it was much more common for eighteenth-century novels to be translated before they were illustrated, a point highlighted by Nathalie Ferrand.[31] Barchas's work on the graphic design of the eighteenth-century novel has begun the important task of exploring the rare visual elements of the novel in this period. As she demonstrates, fantasy travel narratives such as Defoe's *Robinson Crusoe* (1719) and Swift's *Gulliver's Travels* (1726) were more visual than other literary works from this period, and included black and white frontispiece illustrations of their fictional narrators. Swift also printed engraved monochrome maps in the first edition of *Gulliver*, and Defoe included fold-out maps in first editions of Crusoe's *Farther Adventures* (1719) and *Serious Reflections* (1720).[32] Book illustrations as we tend to think of them now, pictures of notable scenes from the text's plot, tended to be later additions to fictional works which had stood the test of time, and which would be sure to sell despite the additional cost of image production.[33] When it came to coloured ink, the pressure was even higher to be able to predict sales of works requiring such investment, so perhaps nursery rhymes, in their ability to continue to shift units beyond their first appearance, were a safer investment. One such example is a children's chapbook recorded as the oldest surviving collection of nursery rhymes, *Tommy Thumb's Pretty Song Book* (1744), printed with illustrations in alternating pages of red and black ink.[34]

If there was a general rule in eighteenth-century book design that first edition literary works would not include colour images, then there is of course one exception: John Kidgell's *The Card* (1755) (Figure 4.2).

Gardeners, 1730). This text included some colour mezzotints, as did John Martyn's *Historia Plantarum Rariorum* (1728–37), illustrated by Jacob van Huysum. See Wilfrid Blunt and William Thomas Stearn, *The Art of Botanical Illustration: An Illustrated History* (New York: Dover, 1994), 133. Nickelsen tells us that Johann Wilhelm Weinmann's renowned botanical work *Phytanthoza Iconographia* (published 1735/45) was one of the first colour-printed works. Nickelsen, 'The Challenge of Colour: Eighteenth-Century Botanists and the Hand-Colouring of Illustrations', *Annals of Science*, 63.1 (2006), 3–23, 5.

[31] Nathalie Ferrand, 'Translating and Illustrating the Eighteenth-Century Novel', *Word & Image*, 30 (2014), 181–3.

[32] Barchas, *Graphic Design*.

[33] See, for example, Sandro Jung, 'The Other *Pamela*: Readership and the Illustrated Chapbook Abridgement', *Journal for Eighteenth-Century Studies*, 39 (2016), Special Issue: *Picturing the Eighteenth-Century Novel through Time*, Christina Ionescu and Ann Lewis (eds.), 513–31.

[34] ['Nurse Lovechild'], *Tommy Thumb's Pretty Song Book*, 2 vols. (London: Cooper, 1744), vol. 2. Only the second volume of this collection has survived.

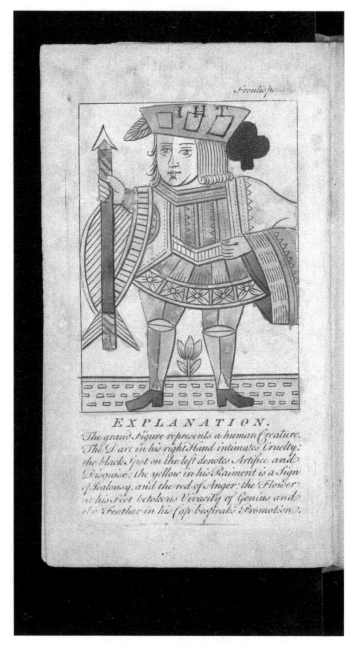

Figure 4.2 Frontispiece and title page of John Kidgell's *The Card* (1755). Image courtesy of Cambridge University Library

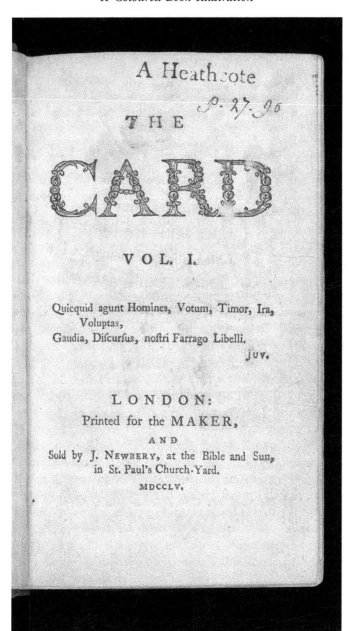

Figure 4.2 *(cont.)*

The image is a hand-coloured copperplate frontispiece, which would have been printed on a different press and added to the book before sewing. The image problematises any easy alignment of text and image, despite its caption:

> The grand figure represents a human Creature. The Dart in his right Hand intimates Cruelty; the black spot on the left denotes Artifice and Disguise; the yellow in his Raiment is a sign of Jealousy, and the red of Anger; the Flower at his feet betokens Vivacity of Genius and the Feather in his Cap bespeaks Promotion.

The caption insists upon the capacity of colour to carry meaning, but the abstract ideas signified here, artifice and disguise (black), jealousy (yellow) and anger (red), bear little if any relation to the epistolary narrative that follows. At least one contemporary reader was confused by this caption, a contributor to the *Monthly Review*, who concluded that 'It would pose an *Oedipus* to unravel this'.[35] As Barchas points out, it is likely that Kidgell was simply invoking playing cards and replicating their colours, red, yellow, blue and black, rather than saying something profound about his fiction.[36] But perhaps he felt that it reflected well upon himself as an author. Colour, Sarah Lowengard has argued, demonstrated the 'technical skills and aesthetic sensibility' of the book's creator.[37] Such an interpretation of *The Card* might be supported by its title page, which claimed the book to be printed for the 'maker' rather than the 'author'. Facing the title page, the arresting colours of the frontispiece marketed Kidgell's novel as craftsmanship, as experimental fiction, but it encouraged sales of a work to readers who were ultimately disappointed, as the reviewer complained: 'A Title so novel, and, to appearance, so inapplicable to any production from the press amounting to two volumes, has, no doubt, prevailed upon many to satisfy their curiosity by purchasing the performance'.[38] In an undoubtedly innovative move, Kidgell's novelty image was a publicity ploy, unlike Sterne's marbled page, which was undiscoverable until page 169 of volume 3.

Unless colour was a component of a particularly collectable text, throughout the eighteenth century it was most often an add-on, and consumers of any book other than *Tristram Shandy* would always have known in advance that the pages of a text they were buying included colour. Unlike Kidgell and the printers of red title pages, Sterne surprised the first purchasers of *Tristram Shandy* by including his marbled page

[35] *Monthly Review*, 12 (1755), 117–21, 120.   [36] Barchas, *Graphic Design*, 233, n. 82.
[37] Lowengard, 'Colour Printed Illustrations', 53–76, 58.
[38] *Monthly Review*, 117; Barchas, *Graphic Design*, 52–3.

towards the end of the third volume of this text. Like Kidgell's frontispiece, Sterne's marbled leaf declares *Tristram Shandy*'s author to have aesthetic taste and proficiency with the tools of book production. But Sterne, much more than Kidgell, was not only 'author' but also 'maker' of a three-dimensional artefact. As the first polychrome illustration of (in the strict sense of having relevance to) a fictional text, the marbled page lights up the black and white world of the eighteenth-century novel in a manner entirely unprecedented, and breaks new ground in its close-knit relationship to the instalment which carries it.

The marbled page is a much more slippery sign than red-inked title pages and hand-coloured engraved frontispieces, which aimed for standardisation. As Lowengard argues, even in scientific works featuring anatomical or botanical images, where consistency and similarity were privileged and colour variations could be 'disastrous', in certain circumstances variations in colouring could also be desirable, enhancing 'the uniqueness of each copy'.[39] Part of the attraction of paper marbling is the fact that the resulting artworks are unique in every copy. Unlike the black-graven outlines of Kidgell's knave, Sterne's image is formless, dependent on the instability of coloured inks in this period and the capacity of the marbling technique in particular to enhance uniqueness in each impression. Sterne draws upon a tradition of using colour illustrations characterised by a desire for stability and standardisation, but he turns it on its head, satirising any quest for scientific accuracy or uniformity through the deliberate unpredictability of his medium.[40] It is therefore the element of his novel over which he was able to exert the least control. But it is not just the uniqueness of his own text, and the story of Walter's difficulty in reconciling contradictory knowledge sourced from coloured medical works, that Sterne illustrates with the marbled page, as the next section will show. He also exploits marbling's predominance in the book trade to illustrate Walter's fascination with his book collection and to bring to life Tristram's creative act of appending this material to his memoir.

III Marbling and the Book

Though marbled paper was widely available, used to bind and preserve texts and, more simply, as wrapping paper, marbling itself was a rare

---

[39] Lowengard, 'Colour Printed Illustrations', 60.

[40] De Voogd has argued that Sterne creates his marbled page in a painterly tradition emerging in the second half of the eighteenth century, which privileged 'the paradoxical principle of accidental design, of carefully planned seeming chaos'. De Voogd, 'Use of Accidents', 281.

practice in eighteenth-century England. The year that Sterne's marbled page appeared in bookshops, 1760, was also an important year in the history of English marbling, when the Society for the Encouragement of Arts, Manufactures and Commerce planned to award a premium for it:

> For marbling the greatest Quantity of Paper, equal in Goodness to the best marbled Paper imported from abroad, not less than one Rheam [*sic*]; to be produced on or before the 2d Tuesday in February, 1760 - £10.[41]

Founded by William Shipley in 1754 through subscription, and still extant today as the Royal Society of Arts, the society awarded cash premiums to entice Englishmen to develop liberal arts, science and manufacturing at home. In 1759 the society began to be concerned that despite marbled paper appearing as binding material for English books since at least the seventeenth century, English stationers imported all of their marbled paper from France and Germany via Holland.[42] That was not to say that England had no marblers; for at least a century English bookbinders had marbled the edges of books, in a bid to copy the latest French fashion.[43] But it would not be until 1766 that Englishman Richard Dymott would claim to have perfected the art.[44] Aware that England had the requisite skills to produce marbled paper but that English marblers had not yet begun to produce enough of it to be self-sufficient, the society sought to help establish large-scale manufacture of marbled paper. The primary criterion for the successful award of the 1760 premium, therefore, was not so much quality as quantity.

The Society for the Encouragement of Arts, Manufactures and Commerce boasted a number of well-known members. In 1760, Laurence Sterne was one of them. He appears in the list of names alongside his friends and associates: John Wilkes, David Garrick, James Dodsley, Elizabeth Montague, Lord Rockingham, Lord Walpole and Thomas Walpole, and Joseph Nollekens.[45] Patterson has been the only

---

[41] Society for the Encouragement of Arts, Manufactures, and Commerce, *Premiums by the Society Established at London for the Encouragement of Arts, Manufactures, and Commerce* (London: by Order of the Society, 1759). See Patterson, 'The Moral of the Next Marbled Page', 27.

[42] Richard J. Wolfe, *Marbled Paper: Its History, Techniques, and Patterns: With Special Reference to the Relationship of Marbling to Bookbinding in Europe and the Western World* (Philadelphia, PA: University of Pennsylvania Press, 1990), 67–70; Patterson, 'The Moral of the Next Marbled Page', 193.

[43] Wolfe sees this as evidence that marbling was happening in England in this period. Wolfe, *Marbled Paper*, 37.

[44] De Voogd, 'Use of Accidents', 285.

[45] Patterson, 'The Moral of the Next Marbled Page', 64–5.

scholar so far to point out that during the year which saw the plight of English marbling raised in a public forum, Sterne was busy producing the only novel ever to have included a marbled leaf within its pages.[46] She notes that because he was a member, Sterne would have known that the society offered hundreds of premiums each year. He would have seen the notices of premiums published in the newspapers, as well as in the society's official publication. He may also have known that the marbling premium advertised in 1759, with a deadline of February 1760, was not awarded, primarily because none of the applicants was able to produce the hefty quantity of paper. But other potential applicants may have been unwilling to engage in the competition, given the size of the prize relative to the quantity of paper required.[47] The society offered larger premiums for smaller quantities of marbled paper in subsequent years, until a sum of fifty pounds was finally awarded to Messrs. Portbury & Smith in 1763.[48] If Sterne had conceived of including a marbled leaf as the 'motly emblem of his work' in volume 3 of *Tristram Shandy* by February 1760, he surely would have been interested in the applicants to, and the outcome of, that first prize for English marbling. Patterson's retracing of this history of English marbling allows us to reveal one of Sterne's major innovations in 1761: at a time when English marbling was in its infancy, and those practising the art unable or unwilling to submit so many reams to the society for recognition, he could locate and contract an English marbler to produce 8,000 marbled pages for *Tristram Shandy*.[49] Sterne also innovated with the style of the page – it has English blotches as opposed to the French style of combing – which would have been unusual at this time. His page is marbled with daubs of bright colour, darker and more defined than John Baskerville's iconic swashes of pastels. The English style of marbling was freer than the French combed style so popular in the period (present in the image of James's Powder in Figure 4.4). Marbled paper by Baskerville and by Sterne's marblers also differed from its European counterparts in being more transparent, leaving the paper visible beneath and around the inks. This meant that the resulting paper was not as thick and glossy to the touch, which could explain why the European style continued to be more successful in the English book trade into the nineteenth century, for its protective qualities. Nevertheless, in his financing and facilitating mass production of the art of marbling, Sterne

---

[46] Patterson, 'Tristram's Marblings and Marblers', *The Shandean*, 3 (1991), 70–97.
[47] Patterson, 'John Baskerville, Marbler', *The Library*, s6–12 (1990), 216.   [48] Ibid., 215.
[49] Day, '*Tristram Shandy*: The Marbled Leaf', *Library*, 27 (1972), 143–5, 145.

helped support home manufactures, in keeping with the aims of the society of which he was a member.

The society's desire to support home-grown marbling arose from its concerns over the English book trade, as bookbinding was by far the most common use for marbled paper in this period. Many eighteenth-century books, in England and across Europe, appeared marbled, and sometimes even the leather of hardbacks was marbled. Three-quarter bindings (paper on boards with leather spines) or half-bindings (with additional leather corners) sometimes displayed marbled-paper boards front and back. For many readers, then, the marbled leaf in *Tristram Shandy* must have connoted the outside, rather than the inside of books. Sterne turns the structure of the eighteenth-century novel inside out, having marbled paper peer out from within a sewn work, instead of (and in some cases as well as) enclosing and preserving the text within. This creative manipulation of the order in which readers usually encountered the structure of the conventional codex plays into Sterne's preference for non-linearity as explored in Chapter 6 on engraved lines. But it is also significant that the page is not simply a piece of French marbled paper, sewn into the book, which would have been an easier and more efficient way to make that statement. Sterne preserves the white margins of the leaf, too, which made the marbler's job considerably more difficult, as they had to ensure that the paper lay perfectly flat in the ink bath to prevent colour seeping up the folded edges of the page. Because the marbled pages carry the same white margins as every other page in *Tristram Shandy*, and they appear in regular pagination, Sterne hints that the novel and its wrapping are one, inseparable, revealing his subversion of traditional practices of eighteenth-century book production. Because his volumes were sold 'sewn' rather than in 'sheets' (that is to say, each volume was sewn together but not yet bound), with the marbled page Sterne shows that this is not just a narrative but a three-dimensional artwork of which he is the designer.

This hand-marbled page is unique in every copy of *Tristram Shandy*. The leaf, pre-cut with its margins folded back, was dipped by an unidentified English marbler into a bath of four colours: red, green, yellow and black.[50] It was then hung up to dry, and the process repeated on the

---

[50] Patterson, 'The Moral of the Next Marbled Page'. Red ink was certainly available locally. In 1760 the *York Courant*, one of Sterne's local newspapers, carried an advertisement for Stephen Wilkinson, a local bookbinder which touted for a journeyman while offering his red ink for sale:

other side. The marbling only appears within the text box, as did the ink of the black page in volume 1. Page numbers were hand stamped onto the top margin (note the slightly larger, less uniform typeface) and then the leaf was sewn or pasted into place in advance of sale.[51] Because volumes were sold sewn, the page very rarely appears in the incorrect place in original bindings.[52] The marbled page required significant forward-planning on the part of the printers; this was no cancel page, which entailed cutting out and replacing one leaf of a gathering in an improvised but common practice responding to error. Such amended gatherings usually include a regular number of pages. Neither is it a paratextual image, like the copperplate illustrations which often appeared in books of this period as additions after the printing of the text, due to their having been printed on a different kind of press. The second edition of *Tristram Shandy* carrying Hogarth's frontispiece is a good example of this. The status of such illustrations as 'extras' is compounded by their lack of pagination. In paginating the marbled leaf as 169 and 170, and inserting it between the fourth and fifth leaves of the 'L' gathering, Sterne has the marbled page added to an octavo sheet, increasing the size of the gathering. Because the marbled page has been inserted into the middle of the sheet, where the fold is, sometimes a little tab folded inwards remains visible in the earliest copies of *Tristram Shandy*. In order to allow for the insertion of the marbled leaf in the centre of the gathering, the printers would have to disrupt the pagination of the forme (Figure 4.3). In requiring his typesetters to paginate the sheet according to Figure 4.3b, Sterne would have upturned conventional practice in the print shop, where habit was key to efficiency. He disrupts the order of the creation of his book – and of the eighteenth-century book more generally – for the addition of the marbled page.

For the bibliographers among his readership, the joke would have been underlined by Tristram's calling upon Saint Paraleipomenon to help his readers understand the marbled page's moral ('read—or by the knowledge of the great saint Paraleipomenon—I tell you before-hand, you had better

A JOURNEYMAN BOOKBINDER, that is a sober careful Man, and understands his Business, may have constant Employment, and suitable Encouragement, by applying to STEPHEN WILKINSON, Bookbinder in the Judges Lodgings, Coney-street, York.
Of whom may be had,
RED INK, as good as any that is made, and of the same Qualities with that used by the Officers in the Customhouse in Newcastle. (*The York Courant*, York City Archives)

[51] I am indebted to W.G. Day for assisting me to come to this conclusion.
[52] Patterson, 'The Moral of the Next Marbled Page'.

| 165 | 172 | 169 | 168 |
| 164 | 173 | 176 | 161 |

Front

| 167 | 170 | 171 | 166 |
| 162 | 175 | 174 | 163 |

Back

Figure 4.3a   A regular octavo sheet featuring pages 169 and 170

| 165 | 174 | 171 | 168 |
| 164 | 175 | 178 | 161 |

Front

| 167 | 172 | 173 | 166 |
| 162 | 177 | 176 | 163 |

Back

Figure 4.3b   The same octavo sheet paginated without 169 and 170

throw down the book at once'). The Christian chronicles produced by Paraleipomenon covered perceived gaps in the Bible, so the term 'Paralipomena' came to mean 'Things omitted in the body of a work, and appended as a supplement'.[53] To invoke the name of Paraleipomenon, therefore, is to reference the practice of appending missing or ancillary text to a narrative. With the marbled page, Sterne physically supplements the codex, adding a page to a gathering, and in the performative act of pasting and/or sewing in the marbled page[54] has the print shop employees enact the very process of supplementation that Tristram discursively undertakes

[53] *OED*, cited in *The Life and Opinions of Tristram Shandy, Gentleman: The Notes*, Melvyn New, Richard A. Davies and W.G. Day (eds.), The Florida Edition of the Works of Laurence Sterne (Gainesville, FL: University Press of Florida, 1984), vol. 3, 269, n. 268.2–3.

[54] Patterson, having seen a copy of volume 3 still in blue wrappers which has the marbled page both hand-sewn and pasted into place, argues that all copies were likely to be produced in this manner. Patterson, 'The Moral of the Next Marbled Page', 124.

throughout his memoir – as in the sermon, discussed in Chapter 3 – and to which he self-consciously draws attention in his reference to the saint.

The chapters including and preceding the marbled page are those most dedicated to Walter's book collecting and to the materiality of these texts. Sterne's disruption of gathering L with the marbled page reflects Walter's coveted book collection and Tristram's desire to incorporate as much as possible of it into his work. Tristram himself enacts this process of supplementation with the words immediately following the marbled leaf, which are a quotation from Erasmus's 'De Captandis Sacerdotiis' in his *Colloquia Familiaria*: *"NIHIL me poenitet hujus nasi,"* quoth *Pamphagus;*—that is—"My nose has been the making of me."——"*Nec est cur poeniteat,*" replies *Cocles;* that is, "How the duce should such a nose fail?"' (3.37.171). That Tristram should include at this point an uncontextualised extract of another work might have been suggested to us by the marbled paper, usually a signifier of the beginning or end of a text. Walter cannot comprehend Erasmus's dialogue, scratching at the paper with a knife to try to make sense of it. He only finds relief by consoling himself with the works of Hafen Slawkenbergius, his copy of which is 'for ever in his hands,—you would have sworn, Sir, it had been a canon's prayer-book,—so worn, so glazed, so contrited and attrited was it with fingers and with thumbs in all its parts, from one end even unto the other' (3.42.200–1). As Jonathan Laidlow points out, Walter's copy of Slawkenbergius's works is incorrectly bound, as Tristram points out that 'the bookbinder has most injudiciously placed it betwixt the analitical contents of the book, and the book itself' (3.38.176).[55] Tristram will appear to bind Slawkenbergius's text within his own novel, as it forms the surprising opening section of volume 4. Sterne's marbled page resembles – in fact, it constitutes – the matter of bookbinding, and its placement in a chapter about Walter's book collection, in an instalment of the novel which details and draws from those works, illustrates in remarkably lifelike ways the process by which Tristram 'binds' together texts on noses within his autobiography.

Marbled bindings were an indication of prestige, but they did not always guarantee that a book's contents were equally reputable, as the anonymous Sternean imitator responsible for *The Life, Travels, and Adventures, of Christopher Wagstaff, Gentleman, Grandfather to Tristram Shandy* (1762) pointed out: 'I must protest against the marble covers, gilt

---

[55] Jonathan Laidlow, 'A Compendium of Shandys: Methods of Organising Knowledge in Sterne's *Tristram Shandy*', *Eighteenth Century Novel*, (2001), 181–200.

backs, pompous frontispieces, and other adscititious embellishments, by
which so many fine books in the libraries of the curious are at once
ornamented and disguised. It is absurd that any thing lettered should
appear about the production of a fool'.[56] But whereas marbled boards
were relatively expensive, marbled paper was often used to create cheap
paperback bindings for short prose works and poetry, or notepads. In
being associated with worthy hardback fiction, with hackwork expensively
bound, and with paperback fiction of varying quality, it is unsurprising
that marbled paper was sometimes invoked to satirise literary value, and
Sterne was not the first author to draw upon the associations of marbled
paper. When annotating the marbled leaf, the Florida editors refer readers
to Eric Rothstein's identification of 'An earlier instance of its use' in Noël-
Antoine Pluche's *Le Spectacle de la nature* (Paris, 1732–42).[57] For
Rothstein, Sterne read Pluche, and he identifies a copy of *Le Spectacle de
la nature* in the sale catalogue of Sterne's library as evidence. The Florida
editors cite Rothstein's footnote: 'Conceivably the marbled paper, with its
mystic meanings, is a reply to Noël-Antoine Pluche, who used it as an
example of meaningless color unconnected to objects'.[58] Rothstein's claim,
present, too, in the annotation of the marbled page by the Florida editors,
misleadingly gives the impression that Sterne is not the first author to
include a marbled page in his work. But Pluche does not 'use' marbled
paper in a literal sense.[59] Rothstein refers us in particular to this passage,
where Pluche does indeed use marbled paper – metaphorically – to argue
for the meaninglessness of random colour:

> comme les couleurs sont destinées à mettre une distinction dans les objèts,
> elles ne plaisent pas long-tems si elles ne tiennent à quelque figure: parce
> qu'alors elles font hors de leur place. Un beau papier marbré & un beau
> point d'Hongrie sont d'agréables couleurs & rien de plus. Le premier coup

---

[56] *The Life, Travels, and Adventures of Christopher Wagstaff, Gentleman, Grandfather to Tristram Shandy*, 2 vols. (London: Hinxman, 1762), vol. 2, 27.

[57] *The Notes*, 270, n. 269–70.

[58] Eric Rothstein, *Systems of Order and Inquiry in Later Eighteenth-Century Fiction* (Berkeley, CA: University of California Press, 1975), 66, n. 6. His reference is to the first Paris edition: *Le Spectacle de la nature*, 9 vols. (Paris, 1732–42), vol. 7, 68.

[59] While we all agree that the catalogue of Sterne's book collection produced after his death (1768) by no means indicates that Sterne himself owned or read any of the books listed there (see p. 183, n. 60), the appearance of Pluche's text in the list increases the chance that he may have read the passage. Editions from 1735, 1736, 1740 and 1750 appear in the library sale catalogue across two separate entries, which increases the chances that Sterne would have owned at least one copy. Having checked these editions as well as the first in English and French, I have found marbled paper only in the bindings. *A Catalogue of a Curious and Valuable Collection of Books, Among which are Included the Entire Library of the Late Reverend and Learned Laurence Sterne*, items 915, 1681a (64) and 2202 (82).

d'oeil n'en déplaît pas: on peut même y chercher d'utiles nuances, & de bonnes combinaisons. Mais si l'on vouloit prolonger ce spectacle inanimé, même en le diversifiant un quart-d'heure de suite, on n'y tiendroit point: l'esprit cherche, non des couleurs, mais des objèts colorés.[60]

Rothstein sees Sterne as countering Pluche's insistence that marbled paper indicates the impossibility of making sense of randomness and hieroglyphs. Rather than borrowing the idea of an inserted marbled page from Pluche, Rothstein actually claims that Sterne took from him, and questioned, the metaphor of 'papier marbré' as a vast expanse of unintelligible material.

Sterne was perhaps more familiar with the use of marbled paper in earlier English examples, as a metaphor for literary value, than from Pluche. The widespread availability of texts bound in marbled paper in the eighteenth century is played upon by a satirical book catalogue found at the close of the anonymous *Serious and Comical Essays* (1710):

> *A Catalogue Of Choice and Valuable Books in Most Faculties, Viz. Divinity, History, Law, Physick, Travels, Voyages, Poetry, &c. Of which the Unlearned, as well as the greatest Scholars, are the Authors; the Raw Country Girl, as well as the best Bred Lady at Court; the Peasant in his Leather Jerkin, as well as a Chaplain in Ordinary; an Old Woman who can never read or write, as well as a Collegiate Physician; and a Poor Illiterate* Yorkshire *Attorney as well as a Serjeant at Law. N.B. The Books may be view'd at any Church, Exchange, University, Park, Playhouse, Inn, Or Conventicle in* England *in Particular; likewise in other Parts* (Lunopolis: Printed for the Man in the Moon, in the Year 1707).[61]

---

[60] Though Rothstein refers us to the first Paris edition, I cite here from the edition most likely to have been seen by Sterne: Noël-Antoine Pluche, *Le Spectacle de le nature, ou entretiens sur les particularités de l'histoire naturelle* (Paris: Estienne, 1746), vol. 7, dialogue 18, 113. The passage was translated in the eighteenth century as follows:

> Colours being appointed to establish a Distinction between Objects, they cannot please long, if they are not connected with some Figure or other: They are out of their Place in that Case. A fine marbled Paper, or a fine Furniture of *Irish*-stitch Tapestry Hangings, are beautiful Colours, and are nothing else. The first Sight of them is not unpleasant: And they may hint to you some useful Shades and Combinations of well-matched Hues. But, if you would prolong this inanimated Scene, though you should vary it for a Quarter of an Hour together, there would be no bearing of it. The Mind is not fond indeed of Colours, but of coloured Objects.

Translation from the third London edition: Pluche, *Spectacle de la Nature: Or, Nature Display'd* (London: Pemberton, 1748), vol. 7, dialogue 18, 85. The London editions used red ink on their title pages.

[61] Bound in the back of *Serious and Comical Essays [. . .], With Ingenious Letters Amorous and Gallant. Occasional Thoughts and Reflections on Men and Manners. Also the English Epigrammatist, And the Instructive Library. To which is added, Satyrical and Panegyrical Characters. Fitted to the Humours of the Time* (London: King, 1710). The catalogue does not appear on the title page or in the index, so it may be an independent publication, though the satirical imprint and running pagination suggests otherwise.

This mock-catalogue is almost convincing, being found at the very end of the text, where publishers would frequently advertise their available stock. At several points, it exploits the catalogue genre's tendency to list the material qualities of the books to underline the satire. Marbled paper functions as paperback bindings for '*Destructio Poesis, ceu Musarum Reuina*: An Oration spoken at *Drury-lane*, by Mr. D'—*ery*, stitcht neatly in Marble Paper', 'Hope in a Hopsack; or Dependance on Promises Labour in vain; a Poem; Dedicated to the Courtiers. Folio; stitcht in Marble Paper', 'The Military Buffoons; a Poem Burlesque, in Three Parts; Dedicated to the chief Officers of the Train'd Bands. Stitcht in Marble Paper' and 'A Satyr on a Footman who stole Brandy out of Closets: By a Lady. Stitcht in Marble Paper'.[62] Marbled paper in the catalogue appears only in conjunction with poetry, indicating that these were slim works, conveniently bound as pamphlets, which happens to make them more ephemeral, too.

Like the mock-catalogue, Montesquieu's *Persian Letters* (1721) also precedes Pluche's *Spectacle de la Nature* in its use of marbled-paper imagery.[63] This satire went through several editions in French as well as in English, and was revived again at mid-century upon the success of Montesquieu's *Spirit of the Laws* (1748). In the *Letters*, Montesquieu pokes fun at the follies of French society by framing his missives as accounts of the travels of Usbek and Rica, two Persian men in France. When a physician at Leghorn writes to Rica asking what he thinks of amulets and talismans, Rica writes that despite their religions (Judaism and Islam, respectively) at times endorsing what could be said to be the supernatural values of objects, especially holy books, he is sceptical of their powers. He encloses a relevant tract for the perusal of his friend: a letter from a French country doctor to another in Paris. In it, the country doctor's insomniac patient refuses to be treated by the physician before enlisting the help of 'a man that never practises Physick, but who has a multitude of Medicines for such as can't sleep': a bookseller.[64] The bookseller prescribes a religious book as a soporific, inspiring the country doctor to open a pharmacy of

[62] 'A Catalogue of Choice and Valuable Books', in *Serious and Comical Essays*, 271, 277, 278.
[63] Montesquieu's *Persian Letters*, Thomas Flloyd (trans.) (London: Tonson, 1762) and *Persian Letters*, John Ozell (trans.) (London: Tonson, 1722) both appear in *A Catalogue of a Curious*, items 1589 (61) and 1738 (66), but only the later edition could have been acquired before Sterne's creation of the marbled leaf.
[64] Montesquieu, *Persian Letters*, Ozell (trans.), 'Letter from a Physician in the Country to a Physician at *Paris*', vol. 2, letter 143, 274. Montesquieu's 'physician', Mr Anis, is a caricature of Jean Anisson, director of the Imprimerie Royale and specialist in religious books. *Persian Letters*, Raymond N. Mackenzie (ed.) (Indianapolis, IN: Hackett, 2014), 274.

alternative remedies. An inventory of the doctor's medicines (books) follows, including an emetic consisting of a warmed infusion of 'a Leaf of marble Paper, which was serv'd for a cover to the Collection of J.F's pieces', or poetry from the Jeux Floraux, or floral games, a still-extant poetry society which holds an annual competition. 'Infuse it the space of three Minutes; heat a spoonful of this infusion, and swallow it'.[65] Here, Montesquieu references the cheaper process of covering sewn pamphlets with sheets of marbled paper: an icon of cheap fiction and an image of the eighteenth-century equivalent of the paperback. For Montesquieu's country doctor, his patients need not read the poetry; simply consuming the cheap marbled paper covers of such hackwork could cause vomiting.

The examples of the mock-catalogue and the *Persian Letters* show Sterne departing from the use of marbled paper as literary imagery to a much more physical (and expensively produced) bibliographical joke on the process of binding. Whether as a joke on the sickliness of popular poetry or as a scientific example illustrating how colour can be uninteresting out of context, marbled paper featured in books before Sterne, but had never been physically bound in with the text, as it is within *Tristram Shandy*. The physicality of the page is unprecedented and surprising, and Sterne exploits the fact that an image of marbled paper could metaphorically stand for bookbinding and literary value, making the joke three-dimensional through his disruption of gathering L.

Exploiting the physical properties of marbled paper in the book trade, Sterne follows much more closely the metaphorical use of marbled paper by Montesquieu and in the mock-catalogue than that by Pluche, by invoking the semantic field of bookbinding. The leaf functions as an illustration of the material appearance of the works Walter obsesses over, while commenting self-consciously on Sterne's practice of incorporating scholarship and mock-scholarship within his volumes in a manner which physically supplements his text. The marbled page therefore heralds Tristram's translation and publication of one of Slawkenbergius's tales, just a few pages later, separated from this book by a volume-break and, as is visible in at least one original binding of the novel, marbled endpapers.[66] As the next section will show, Montesquieu's literary image of marbled paper as a quack nostrum also functions as a significant precursor in helping contextualise Sterne's

---

[65] Ibid., 224 n. 223. Montesquieu, *Persian Letters*, 'Letter from a Physician in the Country to a Physician at *Paris*', enclosed in letter 143, Rica to Nathaniel Levi, a Jew Physician at Leghorn, vol. 2, 278–9.

[66] For example, see the first edition copy held by The Laurence Sterne Trust, accession number CCWSH:0198.

secondary field of reference: the use of marbled paper for wrapping and authenticating quack medicines in this period.

IV   Marbling and Medicine

Sterne's works were always advertised in the most basic manner, never revealing the surprises that each instalment might hold. There was one exception to this rule, however, when the *Dublin Courier* in 1761 made a point of marketing the marbled page as a means of ensuring that customers bought an 'authentic' copy of the novel: 'the public are requested to take notice, that the only compleat edition is printed by Dillon Chamberlaine, and Samuel Smith, on a beautiful Large Type, and fine paper, ornamented with an elegant frontispiece of the Christening, and a curious emblematical Marble Leaf, &c.'[67] Sterne's Dublin publisher drew upon the uniqueness of the patterns created by marbling in order to encourage readers to purchase his own edition, and to authenticate it as genuine. Chamberlaine was drawing from a widespread use of marbling in counter-forgery efforts during the eighteenth century, which scholars have argued Sterne that also referenced. Patterson has been perhaps most forthright in this argument, drawing upon the marbled strips which appeared on some bank notes during the late seventeenth century to support one of her interpretations of the moral of the marbled page as 'do not steal' (intellectual property).[68] The bank notes that Patterson has in mind were made from books of paper marbled in the left-hand margin where the note would be excised from the volume, as in an example of 1694 held in the museum of the Bank of England. Because marbling creates designs impossible to be replicated, a marbled edge on a bank note could be verified as genuine when it was returned to the bank for payment, where it would match the stub in the book, but as the Bank of England points out, while notes were in circulation they were impossible to check.[69] Sir John Clapham has traced the use of these notes to a short window of two weeks in 1695, between 31 July and 14 August, after which the experiment came to an end when it emerged that one had been forged. He calls this episode 'a curiosity with no permanent importance'.[70] Though this was a short-lived practice in the Bank of England, marbling

---

[67] *Dublin Courier*, 4 March 1761.   [68] Patterson, 'The Moral of the Next Marbled Page', 105.
[69] Bank of England, 'Bank Sealed Bill' (1694), object number 124/001.
[70] John Clapham, *The Bank of England: A History, Volume 1: 1694–1797* (Cambridge University Press, 1966), 23, n. 4.

continued to be used for other forms of fraud prevention, as demonstrated by stationer Edmund Parker's advertisement for marbled paper in 1722: 'Paper Marbled by Samuel Pope for Merchants Notes or Bills of Exchange; to prevent Counterfeiting, or any of the Companies Bonds, are now Marbled by him to perfection, and Cheaper than formerly'.[71] In 1731 Samuel Pope was granted the first patent for marbled paper for the prevention of forgery.[72] Marbled paper was used to authenticate medical products, too, being used to package two of the most widely advertised and consumed medicines of the mid-eighteenth century: Dr Robert James's Fever Powders and the Anodyne Necklace, medicines which became iconic on both the medical and the literary marketplaces. Like the Bank of England in the late seventeenth century, and Samuel Pope in the early eighteenth, Sterne exploited the fact that paper marbling created inked patterns impossible to replicate, but rather than its use for financial transactions he may also have had in mind the use of marbling as a fraud-prevention technique in the packaging and marketing of medicines, given the context of medical mishap in the third volume of *Tristram Shandy*.

Advertisements for the Anodyne Necklace, promising to ease childbirth for women and help teething in babies, are a frequent sight in eighteenth-century newspapers, often accompanied by a woodcut logo, making them instantly recognisable.[73] They became increasingly inventive over the first half of the eighteenth century in deploying image and text to market and authorise the Anodyne Necklace.[74] Various pamphlets claiming to demonstrate the necklace's efficacy by scientific principles promoted and accompanied the Necklace, and they were distributed for free; 'There is a Person ALWAYS ready up One pair of Stairs, to GIVE these Books away', boasted the title page.[75] The first of the Anodyne Necklace's promotional publications was *A Philosophical Essay upon the Celebrated*

---

[71] 'Books lately Printed for Edmund Parker' [11pp.], in *The Devout Christian's Preparative to Death*, Robert Warren (trans.), 7th ed. (London: Parker, 1722), 217 [n.p.].

[72] *Abridgements of Specifications Relating to Printing, etc.* (London: Commissioner of Patents, 1859). No. 530, May 20 1731: earliest known patent for marbled paper, issued to Samuel Pope for the prevention of forgery, 85–86. (Rpt. London: Printing Historical Society, 1969).

[73] See, for example, an advertisement for the Anodyne Necklace which happens to be printed alongside one for Sterne's *Sentimental Journey*: *Public Advertiser*, Wednesday, 2 March 1768.

[74] Francis Cecil Doherty's book-length study of the advertising of the Anodyne Necklace explores their visual marketing (the evolving woodcut logo over the course of the century) as well as their literary borrowing. Doherty, *A Study in Eighteenth-Century Advertising Methods: The Anodyne Necklace* (Lewiston, NY: Edwin Mellon, 1992), 28. The logo of the necklace, for example, changed frequently throughout the century but always asserted authority.

[75] Paul Chamberlen, *A Philosophical Essay upon Actions on Distant Subjects*, 3rd ed. (London: Parker, 1715).

Anodyne Necklace. It appeared around 1715, went through upwards of twenty-five editions and continued to be in print in the 1750s.[76] Mrs Garway (at her store near the Exchange), along with three other stockists, had the right to distribute the necklace, but Garway attempted to pass off her old stock of Major John Choke's necklaces as the official 'Anodyne Necklace'. The accompanying pamphlets therefore sought to authenticate the product, carefully describing the packaging for potential customers:

> And before See that your Necklace which you Buy, is Sealed up in Marble Paper, with a Bottle of the foregoing Pain-Easing Cordial Tincture for the Gums along with it: And that it has the Print of this Anodyne Necklace pasted on it, & is sealed with the Seal of this Anodyne Necklace.[77]

Notices describing the outward appearance of the necklace quickly became more and more aggressive in their insistence on the marbled paper and the accompanying publications as authenticating documents, as in The Late Dreadful Plague at Marseilles Compared with that Terrible Plague in London (1721):

> Occasion is here taken to Desire all those Persons who either Go or Send to *the Royal Exchange Gate* to Buy This NECKLACE, *(*Pr. 5s.*)* to See expressly that they have the Right Anodyne Necklace Recommended by Dr *Chamberlen* for Children's TEETH, Given them: And therefore Besure see that it is put up (together with a Bottle of the Liquid Coral to soften and open the Gums withal; and a Stitcht Book of Directions how to order and manage the Child under these afflicting Circumstances, along with it) in a little Red Marbled Paper Box, with not only the Print of this Anodyne Necklace pasted on the outside of it, but is also Sealed up with the very SAME Seal of the Anodyne Necklace which is in the Title Page of this Book.
>
> Or else you have not *This Anodyne Necklace* Given you, but Another instead of it, and which is not *That* you design to buy.[78]

This text was dedicated on its title page to 'Dr Sloane', Hans Sloane, president at this time of the Royal College of Physicians, in a bid to lend

---

[76] Doherty, *Advertising Methods*, 13.   [77] Quoted in ibid., 27.

[78] *The Late Dreadful Plague at Marseilles Compared with that Terrible Plague in London, in the Year 1665* (London: Parker, 1721), 11. One exception is the 1717 *Philosophical Essay* which simply describes the packaging as a small, round, red box:

> Those Persons who go to Mrs. *Garway's* at the *Royal Exchange-Gate* to Buy this NECKLACE, are desired to Ask expressly for *The Anodyne Necklace that is Recommended by Dr. Chamberlen*, which is Sealed up in a little Round Red Box, with the Print of the Necklace curiously Engraved upon it, to prevent Mistaking (instead of it) A Great Redish Necklace, Made of a Root, which is Sold at her Shop'.

Chamberlen, *A Philosophical Essay upon Actions on Distant Subjects* (London: Parker, 1717), 71.

credence to the product. Sloane was also at this point secretary (later to be president) of the Royal Society. As well as underlining the packaging and presentation of the necklace, from the 1717 enlarged edition of the *Philosophical Essay* onwards, advertisers of the Andoyne Necklace had begun a long-term attempt to associate the necklace with the Royal Society, through dedications and testimonials, and by calling upon the identity of Dr Paul Chamberlen. Because physicians such as Dr James vended their own nostrums while also lending their names to remedies invented by others, to this day scholars are unsure whether Chamberlen invented the necklace or was simply the face of the brand. Because his testimonials appeared in advertising materials from the very beginning, it is tempting to read the anonymous pamphlets as if they were written by him. Paul was descended from the Chamberlen dynasty of obstetricians who invented and used the forceps, and during the seventeenth century kept the instrument secret, blindfolding any women subjected to its use.[79] The instrument was finally publicised a century later, in response to William Smellie promoting a rival invention in his *Treatise on the Theory and Practice of Midwifery* (3 vols., 1752–64), the science behind which clearly informs Tristram's traumatic delivery. Because of the branded forceps, the Chamberlen name was a useful one for the promotion of a nostrum promising to help pregnant mothers deliver their children safely and to prevent cot death through curing teething problems, widely believed to be its cause. Though never explicitly mentioned by Sterne, the Chamberlen name, as the contemporary brand associated with the safe delivery and raising of infants, ghosts the novel, present in Walter's wide reading about the forceps and Slop's demonstration of their use. Sterne's third volume, devoted to the after-effects of the damage caused by the forceps, leads the reader directly to the marbled page which imitates the iconic packaging of the latest Chamberlen product. The page's shared qualities with Anodyne wrapping paper bring a sense of irony, as a joke on the failure of medicine to assist Elizabeth Shandy at her time of need, one that forebodes that Tristram may not have an easy start to life.

Walter shares with the Anodyne company his fascination with obstetrics and his obsession with wounded noses. Tristram tells us that his book collection is exhaustive: 'he collected every book and treatise which had been systematically wrote upon noses, with as much care as my honest uncle *Toby* had done those upon military architecture' (3.34.162). In his desire to collect all published documents on noses, we may suppose that Walter owned some of the Anodyne Necklace's promotional publications widely available by the date of Tristram's birth, 5 November 1718. This is

[79] Doherty, *Advertising Methods*, 31, n. 18.

because, through their accompanying pamphlets, the Anodyne company publicised and brought to a popular eighteenth-century readership rhinoplasty, all in the service of selling marbled-paper packets of necklaces. The primary purpose of these pamphlets was to persuade the reader of the remedy's efficacy. Hanging it around the neck, the pamphlets inform us, warms the necklace, releasing its 'Atoms & Effluvia's' which, by 'sympathy', seek out and combat those emitted from the ailing part of the patient. All 'Corners, Fibres and Orifices' of the patient 'hereby are comforted, eased, and imperceptably healed'.[80] Perhaps surprisingly, a frequent method by which these pamphlets demonstrated this 'Sympathetick Effect' was through comic fiction, and one comic essay in particular is frequently reprinted in the service of the Anodyne Necklace. It is a plagiarised version of Richard Steele's *Tatler* essay on the nose joke in Samuel Butler's *Hudibras* (1663–78). Under the Anodyne brand this material becomes *A Dissertation on Noses*, and from 1717 it was deployed to elucidate the way in which the scientific atoms of the necklace worked. The adapted piece glosses the 'Sympathetick Snout' of Samuel Butler's poem, opening with the following epigraph taken from *Hudibras*:

> *So Learned* Talicotius *from*
> *The brawny Part of Porter's Bum*
> *Cut Supplemental Noses, which*
> *Lasted as long as Parent Breech:*
> *But when the Date of* Nock *was out,*
> *Off dropt the Sympathetick Snout.*[81]

At this time, the name 'Taliacotius', or, more accurately, Gaspare Tagliacozzi, was synonymous with rhinoplasty in the public imagination.[82] A sixteenth-century pioneer of rhinoplasty, Tagliacozzi had improved upon older practices of creating new noses which grafted skin stretched down from the forehead or across from the cheek. In a bid to minimise scarring to the face, he invented a procedure which bound the patient's hand to the back of their head so that one end of a flap of skin from the upper arm could be grafted to the wounded nose. His patients, having lost their noses through violence or tertiary syphilis, would have their hands bandaged to their heads for a period of weeks while the skin settled into its

---

[80] Chamberlen, *Philosophical Essay* (1715), 6–7.   [81] Chamberlen, *Philosophical Essay* (1717), 21.
[82] Emily Cock, '"Off Dropped the Sympathetic Snout": Shame, Sympathy, and Plastic Surgery at the Beginning of the Long Eighteenth Century', in Heather Kerr, David Lemmings and Robert Phiddian (eds.), *Passions, Sympathy and Print Culture: Public Opinion and Emotional Authenticity in Eighteenth-Century Britain* (Basingstoke: Palgrave, 2015), 145–64.

new home before the arm would be cut free. In the epigraph, Butler jokes that Tagliacozzi takes the skin from the 'Arse' of a servant rather than the arm of a patient. After this epigraph, the Anodyne company's dissertation on noses launches into comic tales of bottoms supplying flesh for noses in *Hudibras*, before going on to explicate – in a pseudoscientific manner – how and why these noses dropped off when their donor died:

> According therefore to the Law of Nature abovemention'd there was a perpetual *Tendency* and *Inclination* to each other, between the Atoms and Pores of the Porter's Body and the insitious Nose of the Nobleman, as still subordinate to the Porter, and terminated to him as its Relation, Kin and *Whole*, of whom it was notwithstanding its Separation and Distance as truly a Part as before Separation, and as much Respected, Regarded and Tended towards the Porter as to its WHOLE, as ever it did before: [. . .] So that the *Vital Spirit* in the *Part* and the *Whole* not differing in *Nature* and *Quality*, by consequence the *Vital Spirit* being affected in the Porter, it was also at the same Mathematical instant of time affected in the insitious Nose, which altho' grafted on the *Nobleman*'s Face was nevertheless still animated with the *Vitality* of the Porter of whom it was yet truly a Part: For which reason the Parts being affected by the destruction of the Whole, does not depend on any distance or determinate space of Place being not at all *Local*, but on the mutual Vitality, and therefore must be extended according to the reach of this Vitality wheresoever it is. So that the insitious Nose as animated at first, being still inform'ed with the Vitality of the Porter; the Vitality in the *Porter* ceasing, the *Vitality* also of the *Nose* ceased; And consequently the Porter dying altho' at *Bolognia*, the Nose became a dead Nose even at *Brussels*.[83]

The theory of medical sympathy as promoted by the Anodyne Necklace company, which argued that the proximity of the necklace to the body affected its treatment, was beginning to be disputed, and the satiric comedy of this piece is enhanced by medical jargon about the Law of Nature, vital spirits, tendency and inclination, and atoms and pores. The comic story sits awkwardly alongside the quack essays in the collection aiming to seriously promote the benefits of the Anodyne Necklace,[84] and yet this contrast seems to have been a winning formula. In 1733 the company published three similarly repurposed literary works in an

---

[83] Chamberlen, *Philosophical Essay* (1717), 23–4.
[84] This text was first advertised as a distinct publication in *Mist's Weekly Journal*, 31 Aug.–21 Sept. 1728 and *Fog's Weekly Journal*, 28 Sept.–19 Oct. 1728, as noted by Doherty, 'The Anodyne Necklace: A Quack Remedy and its Promotion', *Medical History*, 34 (1990), 268–93, 290, n. 92. The essay on noses appears as chapter 3 in Chamberlen's *Philosophical Essay* (1715) and as chapter 2 in *Philosophical Essay* (1717).

attractively printed free literary anthology, which led with *A Solution of the Question, Where the Swallow, Nightingale, Woodcock, Fieldfare Stork, Cuckow, and other Birds of Passage Go, and Reaside* [*sic*], *when Absent from us*. The text is illustrated throughout, including on the title page, the lower third of which is emblazoned with the Anodyne Necklace logo. The title text, *A Solution of the Question*, is a reworking of Bishop Francis Godwin's early science fiction tale *The Man in the Moon* (1638). The second story in the anthology is the *Travels of a Shilling* (1710), a repurposed version of Steele's popular it-narrative from the *Tatler* with an added episode in which the circulating coin teams up with four of its fellows to purchase an Anodyne Necklace. The final anthologised text, the *Dissertation on Noses*, had long been repackaged by the company. Adapting fashionable texts into pseudoscientific essays promoting the necklace, the Anodyne Necklace company explored and perpetuated tales about fixing wounded noses. While these anthologies promoted the marbled-paper packets of medicinal necklaces, and the use of that packaging as an authenticating device, by mid-century the company, its necklace and its packaging must have been associated in the public imagination with hackwork, plagiarism and cheap adaptations of popular literary works.

Like the marbled packages of the Anodyne Necklace, Sterne's marbled page is also accompanied by the tale of Tagliacozzi's nose jobs. Walter learns about prosthetics through the works of sixteenth-century scientist Ambroise Paré ('Ambrose Paræus' or 'Andrea Paræus', as he alternately appears in *Tristram Shandy*). Tristram expects his learned readers to be familiar with Paré:

> Be witness——
>
> I don't acquaint the learned reader,—in saying it, I mention it only to shew the learned, I know the fact myself.——
>
> That this *Ambrose Paræus* was chief surgeon and nose-mender to *Francis* the ninth of *France*, and in high credit with him and the two preceding, or succeeding kings (I know not which)—and that except in the slip he made in his story of *Taliacotius's* noses, and his manner of setting them on,—— was esteemed by the whole college of physicians at that time, as more knowing in matters of noses, than any one who had ever taken them in hand. (3.3.181–2)

Aside from the joke on masturbation ('taken them in hand'), Tristram's claim to knowledge is comically undermined by the fact that by this time, one need not have read Paré, an expert on prosthetics, to know about rhinoplasty. In part through popular and comic texts such as *Hudribras* and

Steele's *Tatler* essay, reprinted throughout the century and in the Anodyne pamphlets, rhinoplasty was no longer a niche subject, and through these literary jokes the reputation of Tagliacozzi's procedure had been bathetically undermined. Melvyn New has suggested that because Paré mistakenly described Tagliacozzi moulding arm muscle to patients' faces, when it was actually just the skin, Sterne must have been aware of the contradictory accounts of how the procedure had been done, and had probably read Tagliacozzi first-hand. He therefore concludes that when Tristram complains about the 'slip' Paré made 'in his story of Taliacotius's noses, and his manner of setting them on', Sterne was seriously engaging in this debate, 'drawing on a well-known figure in alluding to Tagliacozzi, but in an informed manner unusual for his century'.[85] But there is another, altogether more comic, interpretation of Tristram pointing out Paré's 'slip' when describing nose jobs and Tagliacozzi's 'manner of setting them on', which is not incompatible with a view that Sterne may have read widely on this subject. Rather than referring to the difference between using arm flesh and skin, Sterne may also have been alluding to Tagliacozzi's literary reputation for taking his skin graft from the bottom rather than the arm. As John Ferriar noted in his *Illustrations of Sterne*, the idea that the new nose was acquired from a servant or butler rather than from the patient, and from his backside in particular, 'obtained such currency throughout Europe, that even the testimony of Ambrose [*sic*] Paré in favour of Taliacotius was disregarded'.[86] Sterne's treatment of the scholarship of noses, then, has a doubleness about it. If we accept New's position, Sterne has Tristram question Paré's accuracy in favour of a more authentic account of the medical procedure. But we should bear in mind that alternatively, or perhaps – what is more likely – simultaneously, Tristram may have been disregarding Paré in favour of a version of medical history popularised by fiction, and perpetuated by the Anodyne pamphlets.

The Anodyne Necklace's saturation of the medical marketplace during this period was rivalled only by the success of Robert James's Fever Powder, counterfeit versions of which began to emerge soon after its invention in 1746. After acquiring a patent for his fever powder, James expressed concern in the newspapers that his product was being pirated:

> Four Doses of this Powder are made up in Marble Paper, and to prevent Counterfeits sealed with the Impression in the Margin.

---

[85] *The Notes*, 276, n. 276.16–23.
[86] John Ferriar, *Illustrations of Sterne* (London: Cadell, 1798), 18.

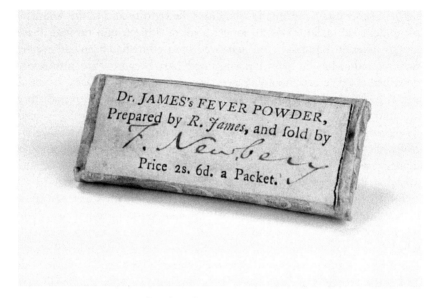

Figure 4.4   An original packet of Dr James's Fever Powder medicine c. 1770,
Museum of the History of Science, Oxford.[87]

    Price *Five Shillings*, or half the Quantity, that is, two Doses, may be had
for *Two Shillings and Six-pence*.
    By Virtue of the Patent abovementioned, I do constitute and appoint
John Newbery my Assignee, and only Vendor of this *Medicine*; and all
Persons are desired to apply for it at his Warehouse at the *Bible* and *Sun*
near the *Chapter-House in St. Paul's Church-Yard*; or at the *Blue Ball* in
George-Yard, Lombard-Street. London.
    R. JAMES.[88]

James was careful to describe where the medicine could be bought and,
most importantly, what it looked like ('made up in Marble Paper, and to
prevent Counterfeits sealed with the Impression in the Margin')
(Figure 4.4).
    When still wrapped, James's parcel looks like an inverted marbled page,
with marbled edges visible under a white rectangular label, reversing the
white margins and marbled rectangle of Sterne's novel. Sterne was familiar

---

[87] Inv. 42170 © History of Science Museum, University of Oxford. Dr James's Fever Powder
Medicine, by R. James, Oxford c. 1770. Accession number: 1930–31.
[88] Robert James, *Dr. Robert James's Powder for Fevers. Published by Virtue of His Majesty's Royal Letters
Patent* (London: 1748?), [n.p.].

with these packets and they therefore should be considered as part of the wider material culture that he drew upon when designing his own graphic innovations.

As a member of the Society for the Encouragement of Arts, Manufactures and Commerce like Sterne, James would have known about the drive to encourage English marbling. As a vendor using marbled paper to package his wares, he would have been especially keen to see English marbling prosper in the hope of reducing his overall costs. As further authentication of his product, James granted only one vendor the right to distribute his fever powder. It was common for booksellers to sell medicines in this period and James chose John Newbery, a fellow member of the Society for the Encouragement of Arts, as his official stockist, using Newbery's signature as a secondary method of authentication.[89] Through him, James's Powders were connected with the literary world, and sold alongside books, newspapers and periodicals.[90] The work for which Newbery is best remembered, the first children's novel, *The History of Little Goody Two-Shoes* (1765), is often attributed to his one-time tenant, Oliver Goldsmith. It subtly helps advertise James's Powders when Miss Margery Goody's father dies a miserable death of 'a violent Fever in a Place where Dr. James's Powder was not to be had'.[91] Newbery gained another literary ally when his step-daughter married Christopher Smart, who dedicated his 'Hymn to the Supreme Being on Recovery from a Dangerous Fit of Illness' (1756) to Dr James, who Smart claimed 'restored me to health from as violent and dangerous a disorder, as perhaps ever man survived'.[92] James's reputation with authors did not last long beyond Goldsmith's death in 1774, however, when pamphlets emerged claiming that the celebrated Fever Powders, in their marbled paper, had killed him. Dr William Hawes's extremely popular *Account of the Late Dr. Goldsmith's Illness* (1774), denouncing the use of the fever powder, went through

---

[89] This process anticipates Sterne's own signing of volumes 5, 7 and 9 to combat fraudulent editions of his work, since mid-century medicines were similarly sold 'signed by the author' to preserve the physician's rights over his tonics. From at least as early as 1759, Dr Hill was signing his tincture of valerian and advertising it as signed, 'to prevent any Mistake', and he went on signing this and his other medicines (his tinctures of sage and spleen wort, and essence of water dock) through to the second half of the century. *London Evening Post*, 1–3 November 1759; *Lloyd's Evening Post*, 6–9 May 1768; *Lloyd's Evening Post*, 11–13 July 1768.

[90] Dorothy Porter and Roy Porter, *Patient's Progress: Doctors and Doctoring in Eighteenth-Century England* (Palo Alto, CA: Stanford University Press, 1989), 110.

[91] Oliver Goldsmith(?), *The History of Little Goody Two-Shoes* (London: Newbery, 1765), 13.

[92] Christopher Smart, *Annotated Letters of Christopher Smart*, Betty Rizzo and Robert Mahoney (eds.) (Carbondale, IL: Southern Illinois University Press, 1991), 67. Chris Mounsey, *Christopher Smart: Clown of God* (Lewisburg, PA: Bucknell University Press, 2001).

several incarnations between 1774 and 1780. Hawes was Goldsmith's apothecary and had attended him at his death. When defenders of Dr James claimed that Goldsmith had died by taking a counterfeit version of the medicine, Hawes's fourth expanded edition included extra passages by witnesses testifying to Goldsmith having taken the real thing, including one by Hawes's servant Mary Pratt, who saw Hawes's journeyman 'take out something wrapped up on MARBLE PAPER, AND A LARGE BROAD SEAL ON IT. I asked him what that was? He broke the seal, and at the same time said, IT WAS JAMES'S POWDER'.[93]

As Roy Porter has shown, quack medicines were among the first brand-name products in Georgian England, and they were highly profitable; Dr James sold 1.6 million units of his fever powders in just twenty years.[94] While it cannot be proven that Sterne had taken James's Powders before 1767, he must surely have known about the most successful proprietary medicine of the century before that date.[95] Sterne had his own health problems to deal with, and in a reply to an enquiry after his health from friends Anne and William James of 21 April 1767, Sterne puns on the James name, pretending to believe in the Dr James brand because of its namesakes:

> My physician ordered me to bed, and to keep therein 'till some favourable change—I fell ill the moment I got to my lodgings—he says it is owing to my taking James's Powder, and venturing out on so cold a day as Sunday— but he is mistaken, for I am certain whatever bears that name must have efficacy with me.[96]

As his illness worsens, it is clear that Sterne does not really invest in the power of James's powder. A fortnight later, in a letter to the Earl of Shelbourne (1 May 1767), he remains weak:

> Death knocked at my door, but I would not admit him—the call was both unexpected and unpleasant—and I am seriously worn down to a shado,— and still very weak, but weak as I am, I have as whimsical a story to tell you

[93] William Hawes, *An Account of the Late Dr. Goldsmith's Illness, so far as Relates to the Exhibition of Dr James Powders*, 4th ed. (London: Hawes, 1780), 19.

[94] Roy Porter, *Health for Sale: Quackery in England 1660–1850* (Manchester University Press, 1989), 45.

[95] James Kelly, 'Health for Sale: Mountebanks, Doctors, Printers and the Supply of Medication in Eighteenth-Century Ireland', *Proceedings of the Royal Irish Academy. Section C: Archaeology, Celtic Studies, History, Linguistics, Literature*, 108C (2008), 94.

[96] Sterne, 'To Anne and William James' (21 April 1767), in *The Letters, Part 2, 1765–1768*, Melvyn New and Peter de Voogd (eds.), The Florida Edition of the Works of Laurence Sterne (Gainesville, FL: University Press of Florida, 2009), vol. 8, letter 205B, 576. No MS exists for this letter.

as ever befel one of my family—Shandy's nose, his name, his sash window are fools to it—it will serve at least to amuse you—The injury I did myself last month in catching cold upon James's Powder—fell, you must know, upon the worst part it could—the most painful, and most dangerous of any in the human body.[97]

While Sterne suggests in his anecdote to Shelbourne that James's powder caused venereal disease, the letter strongly implies that the doctors had used it to treat such an infection. Sterne retells this anecdote in the *Continuation of the Bramine's Journal* (written in 1767 but not published until 1904), where he similarly describes 'catching cold upon James's pouder', after the doctors have diagnosed him as '****':[98] 'poxed' or 'clapt'.[99] The powder had been recommended in medical texts published throughout the eighteenth and nineteenth centuries as a treatment for the symptoms of gonorrhoea as well as syphilis.[100] As New and W.G. Day point out, Sterne's symptoms were more likely to be due to his tuberculosis than to venereal disease.[101] Nevertheless, Sterne seems to retain his later view of the powders as dangerous, expressing relief that John Hall-Stevenson has 'discontinue[d] all commerce with James's powder' in a letter of 11 August 1767,[102] and taking to the pulpit to warn his congregation of the matter in his untitled sermon against murder:

There is another species of this crime which is seldom taken notice of in discourses upon the subject,—and yet can be reduced to no other class:—And that is, where the life of our neighbour is shortened,—and often taken away as directly as by a weapon, by the empirical sale of nostrums and quack medicines,—which ignorance and avarice blend.—The loud tongue of ignorance impudently promises much,—and the ear of the sick is open. —And as many of these pretenders deal in edge tools, too many, I fear, perish with the misapplication of them.[103]

[97] Sterne, 'To William Petty, Earl of Shelbourne' (1 May 1767), in *The Letters, Part 2*, letter 207, 579. No MS exists for this letter.
[98] Sterne, *Continuation of the Bramine's Journal*, in *A Sentimental Journey and a Continuation of the Bramine's Journal*, New and Day (eds.), The Florida Edition of the Works of Laurence Sterne (Gainesville, FL: University Press of Florida, 2002), vol. 6, 177.
[99] Ibid., 'To William Petty, Earl of Shelbourne', 581–2, n. 7.
[100] J. Becket, *A New Essay on the Venereal Disease, and Methods of Cure; Accounting for the Nature, Cause, and Symptoms of that Malady* (London: Williams, 1765), 108. John Hunter was still prescribing it for gonorrhoea in 1786: Hunter, *A Treatise on Venereal Disease* (London: Printed for the Author, 1786), 148.
[101] Sterne, *Continuation*, 'To William Petty, Earl of Shelbourne', 581, n. 5.
[102] Sterne, 'To John Hall-Stevenson' (11 August 1767), in *The Letters, Part 2*, letter 221, 610.
[103] Sterne, Sermon 35, Untitled ['Against the Sin of Murder'], *The Sermons of Laurence Sterne: The Text*, Melvin New (ed.), The Florida Edition of the Works of Laurence Sterne (Gainesville, FL:

Through quack medicines, Sterne argues in the sermon, men 'make merchandize of the miserable,—and from a dishonest principle—trifle with the pains of the unfortunate,—too often with their lives,—and from the mere motive of a dishonest gain', a complaint arising from the visibility of these medicines on the marketplace.[104]

Marbled paper had improved the visibility of the Anodyne Necklace and Dr James's Fever Powder, and Dillon Chamberlaine had clearly thought it would do the same for his edition of *Tristram Shandy*, when his advertisement for *Tristram Shandy* had featured a puff for the marbled page. Upon the publication of the second instalment of Sterne's novel, marbled paper had a heritage in the much-advertised ephemera of ailing bodies and the quack nostrums (and counterfeit nostrums) circulating on the eighteenth-century market which Sterne would eventually decry.

The marbled page could be seen as a reference to the colourful ephemeral packaging of quack nostrums and the contradictory information circulating about them at the time of its surprise appearance near the end of the third volume of *Tristram Shandy*. Certainly, the marbled page's position, sewn or pasted into a volume devoted to wounded bodies, a book collection of mock-learning on noses and concerns over nose jobs, would suggest so. This is a volume entirely concerned with baby Tristram's accident, which happens to be broadly symbolic of impotence in the Shandy patriline. In alluding to the popular refrain by medicine sellers in newspapers and promotional pamphlets that marbled paper indicated an authentic product, Sterne's coloured leaf also raises the question of how far marbled paper can ever protect a designer (like Sterne, James or the Anodyne company) from rival and counterfeit products. In this reading, the page becomes a poignant joke on a notion of copyright ownership as fallible as the human body.

As with many of his print experiments, with the marbled page Sterne takes on older technology and pushes it to new lengths. Marbled paper may have been widespread in eighteenth-century England, but English marbling was not. Sterne therefore innovated with both the style of marbling and the magnitude of its manufacture: 8,000 pages at a time when the Society for the Encouragement of Arts, Manufactures and

University Press of Florida, 1996), vol. 4, 337–8. While this medical element may seem original, New points out that Sterne takes the hint of dangerous medicines from Samuel Clarke's sermon 'Of the heinousness of the sin of willful murder'. *The Sermons of Laurence Sterne: The Notes*, New (ed.), The Florida Edition of the Works of Laurence Sterne (Gainesville, FL: University Press of Florida, 1996), vol. 5, 368, n. 337.28–9. The date of this sermon is unknown.
[104] Sterne, Sermon 35, 338.

Commerce believed mass production in England did not exist. *Tristram Shandy* was a significant landmark in the progress of English marbling. As a unique code, the marbled leaf alludes to the tradition of using marbling as an authenticating device, in bank notes and on the medical marketplace. In having one leaf of his novel marbled, at a time when the most common use for marbled paper would have been bookbinding, Sterne also foregrounded the physicality of the book and the order in which we encounter it, metaphorically and physically. In visually referencing bookbinding, he inverts the order of the novel, turning it inside out. But what has often been overlooked is the way in which Sterne intervenes in the print shop and upsets the physical structure of the printed book in the binding of this leaf; in doing so he pokes fun at Tristram's desire to append texts about noses to the memoir of his life.

In an iconic melange of high and low cultural forms, the marbled page as a surprise colour image illustrates that part of *Tristram Shandy* dedicated to Walter's manner of coping with baby Tristram's wounded nose. The marbled paper helps theorise the broken nose by illustrating Walter's collection of experimental scientific works and perhaps anticipating consumptive adult Tristram's ongoing requirement for doses of marbled-paper medicines, either from fevers arising from his consumption or the hints about his potential suffering from venereal diseases. With the marbled page, Sterne counterpoints Walter's despair – arising from high-minded theory and expensive colour-illustrated book collections – with Tristram's lived experience inside a body which enters the world wounded and needs the kind of medical attention which results in discarded marbled wrappers. Sterne thereby articulates the full range of patient experience for such men as the learned Shandy characters.

CHAPTER 5

Footnotes and Catchwords

The mid-eighteenth-century novel had, relatively recently, acquired a certain look. Readers began to expect print technology to provide them with a framework for the narrative. This framework consisted of elements expected in all kinds of printed documents – page numbers and catchwords – as well as features specific to fiction, such as chapters and footnotes (though notes were not standard in fiction, they were not surprising either). Henry Fielding's dissertation upon chapters in *Joseph Andrews* (1742) is often cited as a self-reflexive comment on the structure of the mid-century novel. In his discussion of the divide and the resulting space between two chapters, which he memorably called 'an inn or resting-place' allowing the reader to take stock of what has passed, Fielding noted that many readers cynically assumed that novelists employed spacing and division merely to bulk out a volume:

> Now for want of being truly acquainted with this Secret, common Readers imagine, that by this Art of dividing we mean only to swell our Works to a much larger Bulk than they would otherwise be extended to. These several Places therefore in our Paper, which are filled with our Books and Chapters, are understood as so much Buckram, Stays, and Stay-tape in a Taylor's Bill, serving only to make up the Sum Total, commonly found at the Bottom of our first Page, and of his last.[1]

Fielding compares the price of a novel appearing on the bottom of its title page with the tailor's total fee at the end of his bill. He equates the tailor's inclusion of minor miscellaneous items ('Buckram, Stays, and Stay-tape', serving to bulk up the bill) with the author's lavish use of white space; both inflate the price of the goods.[2] Sterne may have had this comparison of a

---

[1] Henry Fielding [1742], *The History of the Adventures of Joseph Andrews and of his Friend Mr. Abraham Adams*, in *Joseph Andrews and Shamela*, Thomas Keymer (ed.), Oxford World's Classics (Oxford University Press, 2009), 76.
[2] Ibid.

novel to a tailor's bill in mind when, in *Tristram Shandy*, he suggests that if you want to find out whether his writing is 'clean and fit to be read', your honours and reverences read Tristram's laundry bill (9.8.56). Fielding goes on to demonstrate that, in fact, ordering a work into chapters or books – the 'Art of dividing' – benefits not only authors but also readers by allowing them to chart their progress through the novel, avoiding 'spoiling the Beauty of a Book by turning down its Leaves': 'I will dismiss this Chapter with the following Observation: That it becomes an Author generally to divide a Book, as it does a Butcher to joint his Meat, for such Assistance is of great Help to both the Reader and the Carver'.[3] Through this bathetic metaphor of butchery, Fielding argued that the 'Art of dividing' creates rest stops for the reader, whose progress through the novel he compared to a long journey through endless typographic land-scapes: 'A Volume without any such Places of Rest resembles the Opening of Wilds or Seas, which tires the Eye and fatigues the Spirit when entered upon'.[4] As visual components of the contemporary novel designed to facilitate reading, chapters had become necessary due to the novel's grow-ing size and its digressive capacities. White space, then, made a 'regular' appearance in mid-century fiction. The most common use of white space, chapter breaks, were conventional and expected, and Fielding's joke depends upon the fact that their innovative quality had been quickly forgotten.[5]

Navigational elements in Sterne's works – chapters, pagination, footnotes and catchwords – rarely remain invisible for long. J. Paul Hunter sees Sterne as self-conscious but conventional in his use of chapters, interrogating but ultimately adopting the print conventions of his age: 'Sterne doesn't invent; he notices, points, and revises, leaving the convention intact'.[6] In fact, if we consider Sterne's authorial exper-imentation with chapters alongside his manipulation of longer-standing conventions of the printed page, such as pagination, footnotes and catchwords, we see him upturning readerly expectation, in a manner entirely surpassing the experiments of his forebears. Although scholars such as Christopher Fanning and Christopher Flint have touched on the disruptive capacity of paratexts in *Tristram Shandy*, none has

---

[3] Ibid., 77, 78.   [4] Ibid., 76.
[5] J. Paul Hunter, 'From Typology to Type: Agents of Change in Eighteenth-Century Texts', in Margaret J.M. Ezell and Katherine O'Brien (eds.), *Cultural Artifacts and the Production of Meaning: The Page, the Image and the Body* (Ann Arbor, MI: University of Michigan Press, 1994), 41–69, 50.
[6] Here, Hunter addresses both chapter breaks and the dash in *Tristram Shandy*. Hunter, 'From Typology', 53.

considered Sterne's footnotes and catchwords (especially the latter) in any detail. Of the Greek footnotes in *Tristram Shandy*, Judith Hawley has argued that 'they make a nonsense of the coherence of the text'.[7] Peter de Voogd is perhaps the only one to comment upon Sterne's concern with catchwords. He notes how Sterne's obsession with the aesthetic appearance of his novel led the author to omit them from his most visual pages, such as that depicting Trim's flourish (9.4.17).[8] This chapter develops arguments made by Hawley and de Voogd, suggesting that the layout of Sterne's printed page deliberately obfuscates meaning, and that when Sterne manipulated the navigational elements of his pages he made his texts particularly troublesome to those 'reading straight forwards, more in quest of the adventures' (1.20.130). So far I hope to have shown that Sterne drew his print experiments from a range of printed texts over a variety of genres, but this chapter focuses on forms of prose fiction which lend themselves especially to notes: satire and the novel. It proposes that Sterne's innovations with paratexts combine well-established elements of Scriblerian satire with more subversive, more recent but perhaps lesser-known interventions in Thomas Amory's *Life of John Buncle, Esq* (1756). Amory's footnotes, and the resulting confusion of narrative and delay of catchwords, anticipate Sterne's own experiments with those very paratexts revealing Tristram Shandy to be as equally engaged with its contemporary print context as with that of the previous generation of satirists, if not more so.

I   Rereading Catchwords

The eighteenth century marks a crux in the history of the catchword: it had become an expected convention of the printed text at the same time that printers and authors began to realise that they could get on very well without it. They were sufficiently widespread that Johnson defined them in his 1755 *Dictionary*, proposing that the term 'catchword' arose from the combination of the verb 'catch' and the noun 'word':

---

[7] Judith Hawley, '"Hints and Documents" 2: A Bibliography for *Tristram Shandy*', *The Shandean*, 4 (1992), 49–65, 59.

[8] As Peter de Voogd points out, the first edition omits a catchword on the page depicting Trim's flourish, although the signature and volume number remain. De Voogd, '*Tristram Shandy* as Aesthetic Object', in Thomas Keymer (ed.), *Laurence Sterne's Tristram Shandy: A Casebook* (Oxford University Press, 2006), 116.

CATCHWORD. *n. s.* [from *catch* and *word*. With printers.] The word at the corner of the page, under the last, which is represented at the top of the next page.[9]

The word's etymology reveals the role of the device in catching the eye of the reader. It also invokes a sense of recurrence, as indicated by its use in politics today for a word which is repeated. Tradition holds that the catchword was a reading aid for early religious works, enabling those who read aloud to ensure that they did not skip a page and accidentally blaspheme. But during the eighteenth century, almost all texts appeared with catchwords, not just religious ones. Perhaps the religious catchword was considered so useful in facilitating reading that it was adopted whole-sale. It is, after all, useful in ensuring that we have not accidentally turned over too many pages. However, this theory of blasphemy does not account for the majority of texts which were printed during the seventeenth and eighteenth centuries with catchwords on their verso pages as well as their rectos; surely readers could be trusted to find their way between facing pages? A more popular origin story of the catchword, which certainly sits with its rise to prominence during this period in particular, maintains that rather than serving readers, the catchword helped printers and binders compile pages in the correct order. Indeed, Johnson associated the term 'with printers', as if a general readership need not concern themselves with this piece of industrial jargon. Such an assumption, that the catchword is a paratext without semantic potential, as an almost invisible element aiding the printing process, has remained to the present day, and it remains unquestioned.

The disappearance of the catchword owes something to a growing concern about the appearance of the printed page. David Foxon has demonstrated Alexander Pope's attention to the aesthetics of his works, memorably describing Pope's distaste for italic typeface which appeared to the poet to insult the reader's intelligence while rendering his pages untidy.[10] Lesser known, however, is Pope's omission of catchwords in the *Dunciad*, in what appears to be a much more radical display of the author's intervention in book design.[11] Pope emphasised the difference between the pages of his poem and regular printed pages by having his

[9] catchword, n.s. Samuel Johnson, *A Dictionary of the English Language* (London: Knapton, 1755–56).
[10] David Foxon, *Pope and the Early Eighteenth-Century Book Trade* (Oxford: Clarendon, 1991), esp. 204–5.
[11] Ibid., 190.

prefatory material printed with catchwords as normal when the poem itself had none. Pope's experiments paved the way for mid-century authors who began to see that the catchword was fit for exploitation. In the instances of the black and marbled pages, as in the case of Trim's flourish, Sterne brings forward the catchword 'CHAP.', conveniently improving the aesthetic appeal of those leaves. In his creative omissions of the catchword, Sterne, like Pope, privileged the appearance of the page over its usability.

In the *Dunciad*, Pope's experimentation with catchwords was to omit them. Sterne went much further than Pope, and manipulates the catchwords which remain on his text-filled pages for comic effect. Through creative page breaks in *Tristram Shandy* Sterne tricks the reader. At the moment when Dr Slop breaks Tristram's nose with the forceps, the catchword suggests a bawdier reading than the page overleaf provides. When reading the catchword immediately after the main text, Sterne constructs the following obscenity at the bottom of his page in Susannah's sentence: 'the child is as black in the face as my— | As' (4.14.109). Sterne's open dash (without a full stop) at the end of 'as black in the face as my—' positively encourages us to append the catchword 'As' to Susannah's words. At this point, just before turning the page, we cannot know that Susannah's sentence is incomplete; nor can we predict that the word 'As' is uttered by a different speaker, Walter, who will interrupt Susannah at just the right moment. Moreover, Walter's response ('As your what?') not only reflects his frustration at Susannah's incomplete statement (or, depending which way you read the dash, her muttering under her breath something unsayable) but also comically suggests surprise at the reader's bawdy appropriation of the catchword to suggest 'Ass'.[12] Sterne's play with the catchword catches out the reader, planting in our minds subversive readings of his text through a creative page break. We feel inclined to go back and reread page 109. The catchword, in this instance, becomes visible to the reader not only as a technical device but also as one that carries the potential to manipulate meaning and to alter our reading of the text. Sterne achieves this comedy through playing on catchwords as being simultaneously present and invisible to readers.

Sterne knew that when navigating especially unruly or ambiguous texts with many footnotes, the catchword became a useful, and occasionally essential, reading tool, assisting the reader's negotiation of particularly difficult printed pages. The function of the catchword – a word caught by the eye of the reader – becomes foregrounded when it fails to work. In

---

[12] I am grateful to W.G. Day for this example.

those instances we realise the significance of the device in allowing readers to quickly identify – or catch on to – the word as it is repeated on the next page. Throughout *Tristram Shandy* Sterne uses the catchword to set up and then frustrate the reader's expectations of what appears overleaf. Peter de Voogd has noted this subversion of expectation in Sterne's catchwords:

> Sterne's use of catchwords can be compared with one important feature of rhyme. The skilled reader tries to anticipate what follows while the poet tries to surprise. And in the case of *Tristram Shandy* one not only seldom knows how the sentence (or for that matter the story) will continue, one does not know either what the next page will look like.[13]

In every book other than *Tristram Shandy*, then, if a catchword reads 'CHAP.', there is an element of certainty that overleaf a new chapter will appear. Volume 9 of *Tristram Shandy* differs from the others in being the only one in which Sterne deploys page breaks between chapters. The result is that the reader grows comfortable in the regular appearance of the catchword 'CHAP.' in the bottom right-hand corner of the page, regular due to Sterne's characteristically short chapters. We would expect to be able to predict the end of a chapter with increased ease in this volume, due to this new uniformity of the printed page and the frequent appearance of white space to signal the end of a chapter. However, Sterne surprises the reader in what at first seems to be the most predictable of volumes, manipulating the catchword to question what actually constitutes a chapter.

In volume 9, after chapter 25, Sterne inserts his blank chapters 18 and 19. These chapters, printed on facing pages, constitute the typographic shell of a double-page spread: the text space is blank, but the pages retain the expected paratexts: page numbers, chapter headings, signature and catchwords. Paratextually, everything about these blank chapters is technically in keeping with the rest of the novel. The chapter headings are typographically equivalent to every other chapter heading ('CHAP. XVIII' and 'CHAP. XIX'), abbreviated and employing roman numerals as usual. They feature regular pagination and are preceded by the usual catchword: 'CHAP.' But there is no content – no 'chapters' – to speak of. They are 'non-chapters', and this surprise is entirely unforeseen. By employing the catchword in a technically conventional manner, Sterne manages both to subvert what we expect to see overleaf, and to unavoidably bring to our attention the very paratexts which would usually seem invisible and which

---

[13] De Voogd, 'Aesthetic Object', 116.

we have been informed in the dictionary are not for our use. Sterne reveals to us how dependent we have become as readers upon paratextual conventions and the packaging of the printed page.

Sterne's empty chapters may be seen as a satiric exaggeration of the view of white space Fielding had expressed in *Joseph Andrews*: buckram, stays and stay-tape, that is to say, filler. Sterne had already innovated in this manner, at the point in *Tristram Shandy* when he invites the reader to draw widow Wadman on a blank page provided for that purpose:

> To conceive this right,—call for pen and ink—here's paper ready to your hand.——Sit down, Sir, paint her to your own mind——as like your mistress as you can——as unlike your wife as your conscience will let you—'tis all one to me—please but your own fancy in it. (6.38.146)

The page left blank to provide paper for the creative reader functions almost as empty proforma (Figure 5.1).

When creating the microfilm of one of the British Library copies of volume 6 of *Tristram Shandy*, visible on *Eighteenth-Century Collections Online* (*ECCO*), the blank page for widow Wadman's image is seemingly perceived as an error, and is left out.[14] This may be due to the fact that Sterne – as with his black and marbled pages – omitted all paratextual content except the page numbers; not even catchwords are printed on these visual pages. The blank page differs from the empty chapters in that Sterne sought to emphasise the specific paratext of paper. Calling for his readers to grab writing implements ('here's paper ready to your hand'), it is paper we are looking at in this instance. With the blank chapters, Sterne foregrounds printed paratexts such as chapter headings, catchwords and pagination, especially when Tristram sends us back to look at them:

> When we have got to the end of this chapter (but not before) we must all turn back to the two blank chapters, on the account of which my honour has lain bleeding this half hour——I stop it, by pulling off one of my yellow slippers and throwing it with all my violence to the opposite side of my room, with a declaration at the heel of it——
> ——That whatever resemblance it may bear to half the chapters which are written in the world, or, for aught I know, may be now writing in it— that it was as casual as the foam of Zeuxis his horse: besides, I look upon a chapter which has, only nothing in it, with respect; and considering what

[14] Microfilm Reel#: Eighteenth Century Collections Online: Range 280. Compare to Microfilm Reel#: Eighteenth Century Collections Online: Range 8558.

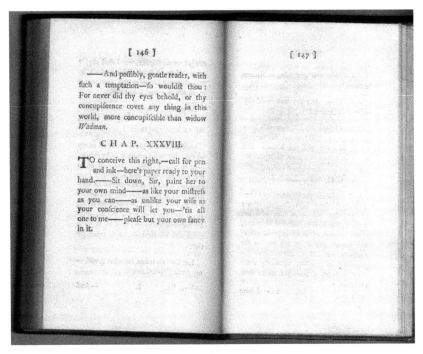

[146]

——And possibly, gentle reader, with
such a temptation—so wouldst thou :
For never did thy eyes behold, or thy
concupiscence covet any thing in this
world, more concupiscible than widow
Wadman.

C H A P. XXXVIII.

TO conceive this right,—call for pen
and ink—here's paper ready to your
hand.——Sit down, Sir, paint her to
your own mind——as like your mistress
as you can——as unlike your wife as
your conscience will let you—'tis all
one to me——please but your own fancy
in it.

[147]

Figure 5.1   The blank page for widow Wadman's portrait (1762). Image courtesy of
The Laurence Sterne Trust

worse things there are in the world——That it is no way a proper subject
for satire—— (9.25.98–9)

Just as when Sterne says he means a nose when he says 'nose', we doubt
that a chapter 'is no way a proper subject for satire'.

Sterne's solely paratextual pages, his blank chapters, may not have
surprised the eighteenth-century reader. Experimental satires of paratexts –
particularly footnotes – had already appeared on the early eighteenth-
century print market. Texts such as *The First of April: a Blank Poem in
Commendation of the Suppos'd Author of a Poem Lately Publish'd, Call'd
Ridotto, or, Downfal of Masquerades* (c. 1724) consisted merely of paratexts:
title, asterisks, printers' daggers, page numbers, footnotes and catchwords
package a blank text space. This poem is very rare, not appearing on
ECCO and residing in only two North American libraries: University of
Pennsylvania's Rare Books and Manuscripts Library and New York
University Library. Whitney Anne Trettien has described this text as a

'conceptual poem that exploits its medium'.[15] In fact, the paratextual packaging of this poem is central to the joke, like Gottlieb Wilhem Rabener's *Hinkmars von Repkow Notes ohne Text* (1743), a text solely consisting of footnotes. The narrator of Rabener's text complains that commentators are more famous than authors, so he sets out to become famous himself by writing a set of footnotes without waiting for an appropriate text to which to key them.[16] An anonymous text contemporary with Sterne's, *A Book without a Title-Page*, seems to have experimented with blankness by omitting the most important paratext of all. A reviewer in the *Monthly Review* for 1761 called it 'An affectation of wit, but void of all meaning whatever, that we can discover. It seems to be one of the silliest attempts to pick the pockets of the unwary purchaser, that we remember to have met with.'[17] As far as paratextual jokes go, it was fleeting, and perhaps self-defeatist in omitting the very paratexts that would ensure its posterity: the book seems not to have survived.

Sterne's empty chapters are more than simply a joke on the medium of the novel, although they rank highly as far as conceptual jokes go. They push the reader out of the narrative to consider the process of book production and the constructed linearity of the novel; the reader has no choice but to contemplate page number, signature, chapter heading and catchword. Later in the volume when, due to a missing catchword, we are unsure what to expect overleaf, we find the missing material from the empty chapters reinserted. Sterne innovates by reincorporating the missing content into the novel, surpassing the experiments of his forebears by continuing to subvert our expectations of chronology and allowing us to go on misreading the novel's paratexts as 'conventional'. When Sterne reinserts 'CHAP. XVIII' and 'CHAP. XIX', he changes the typeface and wording of the chapter headings as follows: 'The Eighteenth Chapter' and 'Chapter the Nineteenth'. The new, apparently revised format of the

---

[15] Whitney Anne Trettien, 'A Blank Poem (1723); or, the Present of Absence', *Diapsalmata*, 29 August 2010, available at http://blog.whitneyannetrettien.com/2010/08/blank-poem-1723-or-present-of-absence.html, last accessed 5 June 2020. See also Sarah Werner, 'Reading Blanks', *Wynken de Worde*, 10 October 2010, available at http://wynkendeworde.blogspot.co.uk/2010/10/reading-blanks.html, last accessed 5 June 2020.

[16] As summarised by Anthony Grafton, *The Footnote: A Curious History* (London: Faber, 1997), 120. For some much later examples of similar texts, see Craig Dworkin, 'Textual Prostheses', *Comparative Literature*, 57 (2005), 1–24.

[17] *Monthly Review*, 24 (1761), 351–2.

chapter headings encourages the reader once again to avoid naively relying upon catchwords as a reading guide; in Sterne's text, we can never be sure that they do not form part of some metatextual joke. At the end of 'The Eighteenth Chapter' Sterne precedes 'Chapter the Nineteenth' with one of the many, regular 'CHAP.' catchwords, of the same typeface as the rest of the text (Caslon), uppercase and abbreviated as elsewhere. While resuming regularity on one level, however, on another Sterne uses the catchword subversively; according to convention it should not feature a full stop to denote abbreviation, and should be represented by sentence case black letter type: 'Chapt.'. For example, words represented in unusual typefaces in *Tristram Shandy*, such as 'BATTERING-RAMS', in small capitals, is preceded by the catchword 'BAT-'. Similarly, the small capitals 'LOVE' appears in the same point size and uppercase typeface as printed overleaf (3.24.129; 8.13.35). Technically speaking, then, the typeface and case of the catchword do not correspond with the title that is overleaf and highlight the reinserted chapter's ambiguous status within the text. At several points throughout the novel, such as the moment of the reinserted chapters, readers are forced to acknowledge Sterne's creative manipulation of paratextual elements usually treated as invisible.

Searching for order at this point in the novel is difficult, because the reinserted chapters have disrupted the linear reading experience. Readers might return to the previous page to reorientate themselves, the final page of chapter 25, to check for some clue or guidance as to how to interpret the material overleaf. Sterne has already taught readers the importance of the catchword, the last word on each page, and how we rely upon it and may flick backwards to it to double-check that we are following the correct chunk of text. But in this instance there is no catchword on the preceding page, and all we have to infer from it, in place of such paratextual guidance, are some instructions in the final line of the paragraph of the main text: 'All I wish is, that it may be a lesson to the world, "*to let people tell their stories their own way*"' (9.25.100). Here, Sterne appears to use the narrative proper to comment on the catchword, or lack thereof. By changing the typeface of the chapter headings, Sterne encourages the reader to see these pasted-in chapters as quite literally out of character, out of numeric chronology. Where, for example, would they appear in a contents list? The last phrase of chapter 25 – in fact, the entire contents of this chapter, most of which is quoted above – deal with Tristram's insistence that the 'blank chapters' were so precisely because he could not compose his text in a linear order.

II Interrupting Footnotes

Footnotes had been central to the design of *Tristram Shandy* since Sterne first proposed his project to Dodsley in 1759. In a letter to his target publisher dated 23 May, Sterne mentions advice he has received on appending notes to his as yet unpublished novel:

> Some of our best Judges here w^d have had me, to have sent into the world—cum Notis Variorum—there is great Room for it—but I thought it better to send it naked into the world——if You purchase the MS.[18]

Sterne alleges that readers of his manuscript, to whom he grants authority through calling them 'Judges', recommend his publishing *Tristram Shandy* as a variorum edition. In this almost throwaway line, Sterne strategically references classic Greek and Latin variorum texts and, perhaps more directly, Alexander Pope's well-known and oft-republished *Dunciad Variorum* (1729), which satirically presented itself as a scholarly edition. In recording that he disagrees with his judges' advice, Sterne simultaneously situates himself as the next major author while stressing that he sees himself as departing from a Scriblerian tradition of satirising textual scholarship through its typographic archetype, the footnote. Though Dodsley's reply to Sterne has not survived, we do know that Dodsley did not wish to purchase the manuscript, but that he nevertheless pursued a conversation with Sterne about how his proposed text should be presented. In a later letter to Dodsley dated 5 October, Sterne writes of the changes he has made to his manuscript since Dodsley's first viewing of it:

> All Locality is taken out of the Book—the Satyr general,—Notes are added where wanted—& the whole made more saleable—about a hundred & 50 pages added—& to conclude a strong Interest form'd and forming on its behalf which I hope will soon take off the few I shall print on this Coup d'Essai.[19]

It appears that, rather than have Sterne send his text 'naked into the world', Dodsley may have recommended some footnotes. The author of the anonymous *Four Satires* (1736) advised that no text should appear without them, recounting his publisher's feedback that his manuscript 'was wanting

---

[18] Sterne, 'To Robert Dodsley' (23 May 1759), in *The Letters, Part 1, 1739–1764*, Melvyn New and Peter de Voogd (eds.), The Florida Edition of the Works of Laurence Sterne (Gainesville, FL: University Press of Florida, 2009), vol. 7, letter 34, 81.

[19] Sterne, 'To Robert Dodsley' (5 October 1759), in *The Letters, Part 1*, letter 36, 97.

[something] very essential, namely Annotations'.[20] Like the fictional publisher of *Four Satires*, Dodsley may have been subscribing to a contemporary view that footnotes in fiction were fashionable.[21] In response, Sterne designed a text which was multi-voiced, fragmentary and interruptive from its very first edition. But unlike the *Dunciad* and *Four Satires*, *Tristram Shandy* is not a satirical poem. Yet it explores and undermines, as those texts do, a binary opposition between literature as wit and notes as dullness, or more broadly between levity and gravity. Sterne's use of footnotes questions the very existence of the boundaries which authors and printers had created on the printed page. While Pope and Swift (as well as our anonymous poet) had used footnotes to target their enemies in particular and textual editing in general, Sterne seems to take the hint from Swift's blurring of the boundaries between the authorial and the printed word, using his notes to comically present to the reader the often-invisible design of the novelistic page as being ultimately under the author's control.

Sterne's uncertainty regarding the need for annotation was understandable given the Battle of the Books which raged during the first half of the century. At mid-century, the usefulness of scholarly notes continued to be debated. Editors of scholarly works were especially anxious about this. Samuel Johnson, for instance, worried that redirection of the reader from the classic text to their paratextual supplements might alter the experience of reading. In his 'Preface to Shakespeare' (1765), he conceived of the reader's movement from text to note as an unsavoury interruption:

> Notes are often necessary, but they are necessary evils. Let him, that is yet unacquainted with the powers of *Shakespeare*, and who desires to feel the highest pleasure that the drama can give, read every play from the first scene to the last, with utter negligence of all his commentators. When his fancy is once on the wing, let it not stoop at correction or explanation. When his attention is strongly engaged, let it disdain alike to turn aside to the name of *Theobald* and *Pope*. Let him read on through brightness and obscurity, through integrity and corruption; let him preserve his comprehension of the dialogue and his interest in the fable. And when the pleasures of novelty have ceased, let him attempt exactness; and read the commentators.[22]

For Johnson, a first reading of a text is one endowed with 'the pleasures of novelty', an idealised experience unmediated by paratexts which would

---

[20] Preface, *Four Satires* (London: Cooper, 1736), viii. Quoted in Roger D. Lund, 'The Eel of Science: Index Learning, Scriblerian Satire, and the Rise of Information Culture', *Eighteenth-Century Life*, 22 (1998), 18–42. 38.

[21] Grafton, *The Footnote*, 121.

[22] Johnson, Preface, *The Plays of William Shakespeare*, 8 vols. (London, 1765), vol. 1, lxix–lxx.

only be tainted by extra-authorial voices in commentary. Johnson believed that 'the general effect of the work is weakened' when one follows the footnotes; readers become unable to fully comprehend dialogue, for example, weakening their ability to appreciate the narrative.[23] The reader's interest, or 'fancy', is better maintained by a fluid text, which would be debased if the reader had to 'stoop' (literally and figuratively) to the foot of the page. Johnson describes this process as refrigerating the mind, figuring footnote-reading as a coolant of readerly desire: 'The mind is refrigerated by interruption; the thoughts are diverted from the principal subject; the reader is weary, he suspects not why; and at last throws away the book, which he has too diligently studied.'[24] In other words, footnotes make an otherwise interesting narrative boring. Johnson warns that diligent readers – those who read footnotes – may be provoked to the point of throwing down the book in a temper. He fears that his own notes may detract from the original work as the author (Shakespeare) intended it.

Johnson's concerns appeared in a preface to the very works which had caused a turning point in the history of the footnote. By 1765, Shakespeare's works had been edited by both Alexander Pope and Lewis Theobald. The latter had applied Richard Bentley's innovative methods of textual criticism to Shakespeare as a reaction to Pope's relatively creative and ultimately erroneous edition of the bard's works. Theobald's chosen title for his edition, *Shakespeare Restored, or a Specimen of the many Errors as well Committed as Unamended by Mr Pope in his late edition of this poet; designed not only to correct the said Edition, but to restore the true Reading of Shakespeare in all the Editions ever published* (1726), coupled with his aggressive tone, provoked Pope to cast him as the hero of the *Dunciad* (1728), in which Theobald became 'Tibbald'. *The Dunciad Variorum* (1729), and later editions such as *The New Dunciad* (1742) and *The Dunciad in Four Books* (1743), incorporated large-scale textual apparatus, functioning as a satiric response to scholastic pedantry. As Chuck Zerby has noted, 'footnotes are *The Dunciad*'s obvious target'.[25] Scholarly footnotes had become the typographic embodiment of scholastic pedantry. By 1765, then, Johnson's reference to 'Theobald and Pope' not only referenced the two major annotators of Shakespeare but also invoked two names forever associated in the *Dunciad*.

Pope was not the first Scriblerian to employ footnotes as satiric revenge. In 1710 Jonathan Swift had memorably copied extracts from William

[23] Ibid., lxx.   [24] Ibid.
[25] Chuck Zerby, *The Devil's Details: A History of Footnotes* (New York: Touchstone, 2002), 54.

Wotton's critical 'Observations on A Tale of a Tub' into the fifth edition of his work in the form of footnotes, making Wotton a pedantic presence in the margins of the very text he criticised. Pope followed Swift in incorporating various voices into his text to satirise his enemies. He emphasises the multi-voicedness of the *Dunciad in Four Books* in his 'Advertisement to the Reader', stating that William Warburton's notes will be added 'to the humorous notes of *Scriblerus*, and even to those written by Mr. *Cleland*, Dr. *Arbuthnot*, and others'.[26] This advertisement, which highlights and identifies the multi-voicedness of the text, ventriloquises Warburton. Despite these attributions in the advertisement, and Warburton's self-attributions after the fact, Valerie Rumbold demonstrates that 'it is overwhelmingly likely that Pope wrote most of the notes himself'.[27]

As a proponent of multi-voiced paratexts and the unstable nature of literary authority, Sterne shares similarities with the Scriblerians. But there are three distinct areas in which he departs from their characteristic use of notes. The first is typographic layout. Like the *Dunciad* and *A Tale of a Tub*, *Tristram Shandy* incessantly interrogates the concept of a printed work, self-reflexively negotiating the space on the page and calling to our attention its layout and origins in the print shop. These texts are crowded with commentary, so much so that the footnotes often take over the *Dunciad*'s pages, encroaching more and more into the space usually allotted for narrative and vying for precedence on the page. But the *Dunciad*'s notes wait at the bottom of the page for the reader to deal with them in their own time, keyed indexically to the line. The appearance of these pages, therefore, differ markedly from those of *A Tale of a Tub* and *Tristram Shandy*, where notes are keyed to typographic symbols such as asterisks and printers' daggers, which interrupt the text proper. Such footnotes are impossible to ignore. Despite the divisive fragmentation of the *Dunciad*'s pages, and the fact that some pages carry more note than text, its notes do not demand to be read with quite the same urgency as those in *Tristram Shandy*, where in some instances they can be essential to the sense of the main text.

A second difference between Scriblerian footnotes and footnotes as they appear in *Tristram Shandy* is time. Johnson's notes to Shakespeare, like those in all critical editions, were a late addition to the text. Many of the

---

[26] Alexander Pope [1743], Advertisement to the Reader, *The Dunciad in Four Books*, Valerie Rumbold (ed.) (Harlow: Longman, 2009), 25.

[27] Ibid., Introduction, 2.

authorial footnotes with which the modern reader is familiar in *A Tale of a Tub* and the *Dunciad* would not have appeared in every eighteenth-century reader's copy of these texts, as the majority were added in later editions. Due to this, *A Tale of a Tub* and the *Dunciad* are shifting and unstable texts, texts which parody and illuminate scholarly editing: they satirise the eternal process of searching for a more perfect and authorially validated edition. Sterne's notes, on the other hand, were produced concurrently with the fiction, allowing meaning to be divided over both planes and encouraging the reader to approach at once all sections of the page in search of meaning. Sterne broke Johnson's golden rule of an uninterrupted first reading, yet he gives pleasure, instead, through mediation, deferral and ambiguity.

The final way in which Sterne's annotation differs from that of his Scriblerian precursors is the extent of their play with authorial identity. Exploiting a Scriblerian instability in both notes and the identities of their originators, Sterne more consistently moves between multiple voices on the foot of his page. Instead of quoting, or pretending to quote, real people, as in most cases did the Scriblerians, Sterne most frequently deploys fictional note-writers: one is Tristram, another Tristram's editor. His footnotes poke fun at Tristram (and, in volume 4, Slawkenbergius), undermining the authority of his narrators. Their main purpose, however, is to undermine the very function of footnotes themselves and thereby to deconstruct the typographic packaging of the eighteenth-century book. Sterne appends thirty-seven notes to *Tristram Shandy*, which can be separated into four categories: thirteen textual references, seventeen footnotes which gloss the text or provide further (digressive) information for the reader, two corrective notes to Slawkenbergius's Tale by Tristram and four corrective notes to Tristram's autobiography by a fictional editor.[28] We may presume that all notes, excluding those composed by the fictional editor, are created by Tristram as author of his autobiography. This is

---

[28] There are thirty-six footnotes in the first edition: 1.20.131–3; 1.23.171; 2.19.172; 3.1.1; 3.10.36; 3.18.79; 4.0.2; 4.0.27; 4.0.29; 4.0.43; 4.0.45; 4.10.98–100; 4.21.139; two at 4.29.193; 4.29.197; 4.29.199; 5.12.61; 5.25.93; three at 5.28.100; 5.28.101; 6.2.7–8; 6.5.14; 7.10.35; 7.17.57; 7.18.62; 7.28.102; 8.1.2; 8.2.6; 8.24.111; 8.26.117; 8.26.120; 9.24.87; 9.26.111. In the second edition Sterne added a footnote to the title of the Memoire presenté à Messieurs les Docteurs de Sorbonne: 'Vide Deventer. Paris Edit. 4to, 1734. p. 366.' Sterne, *The Life and Opinions of Tristram Shandy, Gentleman*, 2nd ed., 2 vols. (London: Dodsley, 1760), vol. 1, chap 20, 134. For further information on the Deventer edition of the Memoire, see New, '*Tristram Shandy* and Heinrich van Deventer's *Observations*', *Papers of the Bibliographical Society of America*, 69 (1975), 84–90, and *The Life and Opinions of Tristram Shandy, Gentleman: The Text*, Joan New and Melvyn New (eds.), The Florida Edition of the Works of Laurence Sterne (Gainesville, FL: University Press of Florida, 1978), vol. 2, Appendix 6, 939–45.

because Tristram reveals himself as author. Two such notes identify Tristram as Walter's son ('* This book my father would never consent to publish; 'tis in manuscript, with some other tracts of his, in the family, all, or most of which will be printed in due time' [5.7.61]; '* This will be printed with my father's life of Socrates, &c. &c.' [8.26.117]). Sterne identifies Tristram as the author of a third footnote by citing John Hall-Stevenson's *Crazy Tales* (1762) as a text written by 'my cousin': '* The same Don Pringello, the celebrated Spanish architect, of whom my cousin Antony has made such honourable mention in a scholium to the Tale inscribed to his name' (7.28.102). Here, Sterne plays upon the capacity of textual apparatus to fictionalise the concept of authorial identity. Hall had publicly taken on the pseudonym Antony Shandy since his *Two Lyrick Epistles* had appeared in 1760 addressed to 'my cousin Shandy' on the title page. In this footnote Sterne advertises Hall's latest publication, in which he and Hall feature as Tristram and Antony Shandy respectively. Furthermore, in directing the reader to Hall's 'scholium', he also draws attention to the very scholium we are reading, encouraging us to recognise that his textual play extends to the very margins of the novelistic page and suggesting a network of well-(self-)glossed texts.

The four pseudoeditorial notes which undermine Tristram as autobiographer and correct his mistakes are particularly ambiguous in terms of authority. A note in volume 2, for example, claims that 'the author' is mistaken on points of historical and lexical accuracy:

> * The author is here twice mistaken;—for *Lithopaedus* should be wrote thus, *Lithopaedii Senonensis Icon*. The second mistake is, that this *Lithopaedus* is not an author, but a drawing of a petrified child. The account of this, published by *Albosius*, 1580, may be seen at the end of *Cordaeus*'s works in *Spachius*. Mr. *Tristram Shandy* has been led into this error, either from seeing *Lithopaedus*'s name of late in a catalogue of learned writers in Dr.——, or by mistaking *Lithopaedus* for *Trinecavellius*,—from the too great similitude of the names. (2.19.172)

The author of this note first picks fault with Tristram's use of the term '*Lithopaedus*', in place of the fuller '*Lithopaedii Senonensis Icon*', changing the suffix in an act of textual emendation. Second, the footnote identifies a factual error in the text. Sterne follows a Scriblerian tradition of satirising scholastic pedantry, parodying notes used for the purposes of textual commentary by correcting a crux in the text through tracing likely sources for the mistake in the author's reading.

Some references in Slawkenbergius's Tale, in Latin, are supposedly written by Slawkenbergius himself (4.0.43; 4.0.45), but Tristram also annotates Slawkenbergius's Tale: '* *Hafen Slawkenbergius* means the Benedictine nuns of *Cluny*, founded in the year 940, by Odo, abbé de *Cluny*' (4.0.27). Here, he supplements and aids the reader's understanding of what is implied to be an inadequate and inaccurate text. Although written in the third person, we are encouraged to read the following note as Tristram's when he acknowledges his own guilt and attempts to excuse the mistake that appears in the text:

> * Mr. *Shandy*'s compliments to orators—is very sensible that *Slawkenbergius* has here changed his metaphor—which he is very guilty of;—that as a translator, Mr. *Shandy* has all along done what he could to make him stick to it—but that here 'twas impossible (4.0.29).

This note reminds us that throughout the interpolated tale, Tristram acts as mediator, editor and translator. In this way, Sterne not only satirises textual editing, as was the project of the Scriblerians, but he also draws from their regular undermining of the supposed authority of the fictional text through Tristram's revelation that he may not have stayed true to the 'original' tale. He admits that in attempting to render Slawkenbergius uniform he has silently emended the original text. Scriblerian-like, Sterne playfully questions the creation of an authentic text.

Sterne makes the footnotes in Slawkenbergius's Tale appear more digressive by combining them with similarly interruptive parentheses. The asterisk is keyed to the text immediately before a set of brackets, where Tristram breaks into Slawkenbergius's narrative:

> By inspection into his horoscope, where five planets were in coition all at once with scorpio * (in reading this my father would always shake his head)
>
> * Haec mira, satisque horrenda.
>
> (4.0.45–6)

With this second interruption, using the 'my father' device to indicate and emphasise Tristram's identity, Sterne points to a plethora of voices fighting to be heard at this point in the novel. He divides the text into three narratives (the main narrative, that within brackets and the one on the foot of the page) which blur and become difficult to attribute to a single authority. The reading process as defined by the typography indicates that we should read the text, then the footnote, but upon returning to the text we are unable to resume reading Slawkenbergius's Tale because Tristram has interrupted the narrative with brackets. Throughout *Tristram Shandy* Sterne exploits the capacity of paratexts to interrupt the text not only on a semantic but also on a visual level.

Both Sterne and the Scriblerians use multiple voices in footnotes to obfuscate meaning, thereby making a statement about textual editing. But whereas the Scriblerians often satirise scholastic pedantry in order to attack specific enemies such as Wootton and Theobald, Sterne parodies scholastic pedantry to draw attention to the book as a constructed artefact by all too human creators. In a sense, Sterne's use of paratexts, though inspired by earlier experiments, differs from that of his precursors in that he creates a text which exploits footnotes in the very first edition, raising questions about literary authority from the outset. While readers of Scriblerian texts must come up against the physical make-up of the printed text, a reader of *Tristram Shandy* must also recognise that such instability did not arise post-publication, and that disruption is rather an integral experience of reading the novel as designed by Sterne. In *Tristram Shandy* Sterne employs footnotes to foster a disruptive reading process in direct contradiction to what was considered ideal. He amplified this sense of dislocation when, alongside interrupting footnotes, he deployed parentheses and, as the previous section explored, catchwords, in an attempt to frustrate the reader's progress, a progress 'in quest of the adventures' (1.20.130), through his novel. By employing the very movement between text and note about which Johnson complained, Sterne preserves ambiguity and sustains the reader's sense of both the comic infallibility of the narrator and the all-pervasive wit of the author.

III   Navigating Unruly Texts

Thomas Amory's *John Buncle* has been associated with *Tristram Shandy* since Clara Reeve grouped the texts together in her 1785 *Progress of Romance* (along with *Don Quixote*, *A Tale of a Tub*, *Gulliver's Travels*, *Citizen of the World*, *Chrysal* and *Arsaces*) as 'Novels and Stories Original and uncommon'.[29] As an anonymously authored and bulky text which describes the fictional autobiography of the title character, *John Buncle* shares with *Tristram Shandy* many striking characteristics, including the incorporation into a fictional text of a wealth of learning. Moyra Haslett has noted Amory's tendency to cite many other texts and

---

[29] Cited in Clara Reeve, *The Progress of Romance*, 2 vols. (Colchester: Keymer, 1785), vol. 2, 53.

to assimilate long passages without reference, as did Sterne in *Tristram Shandy*.[30] That Sterne had read *John Buncle* is highly likely considering his knowledge of mid-century fiction and the text's popularity. Publishing the first volume in 1756, Amory went on to publish a continuation volume (considered by Haslett as a distinct literary work) in 1766. The first volume would continue to be successful after Sterne's death, going through three editions, with two imitations appearing in 1776 and 1782. It was praised in the Romantic period by William Hazlitt and Leigh Hunt, before being largely forgotten.[31]

John Buncle is an important precursor for *Tristram Shandy* because of its unusually complex footnote-laden pages.[32] This novel perhaps devotes more space to footnotes than any other fictional prose work from the period. So much detail appears in Amory's footnotes that the footnote text is itself sometimes footnoted. With such 'sub footnotes' Amory creates layers of divergent narratives competing for precedence on the foot of his page. He frequently keys the footnotes to the main text mid-sentence, redirecting the reader from the text to the footnote, and sometimes, on to a sub footnote, while leaving the sentence in the main text incomplete. He thereby disorientates the reader's position relative to the main text. Such pages, full of competing narratives, reveal the potential for experiment with the catchword, because at such points the device becomes more useful than ever, and therefore more difficult to ignore. When the narrator, Buncle, discovers John Orton's skull he ponders mortality and, through his convoluted incorporation of religious philosophy, his footnotes typographically mirror the knots in his knowledge and the disorder of his soliloquy. In many respects, the typographic layout of the jumbled pages of *John Buncle* corresponds to the rambling digressions of the narrator. *John Buncle* dramatises through creative typesetting the process of unreliable narration, visually and materially reflecting the reader's inevitable alienation from the narrative by forcing us to contend with the book as a constructed material object. In this episode, the note that runs from page 308 to 311 has a sub footnote, which itself runs from page 308 to 310.

---

[30] Moyra Haslett, Introduction, *The Life of John Buncle, Esq*, by Thomas Amory (Dublin: Four Courts, 2011), 18, 23.

[31] Ibid., 33.

[32] Here I only refer to the first volume, which Haslett has described as a standalone novel. The first volume of *John Buncle*, which appeared ten years before the second, separates the footnote text from that of the sub footnote (which is of the same point size) with a thin black rule. The second volume, however, dispenses with this device, which perhaps suggests that Amory preferred a confusion of narratives rather than an attempt to divide and clarify his text. Because of this chapter's focus on the layout of Amory's page, citations are from the first edition unless otherwise noted.

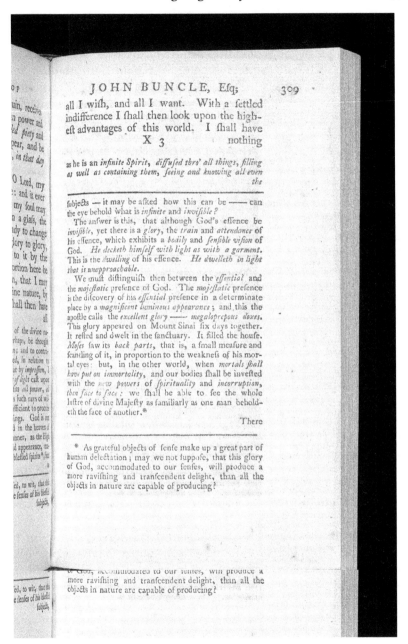

Figure 5.2   Footnotes, sub footnotes and sub footnotes in *John Buncle* (1756). Image courtesy of Cambridge University Library

To this sub footnote is keyed another layer: a second sub footnote, or 'sub sub footnote', self-contained on the foot of page 309 (Figure 5.2). The limitations of the terminology with which we are able to describe phenomena such as footnotes become highlighted in Amory's text, specifically within the first edition. On page 309 he creates a cacophony: four disparate voices offer themselves to the reader. As a result, the signature mark, which would usually appear at the bottom of the page, is pushed into the top fifth of the page, functioning as a typographic divide between the main text and the confusion that lies beneath. A fine black rule divides the footnote from the sub footnote, and the sub footnote from the sub sub footnote. The final words of the main footnote, on the bottom of page 311, serve as an ironic statement upon the disorder of the text: 'I imagine this illustrates the thing. To me it seems reason.'[33] By the time we reach these words, we are bewildered as to the meaning of the 'thing' the narrator proposes to illustrate, and these words appear as an ironic commentary upon the chaos of the page layout. This line prefigures Sterne's memorable statement, discussed above, 'let people tell their stories their own way', which similarly reads as a commentary upon the confusion of the printed paratexts. In *John Buncle*, as in *Tristram Shandy*, readers are forced into a dependence on the catchword. Whichever route they have selected, they must employ catchwords as a reading guide, gradually becoming accustomed to the pattern and layout of consecutive pages. Unlike Amory, who uses catchwords as a much-needed guide to reading his convoluted notes, Sterne plays with the catchword with comic results. What Sterne does draw from Amory is his confusion of footnote and main text, resulting in readers becoming lost in the various narratives, unable to find their bearings. Perhaps Sterne recognised Amory's readers' dependence upon this paratext and, taking his experiments one step further, decided to incorporate into his creative toolkit the one stable factor of *John Buncle* as material text: the catchword.

At times in *John Buncle* we would simply become lost if not for the catchwords. This happens during a convoluted series of narratives across pages 350 to 357, describing Buncle's visit to the private library belonging to the philosophers of Stanemore. The episode concerns a vexed case of authorial attribution, as the narrator debates the authorship of the *Vindiciae contra tyrannos*: 'I asked one of these gentlemen,

---

[33] Amory, *The Life of John Buncle, Esq* (London: Noon, 1756), 311, n. 24.

if he knew who was the author of this book; for it was ascribed to various men.'[34] The authorship of this 1579 text remains contested to this day, but Amory treats this issue at length both in the main text and the footnotes. He employs a footnote (number 30), which we may have guessed would be a long one due to Amory allocating it a marginal summary ('Account of Du Plessis Mornay') to explore the possibility that Philippe du Plessis-Mornay may be the author. Amory ends the main text on page 350 with the fragment of a word: '*D'Au-*', from '*D'Aubigne*', the name of a scholar who supports Buncle's argument. The catchword, as one would expect, reflects the other half of the broken word: '*bigne*', but the only appears seven pages later, as the main text has been entirely usurped by the text of footnote 30 which spreads across the following pages. As we mentally repeat the fragment '*D'Au-*' while searching for the remainder of the word, the fact that the catchword is itself a fragment serves to further emphasise the broken stream of discourse. Amory's lengthy footnotes emphasise the device's interruptive capacity, not permitting us to finish a sentence, or even a word, before being diverted elsewhere. His paratexts dictate an order of reading which must always go backwards in order to proceed in the narrative. The effect of this formal disruption is that readers are forced to acknowledge the presence of – if not actually read – extensive footnote material. Amory highlights his book as a multi-voiced work.

The catchword is only 'caught' after six intervening pages, which display two partial narratives. This time, instead of those halves being text and note, they are actually footnote and sub footnote. This is because Buncle cannot mention the names of 'that wicked fellow, *Paul V.**' and '*Leo XI.*†' in his footnote without needing sub footnotes (keyed to an asterisk and a dagger respectively) to give vent to his digression. This is perhaps the most disorientating part of the novel, because when the word '*D'Aubigne*' is finally completed, another footnote appears (number 31), plummeting the reader back into the margins before the sentence has come to an end. In this typographic display within a narrative context dealing with the instability of literary authority, Amory employs text, footnotes and sub footnotes in a manner which would confuse the most enthusiastic of readers. Most importantly, and most innovatively, at this very point Amory switches the tone of the main text and the footnote, appearing to confuse

[34] Ibid., 350.

the registers he has established in each. Consider the main text, filled with abbreviations and French phrasing:

> *Aubigne* (31), whose word is sterling, affirms it. See here (Mr. Seymour said) the 2d volume of *D'Aubigne's* history, book 2. ch. 2. p. 108, il paroissoit un autre livre qui s'appelloit Junius, on defense contre les tyrans, fait par M. Du Plessis, renommé pour plusieurs excellens livres. --- And, (tom. I. l. 2. ch. 15. pag. 91.) D'Aubigné dits, que M. du Plessis lui a avoué qu'il en estoit l'auteur.[35]

The corresponding footnote, by comparison, reads more like a fuller, central discourse:

> (31) *Theodore Agrippa Aubigne*, the favourite, of *Henry the 4th*, was born in the year 1550, and died 1631, aged 80. He writ several curious things: but his greatest and principal work is his *Universal History, in 3 toms folio*: containing the transactions from 1550 to 1601.——This is a very extraordinary history, and contains many curious relations that are no where else to be found.———He was obliged to fly to France on account of this history, and died at *Geneva*.———His two *satyrs*, called *La Confession de Sancy*—— and *Le Baron de Foeneste*, are fine things.——*The Avantures of the Baron de Foeneste*, (du Chat's edition) are likewise well worth reading: The best edition is a Cologne, 1729, 2 vols. in 12mo.———It is a very curious thing.[36]

The subjective, conversational tone in which Amory describes his sources in the footnote strikes the reader as more in keeping with a main narrative, and the abbreviations, fragmented phrasing and French language phrases which appear in the main text appear more appropriate to the register of the footnote. Amory blends text and paratext through his manipulation of the printed page and his subversive swapping of footnote and main text content.

From the very first footnote in the first volume of *Tristram Shandy* Sterne, like Amory, overthrows the conventional separation of text and paratext, causing us to question what should belong in each. He does so during a riposte to the reader, when Tristram accuses 'madam' of not paying attention to the last chapter:

> How could you, Madam, be so inattentive in reading the last chapter? I told you in it, *That my mother was not a papist.*——Papist! You told me no such thing, Sir. Madam, I beg leave to repeat it over again, That I told you as plain, at least, as words, by direct inference, could tell you such a thing.— Then, Sir, I must have miss'd a page.—No, Madam, you have not miss'd a

---

[35] Ibid., 357–8.   [36] Ibid., 357, n. 31.

word.——Then I was asleep, Sir.—My pride, Madam, cannot allow you that refuge.——Then, I declare, I know nothing at all about the matter.—That, Madam, is the very fault I lay to your charge; and as a punishment for it, I do insist upon it, that you immediately turn back, that is, as soon as you get to the next full stop, and read the whole chapter over again. (1.20.129)

Through Tristram's dispute with 'madam', who swears that Tristram did not inform her that his *'mother was not a papist'*, Sterne encourages the reader to pay close attention to each word on the page, forcing 'madam', and we as readers, to turn back the pages in quest of meaning. This manner of reading, to and fro between chapters, Tristram argues is the best way:

> I have imposed this penance upon the lady, neither out of wantonness or cruelty, but from the best of motives; and therefore shall make her no apology for it when she returns back:—'Tis to rebuke a vicious taste which has crept into thousands besides herself,—of reading straight forwards, more in quest of the adventures, than of the deep erudition and knowledge which a book of this cast, if read over as it should be, would infallibly impart with them—. (1.20.130)

In this exercise in turning back the pages, Tristram discourages us from reading straight forward 'in quest of the adventures' in preference to a more scholarly mode of reading which would impart 'deep erudition and knowledge'. Because of madam's tendency to adopt the former style of reading, Tristram accuses her of failing to read between the lines, of having 'miss'd a page' or 'miss'd a word', misinterpreting the meaning of his phraseology: 'It was *necessary* I should be born before I was christen'd' (1.20.131). He then goes on to explain what madam has been missing: 'Had my mother', he explains, 'been a Papist, that consequence did not follow.*' (1.20.131) Tristram includes an asterisk, directing the reader to a footnote at the bottom of the page which provides all of the relevant scholarly information to support such a claim. Madam, who presumably has not made the connection between Catholicism, birth and baptism, and is in that sense representative of the majority of readers, must read the footnote to comprehend the text. The footnote, which outlines a theory of intrauterine baptism by means of a *'squirt'*, is essential to comprehending the joke.

Using 'Madam' as an example, the main text continues to deplore the want of effective readers, concluding with the following moral anecdote from Tristram: 'I wish [...] that all good people, both male and female, from her example, may be taught to think as well as read' (1.20.133).

Meanwhile, as might be expected, the narrative of the footnote runs on the theme of baptism, displaying scholarly arguments from Thomas Aquinas and the Doctors of the Sorbonne for baptising an unborn baby by injection during a risky delivery. In the absence of a printed rule or ornament separating the main text from the footnote, distinguished from the main text only by its smaller type on subsequent pages (or an inter-rupting signature), the catchwords to both main text and footnote serve as important indicators of where to cast your eye overleaf for quick and effective reading.

Sterne soon exploits our growing dependence on the catchword as we navigate text and footnote. On page 133, we are led to believe that the footnote has concluded because its catchword is omitted (Figure 5.3). On this page, only the main text is supplied with a catchword ('ME-'), indicating that it continues overleaf. It is significant here that this page is a recto (front page, odd numbered), in that we cannot at first see what is overleaf. Upon turning the page we are presented with a full page of the 'MEMOIRE presenté à Messieurs les Docteurs de SORBONNE' (1.20.134). It bears very little relation to the narrative thread of the main text on the preceding page, which concluded on the theme of unruly readers. It more closely corresponds to the theme and closing remarks of that page's footnote:

> If the reader has the curiosity to see the question upon baptism, *by injection*, as presented to the Doctors of the *Sorbonne*,—with their consultation thereupon, it is as follows. (1.20.133)

The open-ended footnote leads us to believe there is something yet to come, but the lack of a catchword simultaneously refutes such a possibility; there is nothing to 'follow', until we turn over the leaf and see the Memoire. In a sense, the content of the marginal note has become centralised in the text. Drawing upon Amory's exchange of registers and themes between text and footnote in *John Buncle*, Sterne also switches registers and themes between main text and note in *Tristram Shandy*.

The final lines of the main text on page 133 elucidate Sterne's textual experiment: 'I wish [...] that all good people, both male and female, from her example, may be taught to think as well as read.' This 'example', of turning footnote into text proper, as a test or task for the reader, serves as a reminder that Tristram had warned us in this very chapter against 'a vicious taste' (from which madam suffers, as well as 'thousands besides herself') 'of reading straight forwards, more in quest of the adventures' (1.20.130). This warning must be borne in mind by readers frustrated in

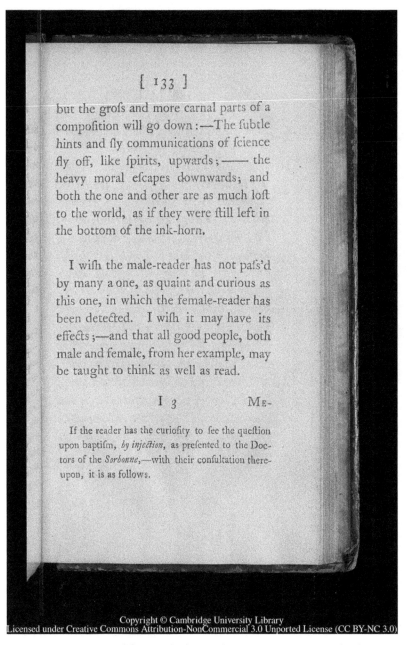

[133]

but the grofs and more carnal parts of a
compofition will go down :—The fubtle
hints and fly communications of fcience
fly off, like fpirits, upwards;—— the
heavy moral efcapes downwards; and
both the one and other are as much loft
to the world, as if they were ftill left in
the bottom of the ink-horn.

I wifh the male-reader has not pafs'd
by many a one, as quaint and curious as
this one, in which the female-reader has
been detected. I wifh it may have its
effects;—and that all good people, both
male and female, from her example, may
be taught to think as well as read.

I 3   Me-

If the reader has the curiofity to fee the queftion
upon baptifm, *by injection,* as prefented to the Doctors of the *Sorbonne,*—with their confultation there-
upon, it is as follows.

Figure 5.3   Main text and footnote leading to the memoire in *Tristram Shandy* (1759).
Images courtesy of Cambridge University Library

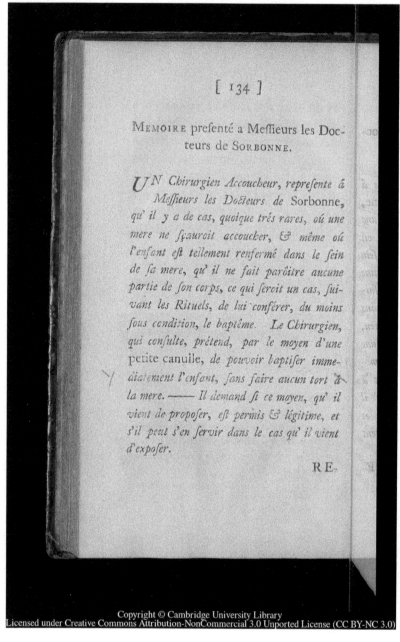

[134]

MEMOIRE preſenté a Meſſieurs les Docteurs de SORBONNE.

UN *Chirurgien Accoucheur, repreſente à
Meſſieurs les Docteurs de* Sorbonne,
*qu' il y a de cas, quoique trés rares, où une
mere ne ſçauroit accoucher, & même où
l'enfant eſt tellement renfermé dans le ſein
de ſa mere, qu' il ne fait paroître aucune
partie de ſon corps, ce qui ſeroit un cas, ſui-
vant les Rituels, de lui conférer, du moins
ſous condition, le baptême.* Le Chirurgien,
qui conſulte, prétend, par le moyen d'une
petite canulle, *de pouvoir baptiſer imme-
diatement l'enfant, ſans faire aucun tort à
la mere.* —— *Il demand ſi ce moyen, qu' il
vient de propoſer, eſt permis & légitime, et
s'il peut s'en ſervir dans le cas qu' il vient
d'expoſer.*

R E.

Figure 5.3 (*cont.*)

their attempts at a linear reading of *Tristram Shandy*. We cannot read Sterne's novel without reading the footnotes, a process which becomes complex due to his creative play with catchwords. Any reading of *Tristram Shandy*, then, is a circuitous one, from text to margins and back again. By placing text apparently belonging to the footnote into the main text, Sterne forces his readers to engage with both text and paratext in a circuitous and non-linear manner.

A further reason to believe that the Memoire belongs to the realm of the footnote is the third-person commentary which immediately follows it:

> Mr. *Tristram Shandy*'s compliments to Messrs. *Le Moyne, De Romigny*, and *De Marcilly*; hopes they all rested well the night after so tiresome a consultation.—He begs to know, whether, after the ceremony of marriage, and before that of consummation, the baptizing all the HOMUNCULI at once, slap-dash, by *injection*, would not be a shorter and safer cut still; on condition, as above, That if the HOMUNCULI do well, and come safe into the world after this, That each and every of them shall be baptized again (*sous condition.*)——And provided, in the second place, That the thing can be done, which Mr. *Shandy* apprehends it may, *par le moyen d'une petite canulle,* and, *sans faire aucun tort a le pere.* (1.20.140)

While the French language remarks allow Tristram to discuss sensitive issues with a semblance of propriety, they also evoke the innovations in Amory's text, specifically his interruption of the main narrative with French statements more akin to the register of the footnote. The third-person opening of this passage in Sterne's main text – 'Mr. *Tristram Shandy*'s compliments to Messrs. *Le Moyne, De Romigny*, and *De Marcilly*' – resembles that of many footnotes in *Tristram Shandy*, as in the one cited earlier in this chapter:

> *The author is here twice mistaken; [...] Mr. *Tristram Shandy* has been led into this error, either from seeing *Lithopaedus*'s name of late in a catalogue of learned writers in Dr.——, or by mistaking *Lithopaedus* for *Trinecavellius*,—from the too great similitude of the names. (2.19.172)

In this commentary Sterne employs a formal tone of narration and the distancing device of the third-person pronoun, unmistakably the register of a footnote. It appears that the footnote has usurped the space of the main body text; the marginal narrative becomes the dominant voice. Here the chapter ends, with the footnote in prime position at the centre of Sterne's novel, in large, main-body-sized type. With his experimentation with footnotes Sterne promotes their centrality to his text, proclaiming the authority of the author over all areas of book design.

IV   Modern Textual Apparatus

Many paratextual experiments in *Tristram Shandy* are lost in modern editions due to digital publishing practices. No modern text represents Sterne's catchwords, although the Florida Edition takes care that the page break allows the Memoire to follow both the footnote and the main text at the same time, gesturing towards while leaving unglossed the ambiguous status of this paratext. Manuel Portela, referring to his Portuguese translation of *Tristram Shandy*, notices several instances in Sterne's first edition where page breaks occur at important moments, affecting the semantics of the text.[37] He argues that in later volumes Sterne began to write with the layout of the printed page in mind, having seen the earliest volumes through the press. An analysis of Sterne's catchwords reveals that Sterne manipulated page breaks from the very first volumes of *Tristram Shandy*, in order to play with the reader's ability to navigate his novel.

Catchwords are central to eighteenth-century reading. This is nowhere more apparent than in the first edition of *John Buncle*. As the reader's only guide, whether they are following the main text, the first footnote or the sub footnote, the catchword directs the eye to the relevant passage on the following page. Due to the sheer magnitude and multitude of these notes and their respective layers, the catchword serves as an important reminder of the last word mentioned in each narrative. It facilitates the difficult task of following Amory's footnotes, especially considering the barely notice-able difference in point size between footnote/sub footnote text and main text. The pages of a text like Amory's are extraordinarily difficult to navigate, and even more so, I would argue, in the scholarly Four Courts Press edition which came out in 2011. This is inevitable, due to modern printing practices, which have no place for catchwords.

Footnotes are necessarily complicated by scholarly editing. In Amory's first edition, sub footnotes are keyed to asterisks, but in the Four Courts Press edition they are keyed to printers' daggers. This is because the editor requires an additional set of notes, for which asterisks are appropriated. This additional editorial commentary appears at the back of the volume as endnotes. Unavoidably, then, Amory's pages feature more typographic interruptions in the scholarly edition than in the first, proffering additional tangents to readers and leading them on into the expanse of editorial

---

[37] Manuel Portela, 'Typographic Translation: The Portuguese Edition of *Tristram Shandy*', in Joe Bray, Miriam Handley and Anne Henry (eds.), *Ma(r)king the Text: The Presentation of Meaning on the Literary Page* (Aldershot: Ashgate, 2000), 291–308.

apparatus at the back of the volume. In certain respects, this amplifies the appearance of Amory's page, in that he appears to have had specific designs for the intertwining narratives offered by the aesthetics of footnotes on the page. The additional option to follow a modern commentary interrupts as it contributes to the complexity of *John Buncle*, highlighting twenty-first-century reading practices and apparatus. An alternative approach taken in *Tristram Shandy* by Melvyn and Joan New, editors of the Florida Edition of the novel, seems both more and less interruptive: the notes appear in a separate volume, keeping the primary text clean, but also requiring the navigation of a second codex. However, it includes an additional paratext which Sterne never intended to utilise; in this edition, scholarly notes are keyed to line numbers printed down the margin of the page.

Sterne, influenced by Amory's experimentation with the footnote, drew from *John Buncle* his fluid interchange between registers of main text and note. But Sterne's own subversion of paratexts takes Amory's experiment to the next level through his additional exploitation of the catchword. With this device in particular, Sterne foregrounds and makes conscious the usually subconscious aspects of reading: page turning, eye movement and conventional expectations of chronology. His experimentation returns the catchword to visibility; he makes the reader read and analyse the device, recognising that it is not necessarily neutral or devoid of meaning. He misuses the catchword, using it to lure the reader into a false sense of the predictability of reading in order to heighten our surprise at what appears overleaf. By manipulating the catchword, he reveals how far the novel is a construct of print and paper, and how we have become blind to that fact.

In *Tristram Shandy* typography becomes a means of producing meaning on the page, with spatial factors and visual signs contributing to the force of the semantic message. Sterne exploits white space, page breaks, typeface, typesetting, chapter headings, footnotes, catchwords – a whole range of paratextual devices – in order to make meaning and to create a reading process which is both non-linear and conscious of the book as a material form. Traditionally considered the realm of the printer rather than the author, paratexts such as the catchword and the footnote become valid ground for the subversion of narrative and print convention, invisible in all but the early editions of Sterne's text. As in 'madam's' ineffective reading, Sterne encourages us to engage with the codex in a self-conscious and reflective manner. He challenges our expectations and in so doing reveals the mechanics of reading and the author's power over those domains.

As in so many of Sterne's seeming innovations in *Tristram Shandy*, with paratexts Sterne develops existing experiments in mid-century print culture. In his use of the footnote we can identify precursors in the Scriblerians' innovations in contesting literary and scholarly authority and their satire of textual editing. But in his play with catchwords Sterne innovates beyond experiments by Alexander Pope and Jonathan Swift. He develops the complexity of the pages of Thomas Amory's *John Buncle*, the successful navigation of which relies heavily upon catchwords in a traditional way. Paratexts, apparently there to facilitate reading – to 'make present' the book – became during the eighteenth century more and more unpredictable. With Sterne, however, they reached a peak of innovation, as his manipulation of the semantics of the traditionally neutral catchword has no comparable forebear. Nevertheless, in Sterne's paratextual self-consciousness we can see him assimilating innovations extant in print and taking them further. Elements of the pamphlets satirising scholarly editions in the first half of the eighteenth century are present in *Tristram Shandy*'s empty chapters, while his complex page breaks and discouragement of reading straight forward chimes with Amory's creative use of the page as a receptacle of competing and contemporaneous passages. In this, too, we see Pope's *Dunciad* and his aesthetic refusal to print catchwords in the margin. Sterne inherits from earlier writers such as Pope a desire to extend his authority into the elements of book production traditionally associated with the printer, for reasons of style but also for creative play with the process of reading. Sterne frequently sought to disorientate the reader in his text, using the catchword – or omitting it – in order to encourage us to go back and look more closely at his work and the way it was produced.

CHAPTER 6

Engraved Lines

Tristram Shandy was rare in being an illustrated novel from its first edition, as this study has shown. Few works of fiction featured images of any kind when first launched. Book illustrations as we tend to think of them now, pictures of notable scenes from the text's plot, tended to be later additions to fictional works which had stood the test of time, and which would be sure to sell despite the additional cost of image production.[1] Janine Barchas's work on the graphic design of the eighteenth-century novel has begun the important task of exploring these texts' rare visual elements. As she demonstrates, fantasy travel narratives such as Daniel Defoe's *Robinson Crusoe* (1719) and Jonathan Swift's *Gulliver's Travels* (1726) were more visual than other literary works from this period, featuring black and white frontispiece illustrations of their fictional narrators. Swift also printed engraved monochrome maps in *Gulliver*, and Defoe included fold-out maps in Crusoe's *Farther Adventures* (1719) and *Serious Reflections* (1720).[2] Sterne's diagrams share with Defoe and Swift's texts a desire to provide cartography for fiction, but instead of mapping his fictional world, Sterne charts his narrator's halting progress in sharing his life and opinions. Sterne's diagrams are characteristically self-reflexive, and instead of representing physical landscapes they indicate narrative movement.

Throughout this monograph I have argued that Sterne was conversant with a range of different book design practices that drew from intertexts which would have been available to – but may or may not have been recognised by – his first readers. This final chapter considers Sterne's use of engraved lines as visual and verbal metaphors for digression,

---

[1] See, for example, Sandro Jung, 'The Other *Pamela*: Readership and the Illustrated Chapbook Abridgement', *Journal for Eighteenth-Century Studies*, 39 (2016), Special Issue: *Picturing the Eighteenth-Century Novel through Time*, Christina Ionescu and Ann Lewis (eds.), 513–31.

[2] Janine Barchas, *Graphic Design, Print Culture, and the Eighteenth-Century Novel* (Cambridge University Press, 2003), 60.

contextualising zigzag lines by examining the print history of dance manuals, by necessity visual texts which had to be ever more experimental in their attempt to teach movement by means of the printed page. Like Sterne's plotlines in volume 6, these attractive volumes self-consciously reflect on the form of the codex, and their diagrams become demystified through labelling and instruction. Trim's flourish in volume 9 shares with the plotlines and with dance notation an alignment of looping lines with motion. The curls of Sterne's engraved lines echo figures that had appeared elsewhere, in manuals and artwork representing the serpentine progress of dances such as the minuet, one of the most popular dances of the mid-eighteenth century. Sterne's engraved lines, when read alongside eighteenth-century dance notation, signify the inability of anyone in Sterne's novel to narrate – or to move – in a straight black narrative line.

I Dance, Digression and Lines

Tristram pauses near the end of the sixth volume to reflect on the progress of his autobiography. Now that he is 'beginning to get fairly into [his] work', he promises to continue his story 'in a tolerable straight line' (6.40.152). With this metaphor Tristram promises what we know he cannot deliver: a linear, chronological narrative. He then, without warning, presents his reader with four engraved lines. The sentence with which he introduces the lines is part type and part diagram, comprising one word ('Now,') and one large woodcut engraving showing the four lines.

Readers returning to *Tristram Shandy* will grasp what these lines mean before they are glossed for us. But what is often overlooked is the fact that the revelation of their meaning is delayed. We do not discover until the next page that the engraved lines provide illustrations of the narratives of Tristram's first four volumes. We remain unable to interpret the lines until the fifth engraved line appears, complete with alphabet labels and instructions:

> By which it appears, that except at the curve, marked A. where I took a trip to *Navarre*,—and the indented curve B. which is the short airing when I was there with the Lady *Baussiere* and her page,—I have not taken the least frisk of a digression, till *John de la Casse's* devils led me the round you see marked D.—for as for *c c c c c* they are nothing but parentheses, and the common *ins* and *outs* incident to the lives of the greatest ministers of state; and when compared with what men have done,—or with my own transgressions at the letters A B D —they vanish into nothing. (6.40.153–4)

With this delayed demonstration of how to read his visual representation of narrative, Tristram leads us from incomprehension to understanding. In the belated inclusion of this information, Sterne forces the reader to diverge from the narrative to revisit the first four engraved lines after the fifth, creating a disordered reading process which complements his digressive narrative. Revisiting the images, we learn to follow the plotlines from left to right and to interpret curves and angles as digressions, reading height and incline as scale and duration of digression.

This *mise en page*, across the spread, is visually arresting. The first four lines appear below the text on the verso, covering over half of the page. On the recto, the fifth line, this one labelled, is sandwiched between two bodies of type. Sterne invites us to consider the print technology that produced these pages: a combination of moveable type and wood block engraving. It is unclear whether Sterne or a wood engraver designed these lines, though the fourth and fifth lines in particular share similarities with the looping squiggles which adorn Sterne's fair copy manuscripts of *A Sentimental Journey* (1768) and the Le Fever episode (vol. 6, 1767) surviving in the British Library; by the time Trim's flourish is printed in volume 9, we can begin to see a sort of house style.[3] The plotlines would have been drawn on paper before being transferred to the smooth surface of wooden blocks of proportionate size to the page. Then the wood would have been engraved relief style, whereby the lines which mark the page remain raised so that when they are inked the rest of the block remains blank. The pages would have been typeset leaving room for the wooden blocks within the forme, which were surrounded by spacers in order to position them below and within the lines of moveable type. The wooden blocks would have been packed into the forme, to raise their surfaces to the same height as the type (or slightly higher, due to the increased pressure required for woodblocks to print effectively). With woodcut printing, both text and image could be printed at the same time using the usual hand press. It was a favoured technique of Sterne's, and many of his first edition fictions include woodcuts, from the fighting cocks in *A Political Romance* (1759) to woodcuts discussed elsewhere in this study (the strikethrough

---

[3] Sterne, 'A Sentimental Journey . . .', the first part; by Laurence Sterne, M.A. The author's corrected draft, prepared for the press; together with the printed preface and woodcut illustrations of the edition by Nichols', British Library, Egerton MS 1610, available at: www.bl.uk/collection-items/laurence-sternes-manuscript-draft-of-the-first-part-of-a-sentimental-journey, last accessed 5 June 2020. Sterne also scores straight lines in the MS of the Death of Le Fever: Sterne, 'Le Fever's Story' [1761–62?], endorsed by Lady Spencer, British Library, Althorp Papers, vol. cdxlv, Add MS 75745.

BRAVO in Chapter 1; the black page in Chapter 2; and Trim's flourish, below).[4] But the pages carrying the plotlines, unlike any other page in Sterne's corpus, have their margins invaded: the images are wider than the text frame, and the zigzag lines stray into the white space. Not even manicules, traditionally marginal print devices, extend beyond the text block in *Tristram Shandy*.[5] Sterne thereby reiterates his graphic control over all aspects of book design. Through invading the margins, the plotlines demonstrate that he is not only responsible for the literary content of a work, usually limited to the substance of the text block, but also for the construction of the book as a physical artefact. This is highlighted by his signing the image with Tristram's initials, '*Inv. T.S and Scul. T.S*' (6.40.153). The Latin abbreviations tell us that Tristram is both artist and engraver, just as in *Tristram Shandy*, Sterne is both author and book designer. But the lines also represent Tristram's narratives of each of the five volumes as sprawling and unruly. As a narrator, Tristram is unable to contain his text. In straying into the margins, the lines accurately reflect Tristram's inability to be concise, with his story frequently running away from him.

By the time the sixth and seventh volumes of *Tristram Shandy* appeared on the literary marketplace in 1762, Sterne's readers came to expect digression. It is, after all, Tristram's 'hobby-horse', which he describes as 'a secondary figure, and a kind of back-ground to the whole' (1.9.32). Fundamentally, Sterne's use of the term 'hobby-horse' in *Tristram Shandy* refers to a pastime which preoccupies the hobbyist to the point of obsession:

> my hobby-horse, if you recollect a little, is no way a vicious beast; he has scarce one hair or lineament of the ass about him—— 'Tis the sporting little filly-folly which carries you out for the present hour—a maggot, a butterfly, a picture, a fiddle-stick—an uncle Toby's siege—or an *any thing*, which a man makes a shift to get a-stride on, to canter it away from the cares and solicitudes of life—'Tis as useful a beast as is in the whole creation—nor do I really see how the world could do without it—— (8.31.131).

---

[4] Sterne, *A Political Romance*, in *The Miscellaneous Writings and Sterne's Subscribers, an Identification List*, Melvyn New and W.B. Gerard (eds.), The Florida Edition of the Works of Laurence Sterne (Gainesville, FL: University Press of Florida, 2014), vol. 9, 108. The coat of arms in *A Sentimental Journey* was printed using a copper plate, which required a different printing press and therefore a laborious and expensive process of overprinting. That image also sits within the text block, not straying into the margins like the plotlines. Sterne, *A Sentimental Journey through France and Italy* (London: Becket and De Hondt, 1768), vol. 2, 38.

[5] See Chapter 1.

Here, a hobby horse can be a diversion of any kind – natural history (maggots and butterflies), art (pictures) or sex (a fiddle-stick) – which, like Toby's obsession with toy wars, allows the hobbyist to temporarily forget the vicissitudes of life. But Tristram's chosen term, 'hobby-horse', held numerous associated meanings at this time, including a horse bred in Ireland (*OED* 1) and a frivolous fellow or lustful woman (*OED* 3b).[6] Less well known are the term's associations with dance. The hobby horse is a traditional character in the morris dance, where one performer wears 'a wicker horse-like frame strapped to his waist', performing 'antics imitating a skittish horse' (*OED* 2a).[7] It also gives its name to a fertility dance performed by women at country mummings in the late seventeenth century (*OED* 2c).[8] Tristram's narration dances around its proposed subject. The term 'hobby-horse' puns on digression's capacity to divert, entertain, and obsess Tristram while associating narration with physical movement.

Sterne uses dance to illustrate his system of digression in *Tristram Shandy* on both visual and metaphorical levels. From his first volume, Tristram finds his autobiography is so digressive that he 'knows no more than his heels what lets and confounded hinderances he is to meet with in his way,—or what a dance he may be led, by one excursion or another, before all is over' (1.14.79). Here, dance can refer to actual dance, digression or deferral. And this is not an isolated image. By the seventh volume, Tristram is literally dancing with Nanette, the 'nut brown maid' with a slit in her petticoat (7.44.159), while attempting to defer his own death (leading the devil a 'dance he little thinks of' across the continent) at the same time that he describes his narrative digression through that very metaphor (7.1.5). When Tristram proudly recaps the extent of his digression during Obadiah's absence from the scene of young Tristram's impending birth to fetch the man-midwife (in fact he only travels to the edge of the Shandy estate), dance is his chosen image. While Obadiah is away, Tristram reminds us that he has narrated Toby's journey from Namur to England, his four years spent in a sickbed at the Shandy London residence and then his subsequent 200-mile journey to Shandy

---

[6] "hobby-horse, n." OED Online, Oxford University Press, www.oed.com/view/Entry/87463, last accessed 5 June 2020.
[7] Ibid.
[8] Ibid. Helen Ostovich, 'Reader as Hobby-Horse in *Tristram Shandy*', in Thomas Keymer (ed.), *Laurence Sterne's Tristram Shandy: A Casebook* (Oxford University Press, 2006), 173. See also David Oakleaf, 'Long Sticks, Morris Dancers, and Gentlemen: Associations of the Hobby-Horse in *Tristram Shandy*', *Eighteenth-Century Life*, 11 (1987), 62–76.

Hall. This, he declares, 'must have prepared the reader's imagination for the entrance of Dr. Slop upon the stage,—as much, at least (I hope) as a dance, a song, or a concerto between the acts' (2.8.120). While likening his extensive narrative digression to music or a dance, Tristram makes clear that digression is key to the progress of his plot and to the preparation of the reader's imagination for receiving the intended effects of his narrative. Celebrating and valorising digression, song and dance as like forms of entertainment, he attempts to get the reader on side while revealing how far he himself is entertained by digression as an art form. Time and again, in *Tristram Shandy*, Sterne uses dance to conceptualise his unique style of literary production.

Dance is a pervasive presence in Sterne's works in the plot, as a motif and a source for his idiosyncratic book design. His references to dance often refer to lines. This is most apparent in Tristram's travels through rural France when Nanette invites Tristram to join in a country dance:

> We want a cavalier, said she, holding out both her hands, as if to offer them ——And a cavalier ye shall have; said I, taking hold of both of them.
>
> Hadst thou, Nannette, been array'd like a dutchesse!
>
> ——But that cursed slit in thy petticoat!
>
> Nannette cared not for it.
>
> We could not have done without you, said she, letting go one hand, with self-taught politeness, leading me up with the other.
>
> [. . .]——Tie me up this tress instantly, said Nannette, putting a piece of string into my hand——It taught me to forget I was a stranger——The whole knot fell down——We had been seven years acquainted.
>
> The youth struck the note upon the tabourin—his pipe followed, and off we bounded——'the duce take that slit!' (7.44.156–7)

Apart from the bounding, we see very little of the dance. We hear the opening notes of the music, but the scene is abstract, composed of imagined serpentine lines: the curving movement of the slit in Nanette's petticoat and her rogue lock of hair. Sterne sexualises these curls, Nanette's slit functioning as a metaphor for her genitalia, heightening the erotic tension of the scene while comically counterpointing Tristram's awkwardness with Nanette's composure. He leaves the dance characteristically incomplete: as soon as Nanette 'capriciously' bends her head to the side, and dances up 'insidious', Tristram decides ''tis time to dance off', so changing only partners and tunes, I danced it away from Lunel to Montpellier——from thence to Pesçnas, Beziers——I danced it along through Narbonne, Carcasson, and Castle Naudairy, till at last I danced myself into Perdrillo's pavillion, where pulling out a paper of black lines, that I might go on straight forwards, without digression or parenthesis, in my uncle Toby's amours——

I begun thus—— (7.44.159–60)

This self-reflexive image of the writer at work relates Nanette's entanglement of Tristram in a circuitous dance to Tristram's tangled writing. Sterne shifts from using dance as textual content to deploying it as a narrative device: Tristram's dance with Nanette begins as a real dance but becomes a figural one, representing both literal travel – from Lunel to Perdrillo's pavilion – as well as his literary digression from his journey in France to Toby's amours in England many years earlier. By manipulating the scene of the dance into a writerly metaphor, Sterne pans away from the country dance, returning Tristram to his study. He also reminds us of his engraved images in volume 6. There, Tristram had prioritised the straight black line, where it seemed to him to represent narrative excellence, as he reflected on that volume's progress:

from the end of Le Fever's episode, to the beginning of my uncle Toby's campaigns,—I have scarce stepped a yard out of my way.

If I mend at this rate, it is not impossible—by the good leave of his grace of Benevento's devils—but I may arrive hereafter at the excellency of going on even thus:

---

which is a line drawn as straight as I could draw it, by a writing-master's ruler (borrowed for that purpose), turning neither to the right hand or to the left. (6.40.154)

He had then proposed to write his 'chapter upon straight lines' (6.40.155). This chapter, perhaps predictably, never appears, for Tristram delights far too much in the dance of digression, and dance itself, to ever write it. Back in Perdrillo's pavilion, in volume 7, Tristram approaches straight lines again, pulling out his ready-printed sheets of writing paper – his 'paper of black lines' – in order to continue his story. This is a characteristic image for Sterne, calling to mind the raw materials of book production and inviting readers to imagine the writing paper on which this text is composed, while reminding them of the 'paper of black lines' memorably printed in the earlier volume. Sterne jokes that such paper will aid

Tristram's apparent desire for linear composition. However, Tristram's promise to avoid digression (and piping, fiddling and dancing), serves only to valorise it:

> —But softly——for in these sportive plains, and under this genial sun, where at this instant all flesh is running out piping, fiddling, and dancing to the vintage, and every step that's taken, the judgment is surprised by the imagination, I defy, notwithstanding all that has been said upon *straight lines** in sundry pages of my book—I defy the best cabbage planter that ever existed, whether he plants backwards or forwards, it makes little difference in the account (except that he will have more to answer for in the one case than in the other)—I defy him to go on cooly, critically, and canonically, planting his cabbages one by one, in straight lines, and stoical distances, especially if slits in petticoats are unsew'd up—without ever and anon straddling out, or sidling into some bastardly digression——In *Freeze-land, Fog-land,* and some other lands I wot of—it may be done——
>
>   But in this clear climate of fantasy and perspiration, where every idea, sensible and insensible, gets vent—in this land, my dear Eugenius—in this fertile land of chivalry and romance, where I now sit, unskrewing my ink-horn to write my uncle Toby's amours, and with all the meanders of JULIA's track in quest of her DIEGO, in full view of my study window— if thou comest not and takest me by the hand——
>
>   What a work it is likely to turn out!
>   Let us begin it.

*Vid. Vol. VI. 152. (8.1.1–3)

Tristram distances himself from his earlier promises to avoid digression, from 'all that has been said upon *straight lines* in sundry pages of my book': with the passive voice, it is as if the pages which carry the plotlines narrate themselves (the footnote directs the reader to the woodcuts). While seemingly denouncing digression and dance (and sex/cabbage-planting) as products of a warm climate, pretending to request that Eugenius save him from such temptations, Tristram simultaneously celebrates them. Dancing and digression are natural and liberating products of warmth, while linear narrative is constrictive and cold. Straight and, by implication, serious narratives might be possible in cooler climates. But under the hot sun, which happens also to be a place of 'fantasy', 'chivalry and romance', filled with 'sensible and insensible' ideas – that is to say, a place of literary inspiration – straight narrative lines are unfeasible. For 'meandering' love stories (Julia and Diego), narratives of sexual attraction (Tristram and Nanette), and in creative work more generally, digressive narratives allow imagination to triumph over judgement, leading to art forms characterised by movement, desire, and experiment ('What a work it is likely to turn out!').

II Cartography and Movement

Sterne was not the first author to use labelled diagrams. Jonathan Swift's map of Laputa, the flying island in *Gulliver's Travels* (1726), includes an alphabetically labelled line indicating its movement.[9] With his maps Swift was exploiting the vogue for travel writing and cartographical works, which had given rise to the success of William Dampier's *A New Voyage Round the World* (1697).[10] The maps in *Gulliver's Travels* have been included in editions published since its first appearance, but they have not always been treated with the same editorial rigour as the text itself, as Nicole E. Didicher notes.[11] They experienced a revival in critical interest in the 1940s and 1950s, when Frederick Bracker pointed out that they 'must certainly be among the most widely circulated maps in our literature'.[12] Didicher shows that in the stability of the maps' errors and inconsistencies across various print runs, Swift underlined his satire on cartographer Herman Moll through a theme which recurs within the text itself: 'the unreliability of supposedly reliable facts'.[13] Swift's satire on facts targets the Royal Society, most memorably in his description of the flying island's scientifically preoccupied occupants. As Pat Rogers points out, Swift parodies the discourse of the Royal Society's transactions when labelling his map of Laputa, and when composing his own plotlines Sterne might have been remembering Swift's 'quasi-geometrical language':[14]

> By this oblique Motion the Island is conveyed to different Parts of the Monarch's Dominions. To explain the manner of its Progress, let *A B* represent a Line drawn cross the Dominions of *Balnibarbi*, let the line *c d* represent the Load-stone, of which let *d* be the repelling End, and *c* the attracting End, the Island being over *C*; let the Stone be placed in the position *c d*, with its repelling End downwards; then the Island will be driven upwards obliquely towards *D*. When it is arrived at *D*, let the stone be turned upon its axle till its attracting end points towards *E*, and then the Island will be carried obliquely towards *E*; where, if the Stone be

---

[9] Jonathan Swift, *Travels into Several Remote Nations of the World. In Four parts. By Lemuel Gulliver, First a Surgeon, and then a Captain of Several Ships*, 2 vols. (London: Motte, 1726), vol. 2, book 3, bound near page 39.

[10] Frederick Bracher, 'The Maps in *Gulliver's Travels*', *Huntington Library Quarterly*, 8 (1944), 59–74.

[11] Nicole E. Didicher, 'Mapping the Distorted Worlds of *Gulliver's Travels*', *Lumen: Selected Proceedings from the Canadian Society for Eighteenth-Century Studies / Lumen: travaux choisis de la Société canadienne d'étude du dix-huitième siècle*, 16 (1997), 179–96, 182.

[12] Bracher, 'The Maps', 61.   [13] Didicher, 'Mapping the Distorted Worlds'.

[14] Pat Rogers, *Documenting Eighteenth-Century Satire: Pope, Swift, Gay, and Arbuthnot in Historical Context* (Newcastle: Cambridge Scholars, 2012), 50; Rogers, 'Ziggerzagger Shandy: Sterne and the Aesthetics of the Crooked Line', *English: Journal of the English Association*, 42.173 (1993), 103.

again turned upon its Axle till it stands in the position *E F*, with its repelling
Point downwards, the Island will rise obliquely towards *F*, where by
directing the attracting End towards *G*, the Island may be carried to *G*,
and from *G* to *H*, by turning the Stone, so as to make its repelling
Extremity point directly downwards.[15]

Swift's engraved line appears regular, uniform and predictable. Unlike
Tristram's capricious circling and plotlines, Swift's island progresses,
albeit in diagonal directions. Swift charts the largely successful motion
of what we are supposed to imagine is a tangible landmass while Sterne
records the invisible progress (and process) of Tristram's convoluted
storytelling.

Rogers's article, 'Ziggerzagger Shandy', in which he briefly posits this
relationship between Swift and Sterne's labelled lines, seeks to contextualise Sterne's plotlines with geometrical diagrams in gardening and
military works from the eighteenth century. It is rare in its consideration
of potential precursors for Sterne's idiosyncratic graphs. Not many
studies consider Sterne's graphic forebears, but those that do invoke
William Hogarth. This line of argument sees Sterne, in his third instalment of *Tristram Shandy*, responding to the engraved illustrations which
the artist had provided for the first two. Thomas Keymer, for example,
sees Sterne mockingly hinting at the inadequacy of Hogarth's pencil by
having the plotlines signed by Tristram in the lower margin in a position
where thus far only Hogarth's name had appeared.[16] Hogarth's
frontispiece had been commissioned after the first edition of volumes
1 and 2 had sold out, though it was available for sale separately as well as
within editions from 1760 onwards and therefore circulated widely. In
the meantime, readers had also encountered the blank single-sided page
in volume 6 reserved for drawing the widow Wadman (6.38.146;
Figure 5.1 in Chapter 5). By the time the plotlines appeared, then,
readers were prompted to question what exactly constitutes an illustration, and what a narrative, and to reflect on Sterne's book design
practices as integral to the work's meaning.

W.B. Gerard and Patrizia Nerozzi Bellman also identify Hogarth's
serpentine line of beauty as a source for the curling lines.[17] Bellman's
article is most interesting for my purposes because in it she makes the
strongest claim so far for the significance of Sterne's use of dance as

[15] Swift, *Gulliver's Travels*, 2.3.39–40.
[16] Keymer, *Sterne, the Moderns, and the Novel* (Oxford University Press, 2002), 78.
[17] Gerard, *Laurence Sterne and the Visual Imagination* (Aldershot: Ashgate, 2006), 15.

literary motif. Bellman argues that Sterne draws upon Hogarth's typography to capture movement through a combination of the visual and the verbal.[18] She compares William Hogarth's labelling of his image of the country dance in *The Analysis of Beauty* (1753) with Sterne's description of 'my Lord A, B, C, D, E, F, G, H, I, K, L, M, N, O, P, Q, and so on, all of a row, mounted upon their several horses' (1.8.25). Both Sterne and Hogarth pun on 'characters', replacing people with letters from the alphabet. But Sterne's alphabet works as a series of labels, riffing on the tendency of novelists and newspapers to abbreviate (and to censor) proper names in print, while Hogarth's alphabet is aesthetic, using the shapes of the letters to illustrate people's postures. Rather than the prancing lords, then, the extract from *Tristram Shandy* that appears most closely to signify the proximity of Hogarth and Sterne's ideas is that which accompanies the plot lines of volume 6. Here, like Hogarth, Sterne invites the reader to interpret the curves he has engraved and labelled.[19] Sterne's labelling of hand-drawn squiggles could certainly be interpreted as a joke on printed manuals, if not Hogarth's text in particular. Sterne was familiar with and certainly referenced Hogarth's concept of the line of beauty, and while scholars such as Leann Davis Alspaugh and Bellman have shown the ways in which he drew from Hogarth, Sterne also shared with the artist an interest in the same source material: innovatively printed dance manuals from the first half of the eighteenth century. Hogarth's country dance image, the large fold-out engraving in the *Analysis of Beauty*, draws from dance manuals' representations and diagrams of the minuet. When faced with the problem of representing movement, both artist and novelist label engraved lines, like so many designers of dance manuals of the period. For the plotlines, Sterne defers annotating his lines to encourage the reader to encounter his digressive text in a looping and non-linear manner. We dance around the text, rehearsing, learning and then perfecting our reading of Sterne's graven lines in time for the final diagram of the novel: an illustration of the sweeping movement of Trim's stick. Digressive narrative, and the

---

[18] Patrizia Nerozzi Bellman, 'Dancing Away: Escape Strategy in *Tristram Shandy* and *A Sentimental Journey*', *The Shandean*, 24 (2013), 135–46, 136–7. See also Judith Hawley, '*Tristram Shandy* and Digression', in Alexis Grohmann and Caragh Wells (eds.), *Digression in European Literature from Cervantes to Sebald* (Basingstoke: Palgrave, 2011), 21–35, on digression, sexuality and Hogarth's serpentine lines.

[19] Leann Davis Alspaugh, "'Howgarth's Witty Chissel': Hogarth's Frontispieces for *Tristram Shandy*', *The Shandean*, 24 (2013), 9–30.

non-linear reading that Sterne directs here, gives the novel a movement akin to the form of the minuet, circling away only to return.

The history of the dance manual is, like that of *Tristram Shandy*, one of innovation. Over the course of the seventeenth and eighteenth centuries they were ever more experimental in their attempt to teach the reader to dance by means of the printed page. The earliest known Italian texts, Fabritio Caroso's *Il ballarino* (1581) and *Nobiltà de dame* (1600), and Cesare Negri's *Le gratie d'amore* (1602) bound together separately printed pages of music notation, textual descriptions of dance steps and engravings illustrating the dancer's gesture and posture. *Orchesographie* by Thoinot Arbeau (real name Jehan Tabourot), the only surviving French manual from this period, was first published in Langres in 1588, and used the same three key ingredients: choreography, music notation and images of dancers indicating elegant carriage. But Arbeau innovated with his presentation of this information. Rather than simply anthologising pages which separately displayed choreography (typeset text), (typeset) music and (wood-engraved) image, he experimented with the format of the book, having the music typeset vertically on the page with the name of each step horizontally beside the note on which it should be danced. Arbeau's experiment was remarkable in terms of indicating timing, and for a long period, his remained the most useful manual for dancing masters across England and France, but it shared with its competitors one significant drawback: readers were as yet unable to visualise the overall shape of the dance. It continued to be difficult to identify where the dance began or ended, and what kind of shape it traced across the floor in between. The overall progress of the dance, its narrative, was yet to be expressed in print.

The eighteenth century witnessed the greatest experimentation with print in dance manuals. It was at the turn of the century that the first dance notation systems were published, such as those devised during the 1680s by French dancing masters Jean Favier and André Lorin. Favier and Lorin considered dance and physical movement to be beyond the power of words to accurately and concisely express, and they codified dance through non-verbal markings to rectify this issue. However, these markings did not catch on. The notation systems offered little beyond existing manuals, and simply replaced verbal choreography with complex markings. The Beauchamp-Feuillet notation system was altogether more successful. It first appeared in print in Raoul-Auger Feuillet's *Chorégraphie, ou l'art de d'écrire la danse* (1700), translated by John Weaver as *Orchesography* (1706), and in Feuillet's *Recueil de contredances mises en chorégraphie* (1706), translated by John Essex as *For the Further Improvement of Dancing* (1710).[20] Beauchamp-Feuillet dance notation was more successful than earlier systems because it indicated the dancers' movement from one spot to another in the ballroom through one engraved line or track. As does Tristram with his narratives in volume 6 of *Tristram Shandy*, Beauchamp and Feuillet desired to express the meandering progress and direction of their dances from beginning to end. The Beauchamp-Feuillet system overlaid the track with dance notation signifying the steps, with the added convenience that, due to the track, readers could infer where in the room those steps should take place. Their pages are illustrations of the shape of their dances with non-verbal language printed over them. While a straight track would indicate movement straight ahead, eighteenth-century dances included many loops and tangents, and Beauchamp-Feuillet manuals are filled with swirling lines indicating the circling progress of the dancer. Tristram's plotlines illustrating the progress of his volumes are similarly tortuous, indicating by means of lines and labels the precise movement of his digressive narrative.

Sterne's narrative, as he illustrates in the swirling tracks of his plot-lines, circles and loops, is continuously deferred. While he and the dancing masters were exploiting an age-old idea of straight lines indicating forward movement, the Beauchamp-Feuillet system of representing both dance steps and movement around the ballroom was an unprecedented experiment in pushing print's capacity for verisimilitude. These books were highly collectable,[21] and the number of booksellers, artists and engravers in the subscription lists for Kellom Tomlinson's *Art of Dancing Explained* (1735), for example, marks out these works as milestones in eighteenth-century book design.[22] To eighteenth-century dancing students, the style of the engraved lines in *Tristram Shandy* would recall a non-verbal system which had become the standard means of teaching and sharing dance routines at mid-century. Sterne, a writer fascinated by the possibilities of print, and who took pride in ensuring

[20] Moira Goff, '"The Art of Dancing, Demonstrated by Characters and Figures": French and English Sources for Court and Theatre Dance, 1700–1750', *The British Library Journal*, 21 (1995), 202–31.

[21] Jennifer Thorp, 'Picturing a Gentleman Dancing-Master: A Lost Portrait of Kellom Tomlinson', *Dance Research*, 30 (2012), 70–9.

[22] 'Samuel Buck, Engraver, for two Setts', 'John Clark Engraver', 'Mr. Ben. Cole, Engraver', 'Mr. W. H. Toms Engraver', and 'Mr. Geo. Bickham junior, Engraver', 'Messieurs Knapton Booksellers' and 'Mr. Henry Lintot Bookseller, three Setts', 'Mr. James Mechel Printer'. Kellom Tomlinson, *Art of Dancing Explained* (London: Printed for the author, 1735).

that his daughter, Lydia, learned to dance,[23] would surely have known about these latest experiments. In printing his plotlines, then, he was drawing upon the aptitude of the most successful short-hand system in the period for representing physical movement.

Only the richest dance pupils in the eighteenth century would have been able to own a Beauchamp-Feuillet dance manual, but, as eighteenth-century newspaper advertisements reveal, dancing masters and boarding schools would have enabled a much wider range of dance students to access these expensive books,[24] and booksellers recommended purchasers to have their pages framed and displayed on the wall of homes and ballrooms, where they could be appreciated by many more viewers.[25] Of the dance manuals available in eighteenth-century York, Kellom Tomlinson's work is perhaps most likely to have been seen or consulted by Sterne. Aside from the fact that Tomlinson had aimed to increase the reach of dancing books by stressing the attractiveness of his plates and boasting that dance notation was now as widespread a skill as reading music,[26] Tomlinson's dance manual had a local connection. He dedicated his book to Catherine, Viscountess Fauconberg, wife of Thomas Belasyse, Lord Fauconberg. Sterne's own parish, St Michael's Church in Coxwold, was the estate church of the Fauconbergs, who lived at nearby Newburgh Priory. Tomlinson named his popular 1753 dance after the punning Belasyse family motto, 'Bonne et belle assez'.[27] Sterne was familiar with these words, which remain emblazoned across the inside wall of St Michael's Church, his living from 1760, and it is likely

---

[23] Sterne, 'To Mrs. F—' (19 November 1759), in *The Letters, Part 1, 1739–1764*, Melvyn New and Peter de Voogd (eds.), The Florida Edition of the Works of Laurence Sterne (Gainesville, FL: University Press of Florida, 2009), vol. 7, letter 41, 105; 'To John Hall-Stevenson' (19 October 1762), in ibid., letter 101, 294. When Lydia attends a party with the Marquis de Sade, Sterne writes to her that he 'would have given, not my gown and cassock (for I have but one,) but my topaz ring, to have seen the *petits maitres et maitresses* go to mass, after having spent the night in dancing'. 'To Lydia Sterne' (24 August 1767), in Sterne, 'To Anne and William James' (21 April 1767), in *The Letters, Part 2, 1765–1768*, Melvyn New and Peter de Voogd (eds.), The Florida Edition of the Works of Laurence Sterne (Gainesville, FL: University Press of Florida, 2009), vol. 8, letter 222, 612.

[24] The second edition of Pierre Rameau's *The Dancing Master*, John Essex (trans.), 2nd ed. (London: J. Essex and J. Brotherton, 1728) was advertised on 19 December 1730 and a third on 7 April 1733 as appealing to boarding schools. *Universal Spectator and Weekly Journal*, 19 December 1730; 7 April 1733.

[25] Tomlinson, *Art of Dancing*, Introduction to Book I, n.p.

[26] Tomlinson, 'Dedication to the Ladies', *Six Dances Compos'd by Mr. Kellom Tomlinson* (London: Tomlinson, 1720), n.p.

[27] Tomlinson also printed the motto alongside Catherine Belasyse's coat of arms on the dedication page of the *Art of Dancing*. Engraved by Francois Morellon la Cave after the 1716 painting by Richard Van Bleeck.

that the Sterne family were familiar with the dance, too, as it was a national success.

Like Sterne's works, Beauchamp-Feuillet dance manuals are beautiful books conscious of their own status as print artefacts. The successful interpretation of these manuals depends on a clear demarcation of space on the page. Feuillet provided instructions in *For the Further Improvement of Dancing* (1710) for interpreting his pages as bird's-eye views of the ballroom floor: 'you must take care to hold always exactly ye upper end of the book against ye upper end of the Roome, so that whatever Motion you make ye book may never come out of its naturall situation'.[28] Unlike Beauchamp and Feuillet, who depicted bird's-eye views of the ballroom floor, Tomlinson used copperplates in the *Art of Dancing Explained* to portray a cross-section of the ballroom, an innovation he stressed was all his own: 'ye steps or Characters are placed upon ye Floor in a perspective Manner intirely new'.[29] The rootedness of the dance manual in the ballroom means that a mark or line which curls to the right indicates that the reader, too, must turn to or move towards the right. Though there is no denying that these texts required advanced levels of a specific kind of literacy, such instructions enabled dancing masters to widely disseminate their routines and for those routines to continue to be re-enacted by dance historians today.

The dance manual's creative use of the printed page to indicate space anticipates Sterne's own typographic play with domestic boundaries in *Tristram Shandy*. Like the Beauchamp-Feuillet system, which requires the reader to orientate themselves in relation to engraved lines, and the book in relation to the room, Sterne frequently requests that we consider our position in relation to typography and the codex, perhaps most famously when Tristram invites us to 'sit down upon a set' (6.1.1). In the first volume of the novel, as he begins a new paragraph, Tristram requests that we shut the door, so that he can impart to the 'curious and inquisitive' reader (1.4.11) sensitive family secrets:

---

[28] Raoul-Auger Feuillet, *For the Further Improvement of Dancing*, John Essex (trans.) (London: Walsh, 1710), 1.

[29] Tomlinson, 'Common Time. The Galliard movement. Triple Time', *Art of Dancing*, Book II, plate vii. Elsewhere in the *Art of Dancing* he does demonstrate some combination steps through a bird's-eye view (e.g. the first, second, eleventh and sixteenth tables), and his six dances published annually between 1715 and 1720 were printed in the traditional bird's-eye view format. Rameau also used a bird's-eye view, though he formed his tracks from swirling handwritten choreography rather than dance notation.

————————————————————————Shut the door.————————————

> I was begot in the night, betwixt the first *Sunday* and the first *Monday* in the
> month of *March*, in the year of our Lord one thousand seven hundred and
> eighteen. (1.4.11)

The phrase 'Shut the door.' is sandwiched between two long dashes or
leadings, creating a printed barrier across the page. In this typographic
representation of space, Sterne has Tristram attempt to create two groups
of readers. Tristram hopes to leave the uninterested reader outside the
room and therefore without access to his history. The line demonstrates
the difference between outside and inside the Shandy parlour, just as the
borders of the Feuillet manuals represent the limits of the ballroom. In
reading on, we all find ourselves in the Shandy parlour, privy to the story
of Tristram's conception. Through this playful engraved line, Sterne
metaphorically delineates domestic space for what seems to be a reading
clique, but in reality, he co-opts all of his readers into the 'curious and
inquisitive' category. We have stepped over the line into the Shandy world.

Tristram's engraved lines around 'Shut the door' might evoke the wall
or door of the Shandy parlour, but the page which carries those lines does
not, as a whole, represent a room. In volume 9 of *Tristram Shandy* Sterne
designs one such page. As in the dance manuals, in *Tristram Shandy* and
the story of Toby's amours, labelled diagrams and bodies become inter-
changeable. In Mrs Wadman's pursuit of Toby, she is justifiably concerned about his virility:

> It is natural for a perfect stranger who is going from London to Edinburgh,
> to enquire before he sets out, how many miles to York; which is about the
> half way——nor does any body wonder, if he goes on and asks about the
> Corporation, &c. – –
> It was just as natural for Mrs. Wadman, whose first husband was all his
> time afflicted with a Sciatica, to wish to know how far from the hip to the
> groin; and how far she was likely to suffer more or less in her feelings, in the
> one case than in the other. (9.26.110)

In this mental image of a route from London to Edinburgh, Sterne aligns
Mrs Wadman's desire to make sense of Toby's war wound with a traveller
wishing to locate the mid-point of his journey, as if on a map. But Mrs
Wadman is not interested in cartography. In researching wounds to the
groin, she had 'read *Drake*'s anatomy from one end to the other. She had
peeped into *Wharton* upon the brain and borrowed *Graaf upon the bones
and muscles; but could make nothing of it' (9.26.110–11). The labelled
diagrams with which the widow is most concerned are found in anatomies,

not atlases. In the footnote, we learn that Graaf wrote upon the pancreatic juices and the parts of generation. The footnote underlines the joke: widow Wadman has been consulting de Graaf's printed illustrations of male genitalia.[30] This slippage of referents between maps and diagrams of bodies anticipates the approaching slippage between the map of Namur and Toby's body. When she asks Toby exactly where he was wounded during the siege of Namur, she is foiled by his naivety, when he indicates on a map where in Namur the accident took place:

> —And whereabouts, dear Sir, quoth Mrs. Wadman, a little categorically, did you receive this sad blow?——In asking this question, Mrs. Wadman gave a slight glance towards the waistband of my uncle Toby's red plush breeches, expecting naturally, as the shortest reply to it, that my uncle Toby would lay his fore-finger upon the place——It fell out otherwise——for my uncle Toby having got his wound before the gate of St. Nicolas, in one of the traverses of the trench opposite to the salient angle of the demibastion of St. Roch; he could at any time stick a pin upon the identical spot of ground where he was standing when the stone struck him: this struck instantly upon my uncle Toby's sensorium——and with it, struck his large map of the town and citadel of Namur and its environs, which he had purchased and pasted down upon a board, by the Corporal's aid, during his long illness——it had lain with other military lumber in the garret ever since, and accordingly the Corporal was detached to the garret to fetch it. (9.26.114-6)

In replacing Toby's groin with the printed map that Trim rushes to collect, Sterne draws upon graphic printing for his humour. The joke becomes a visual one, too, when he includes an illustration page at this point. In so doing, Sterne references the work of his literary precursors, Swift and Defoe, in printing maps in their novels to outline fictional landscapes. But instead of printing a map of Namur, Sterne prints a map of the map of Namur, as it is located in Mrs Wadman's kitchen. This visual page captures the entirety of chapter 27 of volume 9, which consists only of the briefest of sentences, 'My uncle Toby's map is carried down into the kitchen' (9.27.118), and it remains one of the under-analysed print experiments in this novel: this sentence is placed halfway down the page. The centring of the text tells us exactly where the map is: in the middle of the kitchen. As a self-reflexive cartographic joke, this page takes us back to Sterne's illustration of Mrs Wadman's concerns through the image of the halfway point from Edinburgh to London. It is a metaphor for the precise location of Toby's wound, revealing it to be at his mid-point in spite of his

---

[30] See, for example, De Graaf, in James Drake's *New System of Anatomy*, 2nd ed. (London: Innys, 1727), 64–5.

misinterpretation of Mrs Wadman's question; through his allusion to the anatomies, Sterne highlights how far a printed diagram might function as a replacement signifier for Toby's body.

Because the type does not begin at the top of the page, but is lowered to a central position, this chapter-page illustrates Mrs Wadman's kitchen in cross-section. Sterne, like dancing masters and map-makers of all kinds before him, uses white space to signify geographical space. If the map were brought into the middle of Mrs Wadman's kitchen, the page might be seen to recall the bird's-eye views of Feuillet's dance manuals. But Sterne's use of the word 'down' ('Toby's map is carried down into the kitchen') coupled with the text's left alignment directs us to read from top to bottom: this page is a cross-section rather than a bird's-eye view, and is therefore more aligned with Tomlinson's dance manual. The map page retains its page number (like the black and marbled pages) and (unlike them) its catchword, which anchors the limits of the printed page and therefore emphasises the unusual centring of text and this chapter's status as visual conceit. Together, conventional print devices of pagination and catchword act as coordinates, helping to orientate Toby's map. This page is not only a map charting the precise location of Toby's plan of the siege of Namur but, like the dance manuals, also functions as a snapshot of movement. The text's central position, lower relative to where the reader might expect to find it, hints at the 'carrying down' motion of the map into the kitchen. The episode is not just about charting geographies but also about capturing movement between spaces, a movement which Sterne's experimental page represents through drawing upon and further developing experiments with the technology of the book as pioneered by dancing masters before him.

Of course, this is not the only visual device in *Tristram Shandy* to indicate the physical movements of Toby's wooing of widow Wadman. Sterne's choreography of Toby's procession to the house of Mrs Wadman is intricately detailed, culminating in an engraved diagram to assist readers in imagining the progress of the attempted courtship. As Tristram tells us, 'My uncle Toby turn'd his head more than once behind him, to see how he was supported by the Corporal; and the Corporal as oft as he did it, gave a slight flourish with his stick' in encouragement (9.3.13). However, the more the men talk of romantic encounters, the more they become side-tracked. The corporal's reassuring signs with his stick, as he tells Toby 'never fear' (9.3.13), immediately precede the more flamboyant flourish with the same stick (Figure 6.1) which Trim undertakes in praise of singledom:

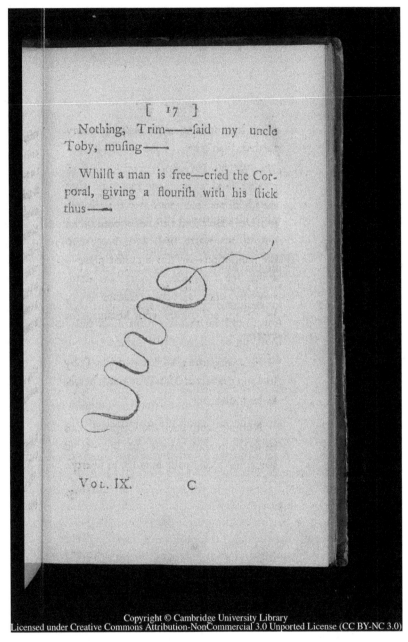

Figure 6.1 Trim's flourish (1767). Image courtesy of Cambridge
University Library

Nothing, continued the Corporal, can be so sad as confinement for life—or so sweet, an' please your honour, as liberty.

Nothing, Trim——said my uncle Toby, musing——

Whilst a man is free,—cried the Corporal, giving a flourish with his stick thus——

[image]

A thousand of my father's most subtle syllogisms could not have said more for celibacy.

My uncle Toby look'd earnestly towards his cottage and his bowling green. (9.4.16–18)

It is clear to see from this image that Trim's hand – holding his stick – appears to wave and circle. Arm circles are represented in the Beauchamp-Feuillet system by a spiralling line (the arm) joined to a straight line with a serif (the body).[31] According to a literal reading of the Beauchamp-Feuillet dance notation, the line would also be read as a wave and loop, revealing the accuracy of the notation and the facility with which engraved lines can illustrate physical movement. Some of the Beauchamp-Feuillet markings which record travelling across the floor also share similarities with the engraving Sterne used to represent Trim's flourish (Figure 6.2) and can be read in similar ways, indicating movement within a set physical space.[32] We read Sterne's line according to the same principles of dancing manuals, interpreting lines swirling left, right, up and down as similar movements off-page.

This engraved line is often claimed as the signature stroke of Sterne's non-verbal experimentation with the form of the printed book, recognised as such in being the logo of the Goldsmiths Prize for original fiction. It is an emblem which stresses just how inadequate words can be when it comes to articulating sex and relationships. And it is a line which demonstrates not progress but deferral. Whether read left to right (as is my preference, and as Tristram would have us do in volume 6) or right to left (top down), this line indicates a reverse movement, starting in one direction, reversing direction many times, before circling back and eventually leaving off in the other. We may also interpret it as the motion of Trim's arm or as a visual euphemism for the gaining and then losing of an erection. We remember Trim's flourish in praise of celibacy because it is visual, but we too easily forget that he has just undertaken a number of smaller (unillustrated) flourishes for the entirely opposite purpose, urging on his master in pursuit

---

[31] Raoul-Auger Feuillet, *Orchesography: Or, the Art of Dancing, by Characters and Demonstrative Figures*, John Weaver (trans.) (London: Meere, 1706).

[32] Ibid., p. 10.

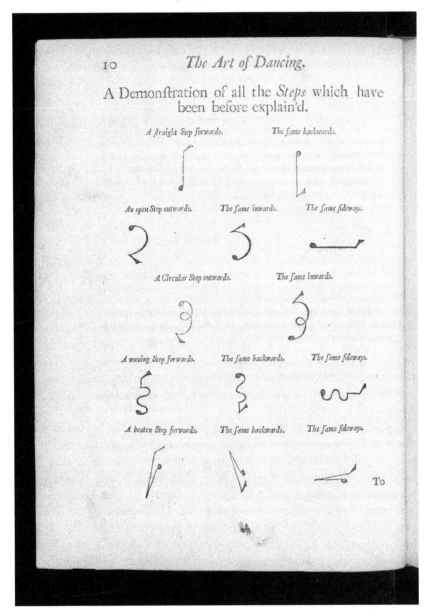

Figure 6.2 Steps in the Beauchamp-Feuillet system of dance notation (1706). Image courtesy of Cambridge University Library

of Mrs Wadman. Trim's squiggle denotes celibacy and male independence, then, as well as literary experimentation more broadly, but it also signifies the men's inability to stick to this idea, indicating Toby and Trim's digressive dialogue which flirts with opposing perspectives. This toing and froing of their conversation is paralleled in the men's quite literal turning on heel and walking in the wrong direction:

> ——whenever that drum beats in our ears, I trust, Corporal, we shall neither of us want so much humanity and fellow-feeling, as to face about and march.
>
> In pronouncing this, my uncle Toby faced about, and march'd firmly as at the head of his company——and the faithful Corporal, shouldering his stick, and striking his hand upon his coat-skirt as he took his first step—— march'd close behind him down the avenue.
>
> ——Now what can their two noddles be about? cried my father to my mother——by all that's strange, they are besieging Mrs. Wadman in form, and are marching round her house to mark out the lines of circumvallation. (9.8.34–5)

After several chapters of digression on Tristram's part, he finally completes the scene: 'When my uncle Toby and the Corporal had marched down to the bottom of the avenue, they recollected their business lay the other way; so they faced about and marched up streight to Mrs. Wadman's door' (9.16.63). Toby and Trim's movement is as digressive as their conversation; they march in opposite directions while dancing from opinion to opposing opinion, and this digression is enacted at the level of narrative, too.

Trim's flourish, as a non-verbal sign indicative of narrative movement and digression, is not only encountered by the reader but is also interpreted within the fiction. The whole time that Trim and Toby pace up and down in front of Mrs Wadman's house, deferring the moment of knocking upon the door in favour of pondering the pros and cons of relationships their movements are closely read by Elizabeth and Walter Shandy. After the flourish, Sterne himself quickly turns on heel and returns to the beginning of this episode to narrate it from their perspectives. Walter proposes watching Toby approach the widow Wadman:

> 'Let us just stop a moment, quoth my father, and see with what ceremonies my brother Toby and his man Trim make their first entry——it will not detain us, added my father, a single minute':
> —No matter, if it be ten minutes, quoth my mother.
> —It will not detain us half a one; said my father.

The Corporal was just then setting in with the story of his brother Tom and the Jew's widow: the story went on—and on——it had episodes in it——it came back, and went on——and on again; there was no end of it——the reader found it very long——

——G— help my father! he pish'd fifty times at every new attitude, and gave the corporal's stick, with all its flourishings and danglings, to as many devils as chose to accept of them. (9.10.39–40)

Trim's story 'went on and on—it had episodes in it—it came back, and went on', but they cannot hear it: Elizabeth and Walter are 'reader[s]'. They see every 'new attitude' that Trim affects, and with every flourishing and dangling of the stick, Walter grows more and more impatient with the men's inability to effect the job that they originally sought to undertake. Trim's flourish, signifying the things with which we have traditionally associated it – celibacy; non-verbal narration; literary experimentation – becomes, when we consider the passages that follow, a mark signifying digressive narrative and deferral. In printing an engraved line of Trim's flourish, Sterne includes us as onlookers to the scene witnessed by Elizabeth and Walter, and we become 'the reader' of Trim's flourishes. As a curving line centred on the page (and Sterne has twice shown that print can represent domestic space), Trim's flourish also resembles the track lines of eighteenth-century dance notation, which mapped the dancer's meandering progress across the floor. Sterne's use of dance in *Tristram Shandy* functions at the level of content, as a metaphor for circuitous narration and, in this reading, as an intertext for visual narrative. Trim's flourish, when read alongside eighteenth-century dance notation, signifies both the one-off movement of his stick and the inability of anyone in Sterne's novel to proceed in a straight, black, narrative line.

Coda: Frontispieces

Given the success of the first volumes of *Tristram Shandy* in 1759, the work's serial publication meant that Laurence Sterne's interventions in the print market of the mid-eighteenth century were regular and high-profile. This study has focused on the elements of that text that he designed himself but before closing explores his wider collaborations in the print market of his day. Sterne's literary celebrity was not only initiated but also perpetuated by the wider book and print trade.

Just hours after Sterne had met James Dodsley to cinch the deal on a second edition, selling the copyright for £450, Sterne was writing to Richard Berenger with a plan to have his novel illustrated. He would exchange both of his ears, he claimed, 'for no more than ten Strokes of Howgarth's witty Chissel, to clap at the Front of my next Edition of *Shandy!*'[1] This letter was composed with a view to Berenger carrying it to his friend Hogarth along with the first two volumes.[2] Sterne's use of the term 'clap' is an interesting play on the verb's secondary meaning, of, as Samuel Johnson defined it, adding one thing to another (usually in haste), while alluding to the noun describing posters for book marketing campaigns as in Alexander Pope's disparagement of 'claps in capitals'.[3] This was a plan which aimed to 'clap' together or combine moveable type and copper plate printing. It was a bid to improve the grandeur and aesthetic appeal of his fiction by having the leading artist of the day illustrate this recent and modish work of fiction: a marketing ploy as bold as 'claps in

---

[1] Sterne, 'To Richard Berenger', London (8 March 1760), *The Letters: Part 1, 1739–1764*, Melvyn New and Peter de Voogd (eds.), The Florida Edition of the Works of Laurence Sterne (Gainesville, FL: University Press of Florida, 2009), vol. 7, letter 48, 130.

[2] Arthur H. Cash, *Laurence Sterne: The Later Years* (London: Methuen, 1986), 9.

[3] 'to clap', *A Dictionary of the English Language: Abstracted from the Folio Edition*, Samuel Johnson (ed.), (London: Knapton, 1755–56). For my discussion of the Pope phrase, see Chapter 4. Sterne acknowledged Scriblerian influence when in the same letter he compared his own request to that of Jonathan Swift, who had requested Pope address an epistle to him through invoking's Cicero's words, '*Orna me*'. See *The Letters: Part 1*, 132–3, n. 7.

capitals'. And it certainly happened in haste, with Sterne's roundabout invitation to Hogarth arriving less than three months after the first publication of *Tristram Shandy*. That very day, the second edition was being advertised as being imminent [footnote reference to the General Advertiser, 8 March 1760] and, when Hogarth complied, the marketing campaign began afresh with announcements appearing in the *London Chronicle* as early as 25 March 1760 of the next edition carrying 'a Frontispiece by Hogarth'.[4] This is a significant moment, being Sterne's first recorded foray into copperplate and rolling press technology. And for all the frontispiece first appeared in the second edition of the first volumes, it was nevertheless an unprecedentedly quick turnaround. *Tristram Shandy* was a novel illustrated by a celebrity artist within weeks of its emergence, and its next instalment, the first edition of volumes 3 and 4, carrying another Hogarthian frontispiece, would make history, making *Tristram Shandy* one of those rare eighteenth-century fictions collaboratively illustrated from its very inception.

Before the advertisements even went to press announcing the Hogarth image, Sterne was sitting for Joshua Reynolds, on 20 March 1760. This was not a standard commission, but rather an ingenious collaboration which saw Reynolds waive the usual fee and retain the resulting portrait for the indulgence of capturing on canvas one of that moment's literary greats. In 1761 and 1768 he would exhibit the resulting work at the Society of Artists, a painting now known as the 'Lansdowne portrait' hanging in the National Portrait Gallery and recognised today as 'a triumph'.[5] It features as the cover image of this monograph. Edward Fisher would create mezzotint engravings of this work, and Simon François Ravenet, who had also engraved Hogarth's frontispiece for volume 1 of Tristram Shandy, would produce the copperplates. Judging by Sterne's hope that the young painter Marie-Geneviève Navarre might copy another portrait, by Louis de Carmontelle, in the form of either a pastel or (what is more likely) engraving, it seems that oil author portraits were particularly valuable for Sterne because of the possibility of their print reproduction:[6] it would

> do her service here—& I w^d remit her 5 Louis—I really believe, twil be the parent of a dozen portraits to her—if she executes it with the spirit of the

[4] Cash, *The Later Years*,12.
[5] W.B. Gerard, *Laurence Sterne and the Visual Imagination* (Aldershot: Ashgate, 2006), 23.
[6] John Kerslake considers engraving most likely given the price (5 Louis d'Ors). John Kerslake, *Early Georgian Portraits* (London: HMSO, 1977).

> Original in y^r hands—for it will be seen by half London—and as my Phyz.
> is as remarkable as my self—if she preserves the Character of both, 'twil do
> her honour and service too—.[7]

The reproduction process would benefit Navarre financially and enhance
the reputation of both parties, ensuring that Sterne's 'phyz' would be seen
by 'half London'. Prints of Sterne's face, like a calling card, allowed his
literary reputation to circulate far beyond what would usually be possible
for authors in this period.

In *Laurence Sterne and the Visual Imagination*, W.B. Gerard sees the
multiple references to paintings and engravings in Sterne's correspondence
as evidence of his interest in their 'power to evoke sympathetic feelings
instead of commonly evaluated elements such as composition, style, or
color'.[8] Certainly the mezzotint engravings were used as emotional aides in
building friendships (with the likes of Holbach) and potential relationships
(as in his exchange with Eliza Draper of a print for a portrait miniature).
Prints seems to have served a sociable purpose, becoming what Gerard calls
a 'proxy' for Sterne in his absence to prospective lovers and far-away
friends. The mezzotints certainly seem to have functioned in that way.
But the copperplate prints of the Reynolds portrait were always already
bookish. While sitting for Reynolds may also have assisted his romantic
endeavours, Sterne would have been well aware that the primary benefit of
the resulting portrait was the fact that he could append it to his next
publication and market the volumes in the press accordingly.[9] The portrait
captured in print Sterne himself, in clerical garb but with wig aslant and a
wry expression which would be adapted by later engravers into a comical
smirk.[10] It also depicted the sitter leaning not on the iconography of his
profession as parson but rather – literally – upon the manuscript of the
most notorious comic novel of the previous year: *Tristram Shandy*. The
resulting copperplate prints thereby symbolised Sterne's shepherding of his
works from manuscript into print through creative technological play.

The Sterne–Reynolds collaboration was a composition designed to
bridge Sterne's profession with his comic writing, and it was destined
and probably always designed to be the frontispiece to his controversially

---

[7] Sterne, 'To Robert Foley', York (11 November 1764), *The Letters: Part 1*, vol. 7, letter 141, 392.

[8] Gerard, *Visual Imagination*, 23.

[9] On the advertisement of Sterne's works in the newspapers, see Siv Gøril Brandtzæg, M-C. Newbould and Helen Williams, 'Advertising Sterne's Novels in Eighteenth-Century Newspapers', *The Shandean*, 27 (2016), 27–57.

[10] On the evolution of this image into caricature, see René Bosch, '"Character" in Reynolds's Portrait of Sterne', *The Shandean*, 6 (1994), 8–23.

titled *Sermons of Mr. Yorick* (1760). Sterne was advertising the first edition of the sermons as ornamented by Reynolds from as early as 19 April 1760, [footnote reference to Whitehall Evening Post], and much of the media furore surrounding that publication arose from the fact that an image of the clergyman followed the title invoking the 'harlequin'.[11] The appearance of Sterne's novel in manuscript form in the image prefacing his sermons created a deliberate slippage between the two texts for which Sterne himself had established the foundations within *Tristram Shandy*. The 'Abuses of Conscience' sermon which he had offered to the world as a 'sample' met with approbation, resulting in 'a handsome volume, at the world's service' (2.17.154–5), ornamented through the securing of Reynolds as partner in book design.[12]

In March 1760 we see Sterne successfully dedicating his time to strategies that facilitated the impression that he was a multimedia sensation, allowing him to appear in oil, mezzotint and copperplate prints at the same time that *Tristram Shandy* became a best-selling novel. As he wrote to Catherine Fourmantel of the print by Fisher: 'There is a fine print going to be done of me—so I shall make the most of myself, & sell both inside and out.'[13] Through collaboration with Ravenet via Hogarth and Reynolds, copperplate engravings become inseparable from Sterne's book design practice, with the Hogarth images becoming and the Reynolds image remaining from the beginning an integral part of *Tristram Shandy* and the *Sermons* respectively. The images naturally follow on from Sterne's own intuitively visual writing style, which incorporates visual effects through commissioning woodcut engravings as an integral part of his typographic narrative and which nods towards and is at times informed by alternative technologies for book production, such as colour printing and mezzotint engraving.[14] The artworks produced by Hogarth and Reynolds were both free-standing as well as bookish images bound within Sterne's works, and served as important marketable visuals to prospective buyers. They are emblematic of Sterne's reaching out to and drawing from media and print sources beyond the novel, his shaping of his work's identity through the print medium, and his construction of an image of the man as well as the book as a print commodity.

[11] As in the essay in the *Scot's Magazine* of 2 March 1761, which accused Sterne of 'mount[ing] the pulpit in a *Harlequin's Coat*' (141).
[12] See Chapter 3.
[13] Sterne, 'To Catherine Fourmantel, Saturday. London [April 5, 1760?]', *The Letters, Part 1*, vol. 7, letter 53, 140.
[14] See, for example, the marbled page, as discussed in Chapter 4.

Bibliography

Primary Sources

Albin, Eleazar, *A Natural History of Birds* (London: Albin, 1731–38).

Anon., *A Book without a Title-Page* (1761?).

    A Catalogue of a Curious and Valuable Collection of Books, Among which are Included the Entire Library of the Late Reverend and Learned Laurence Sterne (York: Todd, 1768).

    The Ceremonial Proceeding to a Private Interrment of Her Late Most Excellent Majesty Queen Caroline (London: Stagg, 1737).

    The Ceremonial of the Coronation of His Most Sacred Majesty Kind George II and of His Royal Consort Queen Caroline (Dublin: Powell, 1727).

    The Clockmakers Outcry Against the Author of the Life and Opinions of Tristram Shandy: Dedicated to the Most Humble of Christian Prelates (London: Burd, 1760).

    The Compleat Letter Writer: or, New and Polite English Secretary, 3rd ed. (London: Crowder, 1756).

    The Dramatic History of Master Edward, Miss Ann, Mrs. LLwhuddwhydd, and Others (London: Waller, 1763).

    An Elegy on the Lamented Death of Poor Truth and Honesty; Who Departed this Life, with the Renowned Paper Call'd the London-Post (London, 1705), National Library of Scotland, Crawford.EB.346.

    An Elegy on the Much Lamented Death of Matthew Buckinger, the Famous Little-Man (without Arms or Legs) who Departed this Life at Cork, Sept 28, 1722 (n.d.), Cambridge University Library, Hib.3.730.1.

    The End of the Lusorium (1798).

    Explanatory Remarks upon the Life and Opinions of Tristram Shandy; wherein The Morals and Politics of this Piece are clearly laid open (London: Cabe, 1760).

    Four Satires (London: Cooper, 1736).

    Gleanings from the Works of Laurence Sterne: Comprising Tales, Humorous and Descriptive, Sermons, Letters &c. (London: Wills, 1796).

    The Late Dreadful Plague at Marseilles Compared with that Terrible Plague in London, in the Year 1665 (London: Parker, 1721).

The Life and Opinions of Tristram Shandy, Gentleman: Vol. IX (London: Durham, 1766).

The Life, Travels, and Adventures of Christopher Wagstaff, Gentleman, Grandfather to Tristram Shandy, 2 vols. (London: Hinxman, 1762).

'A New Method of Multiplying of Pictures and Draughts by a Natural Colleris with Impression', English Patent no. 423 issued to James Christopher Le Blon (5 February 1719).

Serious and Comical Essays [. . .], With Ingenious Letters Amorous and Gallant. Occasional Thoughts and Reflections on Men and Manners. Also the English Epigrammatist, And the Instructive Library. To which is added, Satyrical and Panegyrical Characters. Fitted to the Humours of the Time (London: King, 1710).

A Supplement to the Life and Opinions of Tristram Shandy, Gent.: Serving to Elucidate that Work (London: Printed for the Author, 1760).

Tommy Thumb's Pretty Song Book, 2 vols. (London: Cooper, 1744), vol. 2.

d'Agoty, Jacques Fabien Gautier, 'Two Dissected Heads, on Sacking', after disssections by P. Tarin, *Anatomie de la tête en tableaux imprimés* (Paris: Gautier, 1748), pl. 5. Available at https://wellcomecollection.org/works/a9rcsnxe, last accessed 5 June 2020.

'Muscles of the Back: Partial Dissection of a Seated Woman, Showing the Bones and Muscles of the Back and Shoulder'. Colour mezzotint (1745/1746). Available at https://wellcomecollection.org/works/yec7bmwu, last accessed 5 June 2020.

Amory, Thomas, *The Life of John Buncle, Esq* (London: Noon, 1756).

The Life of John Buncle, Esq, Moyra Haslett (ed.) (Dublin: Four Courts, 2011).

Baillie, John (1736), *The Patriot: Being a Dramatick History of the Life and Death of William the First Prince of Orange*, 2nd ed. (London: Roberts, 1740).

Bank of England, *Bank Sealed Bill* (1694), Object Number 124/001.

Becket, J., *A New Essay on the Venereal Disease, and Methods of Cure; Accounting for the Nature, Cause, and Symptoms of that Malady* (London: Williams, 1765).

Bickham, George, *The Universal Penman* (London: Printed for the author, 1733–41).

Bradley, Richard, *Flower Garden Display'd [. . .] and Coloured to the Life* (London: Smith, 1732).

Buchanan, Robert, *Poems on Several Occasions* (Edinburgh: Moir, 1797).

Butler, Samuel, *Hudibras*, John Wilders (ed.), Oxford English Texts (Oxford University Press, 1967).

Catesby, Mark, *Natural History of Carolina, Florida and the Bahama Islands* (London: Printed at the Expense of the Author, 1731–43).

Centlivre, Susanna, *The Busy Body* (1709), in *The Works of the Celebrated Mrs. Centlivre* (London: Knapton, 1760), vol. 2.

Chamberlen, Paul, *A Philosophical Essay Upon Actions on Distant Subjects* (London: Parker, 1715).

A Philosophical Essay Upon Actions on Distant Subjects, 3rd ed. (London: Parker, 1715).

A Philosophical Essay Upon Actions on Distant Subjects (London: Parker, 1717).

Chambers, Ephraim, *Cyclopaedia, or an Universal Dictionary of the Arts and Sciences* (London: Chambers, 1728).

Clarke, Samuel, *A Demonstration of the Being and Attributes of God, the Obligations of Natural Religion*, 2nd ed. (London: Knapton, 1706).

Cleland, John, *Memoirs of a Woman of Pleasure* (London: Griffiths, 1748–49).

Cockburn, William, *The Symptoms, Nature and Cure of Gonorrhoea* (London: Graves, 1713).

The Symptoms, Nature and Cure of Gonorrhoea, 3rd ed. with additions (London: Strahan, 1719).

The Symptoms, Nature and Cure of Gonorrhoea, 4th ed. with additions (London: Strahan, 1728).

Collier, Jane and Sarah Fielding, *The Cry: A New Dramatic Fable* (London: Dodsley, 1754).

Commissioner of Patents, Abridgements of Specifications Relating to Printing, etc. (London: Commissioner of Patents, 1859). No. 530, May 20, 1731, 85–6. (Rpt. London: Printing Historical Society, 1969.)

Dampier, William, *A New Voyage Round the World* (London: Knapton, 1697).

Defoe, Daniel, *The Farther Adventures of Robinson Crusoe* (London: Taylor, 1719).

The Life and Strange Surprizing Adventures of Robinson Crusoe (London: Taylor, 1719).

Serious Reflections During the Life and Surprising Adventures of Robinson Crusoe with his Vision of the Angelic World (London: Taylor, 1720).

Dodsley, Robert, *The Correspondence of Robert Dodsley 1733–1764*, James E. Tierney (ed.) (Cambridge University Press, 1988).

The King and the Miller of Mansfield: A Dramatick Tale (London: Dodsley, 1737).

The Toy-Shop: A Dramatick Satire (London: Gilliver, 1735).

Drake, James, *New System of Anatomy*, 2nd ed. (London: Innys, 1727).

Fénelon, François de Salignac de La Mothe-, *The Adventures of Telemachus, the Son of Ulysses*, John Ozell (ed.), 2 vols. (London: Innys, 1734–35).

Feuillet, Raoul-Auger, *For the Further Improvement of Dancing*, John Essex (trans.) (London: Walsh, 1710).

Orchesography: Or, the Art of Dancing, by Characters and Demonstrative Figures, John Weaver (trans.) (London: Meere, 1706).

Fielding, Henry (1742), *The History of the Adventures of Joseph Andrews and of his Friend Mr. Abraham Adams*, in *Joseph Andrews and Shamela*, Thomas Keymer (ed.), Oxford World Classics (Oxford University Press, 2008).

The History of Tom Jones, A Foundling, 4 vols. (London: Millar, 1749).

Pasquin: A Dramatic Satire on the Times: Being the Rehearsal of Two Plays, Viz. a Comedy, Call'd the Election; and a Tragedy, Call'd the Life and Death of Common-Sense (London: Watts, 1736).

Florentinus, Paulus, *Breviarum totius juris canonici* (Lyon: Huss, 1484).

Fludd, Robert, *Utriusque cosmi maioris scilicet et minoris metaphysica, physica atque technica historia* (Oppenhemii: de Bry, 1617).

Fordyce, James, *An Essay on the Action Proper for the Pulpit* (London: Dodsley, 1753).

Fuller, Thomas, *The Holy State* (Cambridge, 1642), BL, Add. MSS 694.i.2.

Goldsmith, Oliver(?), *The History of Little Goody Two-Shoes* (London: Newbery, 1765).

Gray, Thomas, *Elegy Wrote in a Country Churchyard* (London: Dodsley, 1751).

Joseph Hall, *Contemplations on the History of the New Testament*, William Dodd (ed.), 2 vols. (London: Davis, 1759).

Harland, S., *The English Spelling-Book*, 3rd ed. (London: Taylor, 1719).

Hawes, William, *An Account of the Late Dr. Goldsmith's Illness, so far as Relates to the Exhibition of Dr James Powders*, 4th ed. (London: Hawes, 1780).

Hogarth, William, *A Harlot's Progress* (London, 1732).

Hunter, John, *A Treatise on Venereal Disease* (London: Printed for the Author, 1786).

Hunter, Joseph, *Journal*, British Library, Add. MSS 24, 879.

Jackson, John Baptist, *An Essay on the Invention of Engraving and Printing in Chiaro Oscuro* (London: Millar, 1754).

  Titiani Vecelii, Pauli Caliarii, Jacobi Robusti, et Jacobi de Ponte, opera selectiora a Joanne Baptista Jackson Anglo, ligno cœlata, et coloribus adumbrata (Venice: Batista, 1745).

James, Robert, *Dr. Robert James's Powder for Fevers. Published by Virtue of His Majesty's Royal Letters Patent* (London: n.p., 1748?).

Jenner, Charles, *The Placid Man; or, Memoirs of Sir Charles Beville* (London: Wilkie, 1770).

Johnson, Samuel (ed.), *A Dictionary of the English Language* (London: Knapton, 1755–56).

  (ed.), *The Plays of William Shakespeare*, 8 vols. (London: Tonson, 1765).

Jones, Phyllis M. and Nicholas R. Jones (eds.), *Salvation in New England: Selections from the Sermons of the First Preachers* (Austin, TX: University of Texas Press, 1977).

Kidgell, John, *The Card* (London: Printed for the Maker, 1755).

Kimber, Edward, *The Juvenile Adventures of David Ranger, Esq*, 2 vols. (London: Stevens, 1757).

Le Blon, Jacob Christoff, 'Préparation anatomique des parties de l'homme' (1721–30). British Museum. Item Number 1928,0310.101. www.britishmuseum .org/research/collection_online/collection_object_details.aspx?objectId=15036 98&partId=1, last accessed 5 June 2020.

Leekey, William, *A Discourse on the Use of the Pen* (London: Ware, [1750?]).

Livie, J. (ed.), *Quintus Horatius Flaccus* (Birmingham: Baskerville, 1762).

Locke, John, *Two Treatises of Government* (London: Churchill, 1690).

MacNally, Leonard, *Sentimental Excursions to Windsor* (London: Walker, 1781).

Marchant, John, *A New Complete English Dictionary* (London: Fuller, 1760).

Martyn, John, *Historia Plantarum Rariorum*, Jacob van Huysum (illus.) (London: Reily, 1728–37).

Montesquieu, Charles-Louis de Secondat, Baron de La Brède et de, *De l'Esprit des loix* (Geneve: Barrillot, 1748).

Spirit of the Laws (London: Nourse, 1750).

Persian Letters, Raymond N. Mackenzie (ed.) (Indianapolis, IN: Hackett, 2014).

Persian Letters, Thomas Flloyd (trans.) (London: Tonson, 1762).

Persian Letters, John Ozell (trans.) (London: Tonson, 1722).

Moxon, Joseph, *Mechanick Exercises* (London: Moxon, 1683).

Palairet, Jean, *A New Royal French Grammar* (London: Nourse, 1733).

Parker, Edmund, 'Books lately Printed for Edmund Parker' [11pp.], in *The Devout Christian's Preparative to Death*, Robert Warren (trans.), 7th ed. (London: Parker, 1722).

Pine, John (ed.), *Horace* (London: Pine, 1733–37).

Pope, Alexander (1743), *Correspondence of Alexander Pope*, George Sherburn (ed.), 5 vols. (Oxford: Clarendon, 1956).

The Dunciad in Four Books, Valerie Rumbold (ed.) (Harlow: Longman, 2009).

'Epistle to Arbuthnot', *The Major Works*, Pat Rogers (ed.), Oxford World's Classics (Oxford University Press, 2008).

Dunciad Variorum, 2nd ed. (London, 1729).

The Works of Shakespeare, 6 vols. (London: Tonson, 1723–25).

Pluche, Noël-Antoine, *Le Spectacle de la nature, ou entretiens sur les particularités de l'histoire naturelle*, 9 vols. (Paris: Estienne, 1732–42).

Spectacle de la nature: Or, Nature Display'd, 7 vols. (London: Pemberton, 1736–48).

Rameau, Pierre, *The Dancing Master*, John Essex (trans.), 2nd ed. (London: Essex, 1728).

Richardson, Samuel, *Clarissa*, 7 vols. (London: Richardson, 1748).

[1740], *Pamela: Or, Virtue Rewarded. In a Series of Familiar Letters from a Beautiful Young Damsel, to her Parents*, 2nd ed. (London: Richardson, 1741).

The History of Sir Charles Grandison, Jocelyn Harris (ed.), 3 vols. (London: Oxford University Press, 1972).

Romaine, William, *Knowledge of Salvation Precious in the Hour of Death* (London: Worrall, 1759).

Rowe, Elizabeth, *Friendship in Death* (London: Worrall, 1728).

Schaeffer, Jacob Christian, *Entwurf einer allgemeinen Farbenverein; oder Versuch und Muster einer gemeinnützlichen Bestimmung und Benennung der Farben* (Regensburg: Weiß, 1769).

Sergeant, John, *Sure-Footing in Christianity* (London, 1665).

Shaw, Thomas, *Travels in Barbary and the Levant* (Oxford: Printed at the Theatre, 1738).

Sheldrake, Timothy, *Botanicum Medicinale* (London: Millan, 1759).

Sherlock, William, *A Practical Discourse Concerning Death* (London: Rogers, 1689).

Smart, Christopher, *Annotated Letters of Christopher Smart*, Betty Rizzo and Robert Mahoney (eds.) (Carbondale, IL: Southern Illinois University Press, 1991).

Smith, John, *The Printer's Grammar* (London: Printed for the Editor, 1755).

Smollett, Tobias, *The Adventures of Peregrine Pickle*, 4 vols. (London: Wilson, 1751).

Society for the Encouragement of Arts, Manufactures, and Commerce, *Premiums by the Society Established at London for the Encouragement of Arts, Manufactures, and Commerce* (London: by Order of the Society, 1759).

Society of Gardeners, *Catalogus Plantarum. A Catalogue of Trees, Shrubs, Plants, and Flowers, Both Exotic and Domestic, Which are propagated for Sale in the Gardens near London* (London: Society of Gardeners, 1730).

Stayley, George, *The Life and Opinions of an Actor*, 2 vols. (Dublin: Printed for the Author, 1762).

Steel, David, *Elements of Punctuation* (London: Printed for the Author, 1786).

Sterne, Laurence, *The Abuses of Conscience* (York: Hildyard, 1750).

    The Case of Elijah and the Widow of Zerephath, Consider'd (York: Hildyard, 1747).

    'Fragment in the Manner of Rabelais: Autograph Manuscript, [1759 Jan-Feb]', Pierpont Morgan, MA1011.

    The Letters, Melvyn New and Peter de Voogd (eds.), The Florida Edition of the Works of Laurence Sterne (Gainesville, FL: University Press of Florida, 2009), vols. 7 and 8.

    The Life and Opinions of Tristram Shandy, Gentleman, 9 vols. (York and London: The Author; Dodsley; Becket, 1759–67).

    The Life and Opinions of Tristram Shandy, Gentleman, 2nd ed., 2 vols. (London: Dodsley, 1760).

    The Life and Opinions of Tristram Shandy, Gentleman, in *The Works of Laurence Sterne*, 7 vols. (London: Printed for the Proprietors, 1783).

    The Life and Opinions of Tristram Shandy, Gentleman, in *The Works of Laurence Sterne*, 8 vols. (London: Printed for the Proprietors, 1790).

    The Life and Opinions of Tristram Shandy, Gentleman, in *The Works of Laurence Sterne*, 8 vols. (London: Mozley, 1795).

    The Life and Opinions of Tristram Shandy, Gentleman, in *The Works of Laurence Sterne*, 8 vols. (Edinburgh: Turnbull, 1803).

    The Life and Opinions of Tristram Shandy, Gentleman: The Text, Joan New and Melvyn New (eds.), The Florida Edition of the Works of Laurence Sterne (Gainesville, FL: University Press of Florida, 1978), vols. 1 and 2.

    The Life and Opinions of Tristram Shandy, Gentleman: The Notes, Melvyn New, Richard A. Davies and W.G. Day (eds.), The Florida Edition of the Works of Laurence Sterne (Gainesville, FL: University Press of Florida, 1984), vol. 3.

    The Life and Opinions of Tristram Shandy, Gentleman (London: Visual Editions, 2010).

    'Penancies', Pierpont Morgan, New York, MS MA 418.

    A Political Romance [1759] (Menston: Scolar, 1979).

A Sentimental Journey through France and Italy (London: Becket and De Hondt, 1768).

A Sentimental Journey and a Continuation of the Bramine's Journal, Melvyn New and W.G. Day (eds.), The Florida Edition of the Works of Laurence Sterne (Gainesville, FL: University Press of Florida, 2002), vol. 6.

Sermons by the Late Rev. Mr. Sterne (London: Strahan, 1769), vols. 5–7.

The Sermons of Mr. Yorick, 4 vols. (London: Dodsley, 1760).

The Sermons of Laurence Sterne, Melvyn New (ed.), The Florida Edition of the Works of Laurence Sterne (Gainesville, FL: University Press of Florida, 1996), vols. 4 and 5.

'Temporal Advantages of Religion', Huntington Library, California, MS HM 2100.

Swift, Jonathan, *A Tale of a Tub*, in *A Tale of a Tub and Other Works*, Angus Ross and David Woolley (eds.), Oxford World's Classics (Oxford University Press, 2008).

Travels into Several Remote Nations of the World, in Four Parts, by Lemuel Gulliver, First a Surgeon, and then a Captain of Several Ships, 2 vols. (London: Motte, 1726–27).

Sylvester, Joshua, *Lachrimæ Lachrimarvm, or the Distillation of Teares Shede for the Untimely Death of the Incomparable Prince Panaretus* (London: Lownes, 1612).

Taylor, John, *Great Britaine, All in Blacke: For the Incomparable Losse of Henry, Our Late Worthy Prince* (London: Wright, 1612).

Tillotson, John, *Sermons Preach'd upon Several Occasions* (London: Gellibrand, 1671).

Toldervy, William, *The History of Two Orphans*, 4 vols. (London: Owen, 1756).

Tomlinson, Kellom, *Art of Dancing Explained* (London: Printed for the author, 1735).

Six Dances Compos'd by Mr. Kellom Tomlinson (London: Tomlinson, 1720).

Tourneur, Cyril, John Webster and Thomas Heywood, *Three Elegies on the Most Lamented Death of Prince Henrie* (London: Welbie, 1613).

Trusler, John, *Twelve Sermons* (London: Legoux, 1796).

Vanbrugh, John and Colley Cibber, *The Provok'd Husband: Or, a Journey to London* (London: Watts, 1728).

Villiers, George, *The Rehearsal* (London: Dring, 1672).

Weinmann, Johann Wilhelm, *Phytanthoza Iconographia* (Regensburg: Lenz, 1735–45).

Williams, Ann and Geoffrey Haward Martin (eds.), *Domesday Book: A Complete Translation* (London: Penguin, 2002).

Wollaston, William, *The Religion of Nature Delineated*, 6th ed. (London: Knapton, 1738).

Woodward, Josiah, *Fair Warnings to a Careless World, or, the Serious Practice of Religion Recommended by the Admonitions of Dying Men [. . .] To which is added, Serious Advice to a Sick Person by Archbishop Tillotson. As also, A Prospect of Death: A Pindarique Essay. With suitable cuts. Recommended as proper to be given at Funerals* (London: Aylmer, 1707).

Periodicals

The Universal Visiter, and Monthly Memorialist (1756).
The Connoisseur (1754–56).
Country Journal or The Craftsman (1726–50).
The Critical Review (1756–1817).
The Daily Journal (1721–37).
Dawks's News Letter (1696–1716).
Dublin Courier (1760–66).
Fog's Weekly Journal (1728–37).
Gentleman's Magazine (1731–1922).
General Advertiser, 8 March 1760.
Lloyd's Evening Post (1757–1808).
London Chronicle (1757–65).
London Evening Post (1727–1806).
London Gazette (1665–1913).
The Monthly Review (1749–1845).
Mist's Weekly Journal (1716–37).
Public Advertiser (1753–90).
The Scot's Magazine, 2 March 1761.
The Spectator (1711–14).
St. James's Chronicle or the British Evening Post (1765–1800).
The Tatler (1709–11).
Whitehall Evening Post, 19 April 1760.
World, 22 September 1790.

Secondary Sources

Aercke, Kristiaan P., 'Congreve's *Incognita*: Romance, Novel, Drama?' *Eighteenth-Century Fiction*, 2 (1990), 293–308.

Allen, Dennis W., 'Sexuality/Textuality in *Tristram Shandy*', *Studies in English Literature, 1500–1900*, 25 (1985), 651–70.

Alspaugh, Leann Davis, '"Howgarth's Witty Chissel": Hogarth's Frontispieces for *Tristram Shandy*', *The Shandean*, 24 (2013), 9–30.

Anderson, Misty G., *Imagining Methodism in Eighteenth-Century Britain: Enthusiasm, Belief, and the Borders of the Self* (Baltimore, OH: Johns Hopkins University Press, 2010).

Ballaster, Ros, '"Bring(ing) Forth Alive the Conceptions of the Brain": From Stage to Page in the Transmission of French Fiction to the English Restoration Novel', in Jacqueline Glomski and Isabelle Moreau (eds.), *Seventeenth Century Fiction: Text and Transmission* (Oxford University Press, 2016), 183–97.

'Satire and Embodiment: Allegorical Romance on Stage and Page in Mid-Eighteenth-Century Britain', *Eighteenth-Century Fiction*, 27 (2015), 631–60.

Bandry, Anne, '*Tristram Shandy*, the *Public Ledger*, and William Dodd', *Eighteenth-Century Fiction*, 14 (2002), 311–24.

Barchas, Janine, *Graphic Design, Print Culture, and the Eighteenth-Century Novel* (Cambridge University Press, 2003).

Bellman, Patrizia Nerozzi, 'Dancing Away: Escape Strategy in *Tristram Shandy* and *A Sentimental Journey*', *The Shandean*, 24 (2013), 135–46.

Berg, Michael Vande, '"Pictures of Pronunciation": Typographical Travels Through *Tristram Shandy* and *Jacques le Fataliste*', *Eighteenth-Century Studies*, 21 (1987), 21–47.

Blunt, Wilfrid and William Thomas Stearn, *The Art of Botanical Illustration: An Illustrated History* (New York: Dover, 1994).

Bosch, René, '"Character" in Reynolds's Portrait of Sterne', *The Shandean*, 6 (1994), 8–23.

  Labyrinth of Digressions: Tristram Shandy *as Perceived and Influenced by Sterne's Early Imitators* (Amsterdam: Rodopi, 2007).

Bourne, Claire M.L., 'Dramatic Typography and the Restoration Quartos of *Hamlet*', in Emma Depledge and Peter Kirwan (eds.), *Canonising Shakespeare: Stationers and the Book Trade, 1640–1740* (Cambridge University Press, 2017), 145–52.

  Typographies of Performance in Early Modern England (Oxford University Press, 2020).

Bowden, Martha F., *Yorick's Congregation: The Church of England in the Time of Laurence Sterne* (Cranbury, NJ: Associated University Presses, 2007).

Bracher, Frederick, 'The Maps in *Gulliver's Travels*', *Huntington Library Quarterly*, 8 (1944), 59–74.

Brady, Frank, '*Tristram Shandy*: Sexuality, Morality, and Sensibility', *Eighteenth-Century Studies*, 4 (1970), 41–56.

Brandtzæg, Siv Gøril, M-C. Newbould and Helen Williams, 'Advertising Sterne's Novels in Eighteenth-Century Newspapers', *The Shandean*, 27 (2016), 27–58.

Bray, Joe, '"Attending to the Minute": Richardson's Revisions of Italics in *Pamela*', in Miriam Handley Bray and Anne C. Henry (eds.), *Ma(r)king the Text: The Presentation of Meaning on the Literary Page* (Aldershot: Ashgate, 2000), 105–19.

Bullard, Paddy and James McLaverty (eds.), *Jonathan Swift and the Eighteenth-Century Book* (Cambridge University Press, 2013).

Campbell, Jill, 'Domestic Intelligence: Newspaper Advertising and the Eighteenth-Century Novel', *The Yale Journal of Criticism*, 15 (2002), 251–91.

Canfield, J. Douglas, *Tricksters and Estates: On the Ideology of Restoration Comedy* (Lexington, KY: University Press of Kentucky, 1997).

Cash, Arthur H., *Laurence Sterne: The Later Years* (London: Methuen, 1986).

Chalmers, Alexander, *The Works of the English Poets, from Chaucer to Cowper* (London: Johnson, 1810).

Clapham, John, *The Bank of England: A History, Volume 1: 1694–1797* (Cambridge University Press, 1966).

Cock, Emily, '"Off Dropped the Sympathetic Snout": Shame, Sympathy, and Plastic Surgery at the Beginning of the Long Eighteenth Century', in Heather Kerr, David Lemmings and Robert Phiddian (eds.), *Passions, Sympathy and Print Culture: Public Opinion and Emotional Authenticity in Eighteenth-Century Britain* (Basingstoke: Palgrave, 2015), 145–64.

Day, W.G., *From Fiction to the Novel* (London: Routledge, 1987).

'*Tristram Shandy*: The Marbled Leaf', *Library*, 27 (1972), 143–5.

'Sterne and Ozell', *English Studies*, 53 (1972), 434–6.

de Voogd, Peter, 'Tristram Shandy as Aesthetic Object', in Thomas Keymer (ed.), *Laurence Sterne's Tristram Shandy: A Casebook* (Oxford University Press, 2006), 108–19.

'Laurence Sterne, the Marbled Page, and the "Use of Accidents"', *Word and Image*, 1 (1985), 279–87.

Descargues-Grant, Madeleine, 'Sterne's Dramatic Persuasion', in W.B. Gerard (ed.), *Divine Rhetoric: Essays on the Sermons of Laurence Sterne* (Newark, NJ: University of Delaware Press, 2010), 207–28.

Didicher, Nicole E., 'Mapping the Distorted Worlds of *Gulliver's Travels*', *Lumen: Selected Proceedings from the Canadian Society for Eighteenth-Century Studies / Lumen: travaux choisis de la Société canadienne d'étude du dix-huitième siècle*, 16 (1997), 179–96.

Doherty, Francis Cecil, *A Study in Eighteenth-Century Advertising Methods: The Anodyne Necklace* (Lewiston, NY: Edwin Mellon, 1992).

'The Anodyne Necklace: A Quack Remedy and its Promotion', *Medical History*, 34 (1990), 268–93.

Downey, James, *The Eighteenth-Century Pulpit: A Study of the Sermons of Butler, Berkeley, Secker, Sterne, Whitefield and Wesley* (Oxford: Clarendon, 1969).

Dworkin, Craig, 'Textual Prostheses', *Comparative Literature*, 57 (2005), 1–24.

Dyson, A.E., *The Crazy Fabric: Essays in Irony* (New York: St Martin's, 1973).

Eisenstein, Elizabeth L., *The Printing Press as an Agent of Change: Communications and Cultural Transformations in Early Modern Europe* (Cambridge University Press, 1979).

Fanning, Christopher, 'On Sterne's Page: Spatial Layout, Spatial Form, and Social Spaces in *Tristram Shandy*', *Eighteenth-Century Fiction*, 10 (1998), 429–50.

'Sterne and Print Culture', in Thomas Keymer (ed.), *The Cambridge Companion to Laurence Sterne* (Cambridge University Press, 2009), 125–41, 133.

Ferriar, John, 'Comments on Sterne', *Memoirs of the Literary and Philosophical Society of Manchester*, 4 (1793), 45–86.

Illustrations of Sterne (London: Cadell, 1798).

Fitzgerald, Percy Hetherington, *The Life of Laurence Sterne*, 2 vols. (London: Chapman, 1864).

Flint, Christopher, *The Appearance of Print in Eighteenth-Century Fiction* (Cambridge University Press, 2011).

'In Other Words: Eighteenth-Century Authorship and the Ornaments of Print', *Eighteenth-Century Fiction*, 14 (2002), 625–72.

Ferrand, Nathalie, 'Translating and Illustrating the Eighteenth-Century Novel', *Word & Image*, 30 (2014), 181–3.

Foxon, David, *Pope and the Early Eighteenth-Century Book Trade* (Oxford: Clarendon, 1991).

Franklin, Alexandra, 'The Art of Illustration in Bodleian Broadside Ballads before 1820', *Bodleian Library Record*, 17 (2002), 327–52.

Gascoigne, Bamber, *Milestones in Colour Printing 1457–1859: With a Bibliography of Nelson Prints* (Cambridge University Press, 1997).

Genest, John, *Account of the English Stage*, 10 vols. (Bath: Rodd, 1832).

Gerard, W.B. (ed.), *Divine Rhetoric: Essays on the Sermons of Laurence Sterne* (Newark, NJ: University of Delaware Press, 2010).

   Laurence Sterne and the Visual Imagination (Aldershot: Ashgate, 2006).

   'Laurence Sterne, the Apostrophe, and American Abolitionism, 1788–1831', in Gerard, E. Derek Taylor, and Robert G. Walker (eds.), *Swiftly Sterneward: Essays on Laurence Sterne and His Times in Honor of Melvyn New* (Newark, NJ: University of Delaware Press, 2011), 181–206.

Gibbons, Alison, 'Multimodal Literature and Experimentation', in Joe Bray, Alison Gibbons and Brian McHale (eds.), *Routledge Companion to Experimental Literature* (Abingdon: Routledge, 2012), 420–34.

Goff, Moira, '"The Art of Dancing, Demonstrated by Characters and Figures": French and English Sources For Court And Theatre Dance, 1700–1750', *The British Library Journal*, 21 (1995), 202–31.

Goldberg, Jonathan, *Shakespeare's Hand* (Minneapolis: University of Minnesota Press, 2003).

   Writing Matter: From the Hands of the English Renaissance (Palo Alto, CA: Stanford University Press, 1990).

Goring, Paul, 'Newspapers, Spectatorship and the Coronation of George III'. Paper presented at After New Historicism: A Seminar Series Organised by Northumbria's Long-Eighteenth-Century Research Group, Northumbria University, 5 April 2017.

   The Rhetoric of Sensibility in Eighteenth-Century Culture (Cambridge University Press, 2005).

Grafton, Anthony, *The Footnote: A Curious History* (London: Faber, 1997).

Hammond, Lansing Van der Heyden, *Laurence Sterne's* Sermons of Mr. Yorick (New Haven, CT: Yale University Press, 1948).

Hawley, Judith, '"Hints and Documents" 2: A Bibliography for *Tristram Shandy*', *The Shandean*, 4 (1992), 49–65.

   '*Tristram Shandy* and Digression', in Alexis Grohmann and Caragh Wells (eds.), *Digression in European Literature from Cervantes to Sebald* (Basingstoke: Palgrave, 2011), 21–35.

   Review, 'The Sermons of Laurence Sterne', *Essays in Criticism*, 48 (1998), 80–8.

Hellinga, Lotte, 'Printing', in Lotte Hellinga and J.B. Trapp (eds.), *The Cambridge History of the Book in Britain, Vol. 3: 1400–1557* (Cambridge University Press, 1999), 65–108.

Holtz, William V., *Image and Immortality: A Study of Tristram Shandy* (Providence, RI: Brown University Press, 1970).

'Typography, *Tristram Shandy*, the Aposiopesis, etc.,' in Arthur H. Cash and John M. Stedmond (eds.), *The Winged Skull: Conference Papers on Laurence Sterne* (Kent, OH: Kent State University Press, 1971), 247–57.

Houlbrooke, Ralph, 'The Age of Decency: 1660–1760', in Peter C. Jupp and Clare Gittings (eds.), *Death in England: An Illustrated History* (Manchester University Press, 1999).

Death, Religion, and the Family in England, 1480–1750 (Oxford University Press, 2000).

Howes, Alan B. (ed.), *Laurence Sterne: The Critical Heritage* (London: Routledge, 1974).

Hunter, J. Paul, 'From Typology to Type: Agents of Change in Eighteenth-Century Texts', in Margaret J.M. Ezell and Katherine O'Brien (eds.), *Cultural Artifacts and the Production of Meaning: The Page, the Image and the Body* (Ann Arbor, MI: University of Michigan Press, 1994), 41–69.

Jung, Sandro, 'The Other *Pamela*: Readership and the Illustrated Chapbook Abridgement', *Journal for Eighteenth-Century Studies*, 39 (2016), Special Issue: *Picturing the Eighteenth-Century Novel Through Time*, Christina Ionescu and Ann Lewis (eds.), 513–31.

Kelly, James, 'Health for Sale: Mountebanks, Doctors, Printers and the Supply of Medication in Eighteenth-Century Ireland', *Proceedings of the Royal Irish Academy. Section C: Archaeology, Celtic Studies, History, Linguistics, Literature*, 108C (2008), 75–113.

Kerslake, John, *Early Georgian Portraits* (London: HMSO, 1977).

Keymer, Thomas (ed.), *The Cambridge Companion to Laurence Sterne* (Cambridge University Press, 2009).

'Jane Collier, Reader of Richardson, and the Fire Scene in *Clarissa*', in Albert J. Rivero (ed.), *New Essays on Samuel Richardson* (Basingstoke: Palgrave, 1996), 141–61.

Sterne, the Moderns, and the Novel (Oxford University Press, 2002).

'William Toldervy and the Origins of Smart's *A Translation of the Psalms of David*', *Review of English Studies*, 54 (2003), 52–66.

King, Kimball, *Western Drama through the Ages* (Westport, CT: Greenwood, 2007).

Kinservik, Matthew J., *Disciplining Satire: The Censorship of Satiric Comedy on the Eighteenth-Century London Stage* (Lewisburg, PA: Bucknell University Press, 2002).

Kita, Sotaro (ed.), *Pointing: Where Language, Culture, and Cognition Meet* (London: Erlbaum, 2003).

Konigsberg, Ira, *Samuel Richardson and the Dramatic Novel* (Lexington, KY: University of Kentucky Press, 1968).

Krivatsy, Peter, 'Le Blon's Anatomical Color Engravings', *Journal of the History of Medicine and Allied Sciences*, 23.2 (1968), 153–8.

Laidlow, Jonathan, 'A Compendium of Shandys: Methods of Organising Knowledge in Sterne's *Tristram Shandy*', *Eighteenth Century Novel*, (2001), 181–200.

Lamb, Jonathan P., 'Parentheses and Privacy in Philip Sidney's *Arcadia*', *Studies in Philology*, 107.3 (2010), 310–35.

Leeuwen, Henry G., *The Problem of Certainty in English Thought 1630–1690* (London: Springer, 2013).

Lennard, John, *But I Digress: The Exploitation of Parentheses in English Printed Verse* (Oxford: Clarendon, 1991).

Levenston, Edward A., *The Stuff of Literature: Physical Aspects of Texts and Their Relation to Literary Meaning* (New York: State University of New York Press, 1992).

Lowengard, Sarah, 'Colour Printed Illustrations in Eighteenth-Century Periodicals', in Christina Ionescu (ed.), *Book Illustration in the Long Eighteenth Century: Reconfiguring the Visual Periphery of the Text* (Newcastle: Cambridge Scholars, 2011), 53–76.

Lund, Roger D., 'The Eel of Science: Index Learning, Scriblerian Satire, and the Rise of Information Culture', *Eighteenth-Century Life*, 22 (1998), 18–42.

Lupton, Christina, 'Creating the Writer of the Cleric's Words', *Journal for Eighteenth-Century Studies*, 34 (2011), 167–83.

Lüthi, Louis, *On the Self-Reflexive Page* (Amsterdam: Roma, 2010).

Lynch, Jack, 'Reading and Misreading the Genres of Sterne's Sermons', in W.B. Gerard (ed.), *Divine Rhetoric: Essays on the Sermons of Laurence Sterne* (Newark, NJ: University of Delaware Press, 2010), 83–100.

Margócsy, Dániel, *Commercial Visions: Science, Trade, and Visual Culture in the Dutch Golden Age* (University of Chicago Press, 2014).

Marks, Sylvia Kasey, Sir Charles Grandison: *The Compleat Conduct Book* (Lewisburg, PA: Bucknell University Press, 1986).

Marsden, Jean I., 'Dramatic Satire in the Restoration and Eighteenth Century' in Ruben Quintero (ed.), *A Companion to Satire: Ancient and Modern* (Oxford: Blackwell, 2008), 161–75.

Maruca, Lisa, 'Bodies of Type: The Work of Textual Production in English Printers' Manuals', *Eighteenth-Century Studies*, 36 (2003), 321–43.

McGuire, Kelly, 'Mourning and Material Culture in Eliza Haywood's *The History of Miss Betsy Thoughtless*', *Eighteenth-Century Fiction*, 18 (2006), 281–304.

McKitterick, David, *Print, Manuscript and the Search for Order, 1450–1830* (Cambridge University Press, 2003).

McLaverty, James, *Pope, Print, and Meaning* (Oxford University Press, 2001).

McPharlin, Paul, *Roman Numerals, Typographic Leaves and Pointing Hands: Some Notes on their Origin, History and Contemporary Use*, Typophile Chap Books, 7 (New York: Typophiles, 1942).

Meyers, Amy R.W. et al. (eds.), *Empire's Nature: Mark Catesby's New World Vision* (Chapel Hill, NC: University of North Carolina Press, 1998).

Monkman, Kenneth, 'Sterne and the '45 (1743–8)', *The Shandean*, 2 (1990), 45–136.

Moss, Roger B., 'Sterne's Punctuation', *Eighteenth-Century Studies*, 15 (1981–82), 179–200.

Mounsey, Chris, *Christopher Smart: Clown of God* (Lewisburg, PA: Bucknell University Press, 2001).

New, Melvyn, 'Reading the Occasion: Understanding Sterne's Sermons', in W.B. Gerard (ed.), *Divine Rhetoric: Essays on the Sermons of Laurence Sterne* (Newark, NJ: University of Delaware Press, 2010), 101–19.

'Richardson's *Sir Charles Grandison* and Sterne: A Study in Influence', *Modern Philology*, 115 (2017), 213–43.

'*Tristram Shandy* and Heinrich van Deventer's Observations', *Papers of the Bibliographical Society of America*, 69 (1975), 84–90.

Newbould, M-C., *Adaptations of Laurence Sterne's Fiction: Sterneana, 1760–1840* (Aldershot: Ashgate, 2013).

Newstok, Scott L., *Quoting Death in Early Modern England: The Poetics of Epitaphs beyond the Tomb* (Basingstoke: Palgrave, 2009).

Nickelsen, Kärin, 'The Challenge of Colour: Eighteenth-Century Botanists and the Hand-Colouring of Illustrations', *Annals of Science*, 63.1 (2006), 3–23.

Draughtsmen, Botanists and Nature: The Construction of Eighteenth-Century Botanical Illustrations, New Studies in the History and Philosophy of Science and Technology (Dordrecht, Netherlands: Springer, 2006), 167–70.

Oakleaf, David, 'Long Sticks, Morris Dancers, and Gentlemen: Associations of the Hobby-Horse in *Tristram Shandy*', *Eighteenth-Century Life*, 11 (1987), 62–76.

Oakley, Warren L., *A Culture of Mimicry: Laurence Sterne, His Readers and the Art of Bodysnatching* (London: MHRA, 2010).

Ostovich, Helen, 'Reader as Hobby-Horse in *Tristram Shandy*', in Thomas Keymer (ed.), *Laurence Sterne's* Tristram Shandy: *A Casebook* (Oxford University Press, 2006), 171–90.

Patterson, Diana, 'John Baskerville, Marbler', *The Library*, s6–12 (1990), 212–21.

'The Moral of the Next Marbled Page in Sterne's Tristram Shandy' (PhD thesis, University of Toronto, 1989).

'Tristram's Marblings and Marblers', *The Shandean*, 3 (1991), 70–97.

Parnell, Tim, 'Sterne's Fiction and the Mid-Century Novel: The "Vast Empire of Biographical Freebooters" and the "Crying Volume"', in Alan Downie (ed.), *The Oxford Handbook of the Eighteenth-Century Novel* (Oxford University Press, 2016), 264–81.

'*The Sermons of Mr. Yorick*: The Commonplace and the Rhetoric of the Heart', in Thomas Keymer (ed.), *The Cambridge Companion to Laurence Sterne* (Cambridge University Press, 2009), 64–78.

Payne, Deborah, 'Comedy, Satire, or Farce? Or the Generic Difficulties of Restoration Dramatic Satire', in James E. Gill (ed.), *Cutting Edges: Postmodern Critical Essays on Eighteenth-Century Satire* (Knoxville, TS: University of Tennessee Press, 1995), 1–22.

Peters, Julie Stone, *The Theatre of the Book, 1480–1880: Print, Text, and Performance in Europe* (Oxford University Press, 2003).

Pooley, Roger, *English Prose of the Seventeenth Century, 1590–1700* (London: Routledge, 2014).

Portela, Manuel, 'Typographic Translation: The Portuguese Edition of *Tristram Shandy*', in Joe Bray, Miriam Handley and Anne Henry (eds.), *Ma(r)king the Text: The Presentation of Meaning on the Literary Page* (Aldershot: Ashgate, 2000), 291–308.

Porter, Dorothy and Roy Porter, *Patient's Progress: Doctors and Doctoring in Eighteenth-Century England* (Palo Alto, CA: Stanford University Press, 1989).

Porter, Roy, *Health for Sale: Quackery in England 1660–1850* (Manchester University Press, 1989).

Range, Matthias, *British Royal Funerals: Music and Ceremonial since Elizabeth I* (Woodbridge: Boydell, 2016).

Rogers, Pat, *Documenting Eighteenth-Century Satire: Pope, Swift, Gay, and Arbuthnot in Historical Context* (Newcastle: Cambridge Scholars, 2012).

  'Ziggerzagger Shandy: Sterne and the Aesthetics of the Crooked Line', *English: Journal of the English Association*, 42.173 (1993), 97–107.

Rose, Mark, 'The Author in Court: Pope v. Curll (1741)', *Cultural Critique*, 21 (1992), 197–217.

  Authors and Owners: The Invention of Copyright (Cambridge, MA: Harvard University Press, 1993).

Rothstein, Eric, *Systems of Order and Inquiry in Later Eighteenth-Century Fiction* (Berkeley, CA: University of California Press, 1975).

Rowe, Katherine, *Dead Hands: Fictions of Agency, Renaissance to Modern* (Palo Alto, CA: Stanford University Press, 1999).

Scott, Walter, 'Preface to Sterne', *The Novels of Sterne, Goldsmith, Dr. Johnson, Mackenzie, Horace Walpole, and Clara Reeve* (London: Hurst, 1823), vol. 5.

Sherman, William H., *Used Books: Marking Readers in Renaissance England*, Material Texts (Philadelphia, PA: University of Pennsylvania Press, 2008).

Solomon, Harry M., *The Rise of Robert Dodsley: Creating the New Age of Print* (Carbondale, IL: Southern Illinois University Press, 1996).

Stedmond, John, *The Comic Art of Laurence Sterne* (University of Toronto Press, 1967).

Swearingen, James, *Reflexivity in* Tristram Shandy: *An Essay in Phenomenological Criticism* (New Haven, CT: Yale University Press, 1977).

Tadié, Alexis, *Sterne's Whimsical Theatres of Language: Orality, Gesture Literacy*, Studies in Early Modern English Literature (Aldershot: Ashgate, 2003).

Tallis, Raymond, *The Hand: A Philosophical Inquiry into Human Being* (Edinburgh University Press, 2003).

  Michelangelo's Finger: An Exploration of Everyday Transcendence (New Haven, CT: Yale University Press, 2010).

Terry, Richard, *The Plagiarism Allegation in English Literature from Butler to Sterne* (Basingstoke: Palgrave, 2010).

  Poetry and the Making of the English Literary Past: 1660–1781 (Oxford University Press, 2001).

Thorp, Jennifer, 'Picturing a Gentleman Dancing-Master: A Lost Portrait of Kellom Tomlinson', *Dance Research*, 30 (2012), 70–9.

Timperley, C.H., *A Dictionary of Printers and Printing* (London: Johnson, 1839).

Tobin, Terence, 'A List of Plays and Entertainments by Scottish Dramatists 1660–1800', *Studies in Bibliography*, 23 (1970), 103–117.

Toner, Anne, *Ellipsis in English Literature: Signs of Omission* (Cambridge University Press, 2015).

Trettien, Whitney Anne, 'A Blank Poem (1723); or, the Present of Absence', *Diapsalmata*, 29 August 2010, available at http://blog.whitneyannetrettien .com/2010/08/blank-poem-1723-or-present-of-absence.html, last accessed 5 June 2020.

Trumble, Angus, *The Finger: A Handbook* (New York: Farrar, 2010).

van Leewen, Eva C., *Sterne's* Journal to Eliza: *A Semiological and Linguistic Approach to the Text*, Studies and Texts in English 2 (Tübingen: Narr, 1981).

Walsh, Marcus, 'Text, "Text", and Swift's *A Tale of a Tub*', *Modern Language Review*, 85 (1990), 290–303.

Watt, Ian, 'The Comic Syntax of *Tristram Shandy*', in Howard Anderson and John S. Shea (eds.), *Studies in Criticism and Aesthetics 1660–1800: Essays in Honour of Samuel Holt Monk* (University of Minneapolis Press, 1967), 315–31.

Werner, Sarah, 'Reading Blanks', *Wynken de Worde*, 10 October 2010, available at http://wynkendeworde.blogspot.co.uk/2010/10/reading-blanks.html, last accessed 5 June 2020.

Wilkinson, Hazel, *Compositor* (formerly *Fleuron*), available at https://compositor .bham.ac.uk/, last accessed 5 June 2020.

'Printers' Flowers as Evidence in the Identification of Unknown Printers: Two Examples From 1715', *The Library*, 14 (2013), 70–9.

Williams, Helen, '"Looking and Reading Simultaneously": APFEL on *Tristram Shandy*', *The Shandean*, 23 (2012), 129–35, 134.

Wolfe, Richard J., *Marbled Paper: Its History, Techniques, and Patterns: With Special Reference to the Relationship of Marbling to Bookbinding in Europe and the Western World* (Philadelphia, PA: University of Pennsylvania Press, 1990).

Woodmansee, Martha, 'The Genius and the Copyright: Economic and Legal Conditions of the Emergence of the "Author"', *The Printed Word in the Eighteenth Century*, special issue of *Eighteenth-Century Studies*, 17 (1984), 425–48.

Zerby, Chuck, *The Devil's Details: A History of Footnotes* (New York: Touchstone, 2002).

Zimmerman, Everett, '*Tristram Shandy* and Narrative Representation', *The Eighteenth Century*, 28.2 (1987), 127–47.

Index